Samuel Graham Wilson

Persia

Western Mission

Samuel Graham Wilson

Persia
Western Mission

ISBN/EAN: 9783743305182

Manufactured in Europe, USA, Canada, Australia, Japa

Cover: Foto ©ninafisch / pixelio.de

Manufactured and distributed by brebook publishing software (www.brebook.com)

Samuel Graham Wilson

Persia

geographical, but express in a general way their relative positions.

The history of the Eastern Persia Mission is sketched by the Rev. James Bassett, in "Persia: Eastern Mission." The present volume relates for the most part to mission work among non-Mohammedan peoples in Western Persia. In the author's "Persian Life and Customs," the field is described and the social and religious conditions of the people detailed. In the following pages, the history of Christianity in Persia and the conditions of religious liberty are sketched; and the narrative of the mission work, the equipment for its prosecution, the methods pursued, the obstacles, persecutions, and triumphs are detailed with reference to Nestorians, Armenians, and Jews. The author's residence and work have been among Armenians in Tabriz. This has given him special interest in this race and opportunity to observe them. The massacre of tens of thousands of them in Turkey has lately drawn the attention of the world to the Armenian Question. For these reasons several chapters are devoted to the race, religion, condition and customs of the Armenians as well as to the prospects of religious reformation among them. The condition of the Jews in Persia is given in some detail. On the other hand the tenets and history of the Nestorians, together with the narrative of the Mission to the Nestorians (1835–1871) is passed over, as a considerable literature on this subject is accessible. The present condition and equipment of the mission at Urumia and Mosul is enlarged upon. Medical missions and Bible distribution are shown to be of special importance for the development of the kingdom of Christ in Persia; and the ravages of famine, cholera and intemperance are described in relation to the efforts of the missionaries for the relief of suffering. A chapter is devoted to the work of other missions, including the Catholic and Anglican missions.

While these pages have been in press, Persia has passed through a severe crisis. Shah Nasr-i-Din was assassinated on May 1st, 1896, at the shrine of Shah Abdul Azim. He had gone to this celebrated golden-domed mosque in the vicinity of the capital, to worship on Friday, the last occasion of the kind before his anticipated jubilee, which was to be celebrated on May 6th. Within the precincts of the mosque a sayid, Mirza Mohammed Reza, presented a written petition. While the shah was reading it, he was shot by the sayid and died within an hour. The assassin seems to have been prompted by political agitators. The chief instigator seems to be Sayid Jamal-i-Din, a political pamphleteer and quondam editor of newspapers in Bombay and Paris.

It was a tragic ending to a long and prosperous reign. Pathos was added to the event by the fact that all the preparations had been made for a joyful jubilee, with grand and imposing ceremonies. Representatives from all the provinces were *en route* for the capital, bearing magnificent gifts; the colors and standards of the various regiments had been sent to be renewed; new coins had been struck and were ready to be issued, commemorating the reign of fifty years; the cities of the kingdom were being swept and garnished and decked in holiday attire; everywhere from the Caspian to the Persian Gulf, from Mount Ararat to the confines of Baluchistan, preparations were being made for illuminations and celebrations beyond all precedent, and Nasr-i-Din Shah was happy in anticipation of universal congratulation,—but the bullet shattered all these plans.

"The king is dead! Long live the king!" Tabriz, where the crown prince resided, was soon astir with joyous throngs, its bazaars were decked and its houses and streets illuminated in a gorgeous manner. All the shops displayed their finest and most gaudy materials, the arched roofs were festooned with rich fabrics; bright-colored goods were hung on ropes from side to side; pictures, chinaware, rich carpets, transparencies and mottoes covered the walls; lamps and candelabra in great profusion illuminated the usually dusky arcades; tens of thousands of torches covered the flat roofs of the houses. With such rejoicings Shah Mezaffir-i-Din was welcomed to his throne. His majesty was invested with the insignia of sovereignty by the chief mujtihids. One mujtihid placed an aigrette of gold and feathers upon his hat, another bound on his sword with full-jeweled sheath, another suspended the rose-colored scarf and the picture of

Ali on his breast, while two others assisted him to mount his throne. He was again formally invested on his arrival at Teheran. The country passed through the crisis in quietness and without the anticipated disturbances.

It concerns us greatly to know what the relation of the new shah will be to missionaries and mission work. His majesty is a religious man and much under the influence of the Ulema. At the same time he is friendly to Christians. He will no doubt protect and favor his Armenian and Nestorian subjects. His relation with missionaries has been most pleasant. For several years, Dr. G. W. Holmes, of the mission, was his confidential physician, and since his accession he has repeatedly requested him to resume the position and attend him at Teheran. The princesses, who remain in Tabriz, until the thousand inmates of the harem of the late shah can be disposed of, have been specially committed to Dr. W. S. Vanneman, with the request that he accompany them to the capital. The American missionaries in a body were honorably received by his majesty. All these marks of regard lead us confidently to expect the same protection and favor as in the reign of Nasr-i-Din and even to hope for enlarged privileges. There is no reason to anticipate any backward steps in religious liberty nor any new hindrances being placed in the way of missionary work.

CONTENTS.

CHAPTER I.
	PAGE
Christianity in Persia	11

CHAPTER II.
The State of Religious Liberty	22

CHAPTER III.
Urumia—The Mission to the Nestorians	43

CHAPTER IV.
Mosul and the Mountains—The Mission to the Nestorians	83

CHAPTER V.
The Armenians and the Gregorian Church	104

CHAPTER VI.
Armenian Wedding Customs	130

CHAPTER VII.
Tabriz and Salmas—The Mission to the Armenians	143

CHAPTER VIII.
Mission Schools in Tabriz and Salmas	197

CHAPTER IX.
Reform of the Gregorian Church	222

CHAPTER X.

Mission Work Among the Jews.................. 237

CHAPTER XI.

Medical Missions 258

CHAPTER XII.

Drought and Famine 291

CHAPTER XIII.

The Cholera Epidemic of 1892.................. 295

CHAPTER XIV.

Bible Translation and Distribution............ 315

CHAPTER XV.

The Missions of other Churches................ 342

CHAPTER XVI.

Intemperance in Persia........................ 352

PERSIA: WESTERN MISSION.

CHAPTER I.

CHRISTIANITY IN PERSIA.

ON the day of Pentecost there were at Jerusalem Parthians and Medes and Elamites and dwellers in Mesopotamia. These, doubtless, scattered, planting the seeds of Christianity in Persia. Tradition says that Peter and Thomas preached the gospel in the Parthian empire. Thaddeus and Bartholomew and Adeus of the Seventy came to the races of the East in Armenia and Persia. Marius, a Persian noble, and his wife Martha, suffered martyrdom under Claudius A. D. 53.

A writer in the reign of Marcus Aurelius notices the spread of Christianity in Parthia, Media, Persia and Bactria. According to Mr. Thomas' interpretation of the Sassanian inscription at Hajiabad, Shapur I. was a Christian king. The name of Jesus is found in the superscription. In the latter part of the third century, Manes, a Magian, famed as a mathematician, astronomer and painter, became a Christian and a presbyter. Afterwards he founded a new religion or heretical Christianity, composed of elements of Christianity, Parseeism, and Buddhism, claimed to be the Paraclete, and gained many converts in Persia and the Roman empire. He was flayed alive by the Magian king.

Christianity steadily increased among all ranks. In A. D. 300 the Parthian capital, Ctesiphon, was the seat of the chief bishop. In A. D. 334 a bishop was settled at Tus (Meshed). Elisha says that Christianity had extended to the eastern borders of the Caspian Sea and the confines of India. At the council of Nice, John was present as bishop of India and Persia. Theodoret says, " I rejoice exceedingly to hear that multitudes have become Christians and that the finest provinces of Persia are honored with their residence." A prominent Mobed embraced Christianity and wrote a defense of it and in condemnation of Magianism. The book had great influence. Its author was stoned to death. The prosperity of Christianity and decline of Magianism, the multiplication of splendid churches, the friendliness of the Christians to the Roman emperor, the intrigues of the Magi and Jews gave rise to a terrible persecution against the Christians.* It was begun in 343 by Shapur II. He first required the Christians to pay a tax made so exorbitant that they might be compelled to deny their

---

* See Sozomen's Ecclesiastical History, Book II., Chaps. VIII. and XV., and Theodoret, Book I., Chapter XXV.; Neander, P 125-131.

with the Christians in Hamadan.* His brother, who succeeded him, is said to have been baptized in his youth with the name Nicolas. But he became a Mussulman under the name of Ahmad Khan and persecuted the Christians. He destroyed all the churches and ordered that every Christian should be banished from his dominions. He also persecuted the Mongols. Complaint was made to the Khan of Tartary and he was put to death. Argun, son of Abaka, succeeded him. Argun removed the capital to Tabriz. He was very favorable to the Christians, and sent embassies to and received them from Pope Nicolas IV., Edward I. of England, and the king of France.† A Mussulman writer says, "True believers trembled lest the sacred temple of Mecca should be converted into a Cathedral." Sham Ghazan, his son, toward the end of his life became a Mohammedan, drawing with him one hundred thousand of his Tartar followers. But he treated the Christians favorably and was in alliance with the crusaders. After him (A. D. 1300) all the Mongol Khans were Mussulmans.

Then came the scourge, the fierce Tamurlane. He regarded himself as appointed to exterminate the Christians. The Nestorians were forced to accept Islam, or be put to death or driven from the land. They took refuge in the mountains of Kurdistan, creeping down afterwards into the plains of Urumia

* Markham, p. 169, 170.
† Malcolm I., 268, Markham, pp. 170.

and Salmas. Some of the Armenians found refuge in Karadagh. Many were slain. Four thousand were buried alive at one time. Henceforth Christianity in Persia existed only in small and scattered remnants.

For twelve or fourteen centuries Christianity had been known in Persia. For a considerable part of this time, Christians continued their efforts to gain the ascendency and to turn the people and government to Christ. First Christianity attacked the revived and vigorous Mazdeism, then it was called to meet the fresh life and force of Islam. A new opportunity came to it when the Mongols arrived upon the scene. But the spiritual power of a degenerate Christianity was not equal to the effort. Several times it seemed on the point of triumphing. Kings, queens and princes accepted or inclined to Christianity, but adverse influences were too strong.

For the last five centuries, Christianity has been simply a tolerated but oppressed and despised sect. From the invasions of Tamurlane until the accession of Abbas the Great (A. D. 1582), a period of 200 years is almost a blank. In A. D. 1603 some Armenian chiefs appealed to Shah Abbas for protection against the Turks. He invaded Armenia, and in the midst of the war decided to devastate it, that the Turks might be without provisions. From Kars to Bayazid the Armenians were driven before the Persian soldiery to the banks of the Arras, near Julfa. Their cities and villages were depopulated. From every place of concealment they were driven forth. Convents were emptied and plundered. The captives were forced to cross the Arras without proper transports. Many women and children, sick and aged, were carried away by the swift current. Two chiefs were beheaded to hasten the progress. Women were captured for the Persian harems. Through unfrequented paths and with untold hardships, they reached their destinations. The principal colony of five thousand was settled at New Julfa near Ispahan. There they were granted many privileges. Many, both Armenians and Georgians, were scattered through Central Persia, and some of their descendants are villagers in the Bakhtiari country. A colony of seven thousand was planted at Ashraf, in Mezanderan. Shah Abbas remarked "that this would be a paradise for Christians, as it abounded in wine and hogs." It proved quite the contrary, however, as the malaria destroyed the greater portion of the colonists, and the remnant were restored to Armenia in the reign of Safi Shah. The colony at Julfa prospered greatly and became very wealthy by trade and the arts.

Shah Abbas again renewed intercourse with the sovereigns of Europe, with Spain, Portugal and England under James I. Sir Dodmore Cotton, ambassador from England, came in great state to Persia.

Under the Safavean kings, the Christians of Azerbaijan and Transcaucasia suffered much from the wars of the Turks and Persians. Both banks of the Arras were generally in the hands of the Persians. Some of the Shahs were tolerant, and the Christians prospered. Some overtaxed them. The last one, Shah Sultan Husain, oppressed them. He repealed the law of retaliation, whereby a Christian could exact equivalent punishment from a Mussulman criminal. He enacted that the price of a Christian's blood should be the payment of a load of grain.

Julfa was subjected to great suffering at the time of the invasion of the Afghan Mahmud. It was captured and a ransom of seventy thousand tomans and fifty of the fairest and best-born maidens exacted. The grief of the Armenians was so heartrending that many of the Afghans were moved to pity and returned the captives. When Mahmud subsequently became a maniac, the Armenian priests were called to pray over him, to exorcise the evil spirit. Nadir Shah continued to oppress the Armenians, ostracized them, and interdicted their worship. On this account many emigrated to India, Bagdad, and Georgia. About eighty villages remained between Hamadan and Ispahan.

Under the Kajar dynasty the state of the Christians is better known. Notices of them abound in the narrations of travelers of the period. Aga Mohammed, the founder of the Kajar Shahs, sacked Tiflis and transported many Georgians into Persia. Others came because of their enmity to Russia. Their descendants, mostly Mohammedans, are frequently met occupying high positions in the government. At the time of the

Russian war (A. D. 1828) nine thousand families of Armenians and many Nestorians emigrated from Azerbaijan. Some were induced to come back by Abbas Mirza, under the protection of the English. Those in Tabriz were exempted from taxes and had the right to appeal to the British consul. This right of protection was afterwards withdrawn, and finally, after many vain protests on the part of the Armenians, the exemption from taxes was annulled in A. D. 1894. The condition of Christians under Nasr-i-Din Shah will be described in the following chapter.

CHAPTER II.

THE STATE OF RELIGIOUS LIBERTY.

THERE are in the religious condition of the Shiahs certain circumstances which tend to modify materially the inherent intolerance of Islam. The Shiahs are a sect suffering from the Sunnis the opprobrium of heterodoxy, and occupying the position of a minority in a religious contest. They have in the school of experience learned what it is to maintain opinion and faith against superior numbers. Having had to contest their right for liberty to differ, they would naturally be more able to appreciate the feelings of others in similar circumstances.

Shiah Islam is a most tolerant organization to its own. It has developed a broad-churchism which tolerates diverse forms of belief. Not to mention the large class of *Dahris* or skeptics, there are the Sufis, who mystify all the rites and ceremonies of Islam; the Arifs, who refuse any special honor to Mohammed or any other prophet, except as they were men who benefited their race; the Ali Allahis, who hold Ali above Mohammed, and are popularly said to regard him as God, the Aylauts or Nomadic tribes, some of whom live without Mollah or Korans, know not even the forms of prayer, and disregard the laws of clean and unclean; the Sheikhis and Mutasharis, and others of many names, with views divers like the colors and kinds of goods in an oriental bazaar; yet all dwell at peace and tolerate each other's opinions. It might be claimed that the terrific persecution of the Babis is in direct contradiction to this. But the Babis were not attacked on purely religious grounds. Their success seemed to imply the subversion of the State; they became involved in political issues and were treated as the enemies of the king, the fanaticism of the people being aroused and opposed to the fanaticism of the new sect. Their slaughter with fire and sword, with torture and inquisitorial cruelty, was for reasons of statecraft, especially after the attempt to assassinate the Shah. Notwithstanding this exception, the Shiahs are remarkably tolerant to all varieties of opinion among themselves.

The treatment which Jews and Christians have received in the past in Persia is shown in other chapters. Their treatment under the Kajar dynasty has been liberal and humane. Christian subjects are rightly grateful to Nasr-i-Din Shah. But, notwithstanding the favor of the king, they have suffered from the quiet and constant repression arising from their state of subjection, trampled upon as weak, despised as unclean, hated as infidels. They have been exposed in the villages to such discomfort and oppression as the true believers have seen fit to inflict, and often have been helpless to obtain redress for their grievances. They have been proscribed in not a few of the avocations of life, excluded in some places from the bazaars and the best positions in trade. Their evidence in law was either unheard or unheeded, their property at the mercy of defrauders, or the legal inheritance of any renegade pervert to Islam. They have, even while enjoying peace, purchased it at the price of a cringing submission, which has subdued their spirits and reduced them, in some cases, to a state of groveling and timidity. There has been, however, great advance in liberty for the Christian *rayats* or peasants in the present reign. Fifty years ago, if a peasant wished to go to a feast, he put on an old coat over his new one, that he might not excite the cupidity of the Mohammedan. The farmers were subject to many hardships, and their daughters were liable to be abducted. An open confession of the divinity of Christ was dangerous. A pastor told me how his grandfather was asked by some Mohammedans if he believed that Christ was God, and on confessing his faith he was thrown into the river. He escaped unharmed. At that time a Nestorian could not ride a horse in a Mohammedan city or village. A bishop was even stripped of his turban in public in the streets of Urumia in 1837.

Through the kindly intervention of Christian Governments, especially by the personal interest of Her Majesty Queen Victoria, calling attention of His Majesty the Shah to certain inequalities, a decree was issued in 1881 regulating the relations of Christian subjects to Mohammedans. The substance of some of its provisions is as follows:—

1. The former law permitted the owner of the village to take one load of fuel and one day's labor from the rayats. This seems harmless, but it was made the occasion of unlimited oppression and extortion, and to check this the law was repealed.

2. The rights of property of the rayat in relation to the landlord were adjusted and defined so as to allow of personal ownership of buildings, etc., by the peasant.

3. The penalty for plundering traveling Nestorians was increased. Sometimes Nestorian laborers going to Russia and returning from their work have been much defrauded by officials at the frontier.

4. Converts to Islam, who may wish to return to Christianity, were given permission. This was a great step in advance. It was, however, a secret provision, *open* revision of existing laws being declared impossible in a Moslem country as against the Koran, but orders were sent to the governors that each case of such return should be referred to Teheran and it would be forgiven. This has been carried out. Three years ago a notable instance occurred when a Nestorian who had become a Mohammedan, came to Tabriz, telegraphed to the Shah that he wished to return to Christianity and an answer was returned giving him full permission, and promising him immunity. In 1893 a Chaldean Catholic who had lived for some

years as a Mohammedan, was brought, at his own request while very ill, and thrown down before my door. He professed deep contrition saying that he had returned to die a Christian. We took him into a room, and Dr. Vanneman attended him during his last days. After his death the brethren buried him and no objection was made by any Mohammedans.

5. A still greater advance was made in regard to the inheritance of Christians who turn Mohammedans. They are no longer to be allowed to confiscate all their relatives' property, but only such a portion is to be allotted to them as would have been theirs if they had remained Christians.

6. In regard to evidence in judicial cases where Christians and Moslems are concerned, as no religious judge could receive the word of a Christian against a Moslem, it was ordered that all such cases shall be tried before the civil courts and that the evidence shall be weighed on its own merits.

These orders were obtained by the British minister, and communicated to the missionaries "that they might report any violation of them." For Nestorians and Armenians alike they have had a beneficial effect. They had special relation to the Nestorians, since a larger proportion of them are cultivators of the soil and so more exposed to oppression than the Armenian merchants and mechanics, especially as quite a number of Armenians have the shield of Russian protection.

The Shah has granted privileges to the Armenians

of Karadagh and Solmas, through the petition of their bishops, regarding the payment of their taxes, which give them almost local self-government. Agitations of fanatics against Christians are forcibly repressed. In 1889 Haji Sayid Ali Akbar, of Shiraz, raised a disturbance by preaching against Christians. A riot occurred in which several lives were lost. The Sayid was expelled from the city.

The Parsees, too, who found scarcely a resting-place in the land of their ancient altars, have had their condition alleviated by the Shah. In 1854 the prosperous Parsees of Hindustan deputed Mr. Manockji as their representative to look after the interests of the Fire-worshipers in Persia. There are about seven thousand of them residing in Yezd, Kerman, and Teheran. They were relieved of many oppressions, and lastly, by a special petition, of the Jazia tax of eight hundred and forty-five tomans on them as Fire-worshippers. In view of this a special Jasan ceremony was held in Teheran on December 18th, 1883. This Zoroastrian prayer service was attended by Persian officials, European and Turkish officers of the Embassies, Armenian merchants and many Parsees. It was the first gathering of such a kind among the Parsees in Persia since the fall of the ancient Persian empire.

Coming now to the considerations of liberty for missionary work, we see that much liberty has been enjoyed. In 1842 it was ordered that no native Christian should be proselyted from one sect to another. In

1851 this was rescinded. About the same time an attempt was made to overthrow our work among the Nestorians. The governor of Urumia, who was engaged in the attempt, was shortly assassinated by the Kurds, and the governor-general at Tabriz, who was encouraging him, was driven out by the Tabriz populace for extortion. The opposition was never renewed. When Dr. Perkins and some Nestorian priests were attacked by drunken *lootees*, the government punished their assailants severely. A series of misfortunes befell their relatives. A feeling of awe grew up and a sentiment developed that the Lord would punish those who would harm the missionaries. This sentiment even now extensively prevails. Missionaries have never been maltreated in the prosecution of their work. The mishaps which have come to them, such as highway robberies, being such as happen to any traveler. Of all the local riots and disturbances in the kingdom, none have been directed against the missionaries.

Since the time above referred to work among nominal Christians and Jews has been freely permitted. Any opposition has been local. It has been repeatedly declared that Christians changing the form of their faith, or Jews becoming Christians, or vice versa, shall not be molested, and shall be protected. In this work intolerance is met from a different quarter, viz.:—from the ecclesiastics of the old churches and the rabbis. This is at times very severe; and because priests, rabbis and bishops are often men of influence and have the means of corruption, they procure the coöperation of the governors. Rev. Dr. Bruce, of Ispahan, writes: "During all my missionary life among Mohammedans, every persecution and opposition to our work, from which we have suffered, has been set on foot, not by Moslems, but by nominal Christians." Of late more difficulties have been made about the opening of new schools and building new churches, but they seem to originate in a desire for fees for building permits, and to be prompted, not from the central government, but from opposing ecclesiastics.

With reference to the distribution of literature, the law, as promulgated in the Revised Police Regulations, Art. 8, is: "Whoever disseminates a book against the religion of the State or the faith shall be imprisoned from five months to five years." Besides this, there are a number of proscribed works, such as the *Mezan-al-Hak*, or Balance of Truth, by Dr. Pfonder. Our mission has published no controversial works. To general Christian literature, especially as most of it is in the Syriac or the Armenian language, no objection has been made. We have large liberty for the distribution of the Scriptures and religious books not controversial. They are imported, passing under the inspection of the officials. Book rooms and Scripture depots are open in many of the principal cities and towns of the kingdom. Occasionally an effort is made, as in Urumia in 1881, to exclude them from the bazaars, but generally wherever there is an Armenian or Nestorian population, their sale is freely allowed, under the principle that they are entitled to buy or sell their own sacred books. Colporteurs go everywhere, and are scattering the word of God far and wide. They always go with some risk to their persons and lives, and are frequently maltreated, but in the main they have free course, hawking through the bazaars, visiting the houses of the governors themselves, or going wherever there is an opportunity for sale. Instances will be found in the chapter on Bible Work.

With reference to the evangelization of Mohammedans, it is well known that the law of the Koran commands that one who forsakes the faith of Islam shall be put to death. It was hoped that the influence of modern thought and civilization, and the example of all enlightened governments would modify and restrain any desire of the rulers or people to see this law executed. The spirit of indifference and skepticism which has taken hold of some of the ruling class would tend to make them disinclined to enforce it. Indeed, the former Sipah Silar definitely declared, "that if any Mussulman became a Christian from conviction, he would be protected." The foreign agent told us that if we would open a good school he would send his own children. When we had conducted a school for Mussulmans a few years in Tabriz, the government gave orders for us to cease teaching Mussulmans. At the same time an official told us that they had no desire to interfere with us, but had given the order to satisfy the demands of some zealots. Sometimes men who came to preaching service were arrested. But finally the government settled upon an order that "we should not allow women or children to come to our churches or schools." This was intended to imply that men might come to church under the idea, doubtless, that they could get no harm from listening to a sermon.

The attitude of the government towards a Mussulman who confesses himself a convert to Christianity was seen in the case of Mirza Ibrahim. He was a Mohammedan of Khoi, in middle life, who had been seeking peace to his troubled soul and could not find it. He came to see if in the religion of Jesus there was that peace he sought. He found Jesus as a Saviour who gives rest to the soul. He publicly confessed his faith in Christ as the divine Redeemer, in 1890. When asked, "Are you not afraid that your friends will kill you for leaving their religion?" he answered, "They can kill only my body; they cannot harm my faith." After his baptism considerable excitement arose, but the governor paid no attention to the accusations. The Mollahs reasoned with Mirza Ibrahim, threatened him, offered him a comfortable post in one of their shrines. His wife left him, taking all the property, and his son and daughter. He had hoped that his daughter would join him in his love for

Jesus, but she became his most bitter and reviling enemy.

Suffering from a sore foot, he not long after these troubles went to the Urumia hospital.* After he became better, he was accustomed to tell of his new-found faith through the villages. One night some police came to a village where he was. He preached Christ to them. In the morning they arrested him and took him before the *Suparast*, the governor of the Christians in Urumia. The Suparast in the presence of a number of Mollahs and other Mohammedans inquired of him, "Why are you, a Moslem, teaching the Christian doctrines?" Mirza Ibrahim took his Testament from his pocket and said, "Is not this Injil a holy book?" The Suparast said it was. "Then am I not right in reading it and teaching it?" "But how about Mohammed?" "That is for you to say. My faith is in Christ and his word. He is my Saviour." At this the command was given, "Beat him." He was beaten, kicked, and reviled. His face shone, as he said, "So was my Saviour beaten." Some of the crowd demanded his blood. He was then taken before the governor of Urumia, and again boldly testified of his faith in Christ. Rich men offered to give him a purse of money, if that was what he needed. He was thrown into prison, heavily chained and his feet bound. The city was in an uproar, a mob was at the prison gates

---

* Note.—The first part of this narrative is according to the letters of Rev. J. C. Mechlin and Dr. J. H. Shedd.

threatening him. His word to them was, "You may shoot me from the cannon's mouth, but you cannot take away my faith." Because of the danger of mob violence, word was telegraphed to Tabriz and the prisoner was ordered to be sent there. Christian friends gave him provisions. The soldiers who were to guard him on the way, told him to wrap them up for the journey. He replied, "No, I have a Master who will provide for me. I must leave this bread for the poor prisoners left here." He then turned to his fellow-prisoners and said, "I have talked with you of Mohammed and have shown you that he can never save you, and I have shown to you Christ the all-sufficient Saviour. You have learned enough of truth to save you if you will only receive it." "They all rose with heavy chains on their necks and bade him go in peace, while they prayed that his God and the Saviour whom he trusted would protect him. As he left the prison he turned, and raising his hands, solemnly called God to witness that if, on the judgment day, he should meet any of these souls unsaved, he had declared unto them the way of life and was free from their blood. He was then escorted by eight soldiers to the house of the general."* A crowd of two hundred Mussulmans followed him into the yard of the governor. An officer came out of the house and told them, "This is a wonderful man. He is as brave as a lion. A Mollah has just been trying to convince him of his error, but

* Dr. Shedd.

he replies to everything, and the Mollah has gone away with his head hanging down. He says that Mohammed is not a prophet, and that unless they can prove that he is, from the Holy Books, he will not give up his faith in Christ, even if they cut off his head." A Christian brother Absalom then came to see him. He asked him, "Does your faith continue strong?" He replied, "It seems to me stronger every day." "Are you not afraid to die?" "I know I must die some time, why should I fear to die now?" Absalom said, "It is not man who sends you to Tabriz; it is God. You are to bear witness to the guards, to the governor, may be to the Crown Prince. Stand firm!" Mirza said, "Tell my friends to pray that God increase my faith. I have no power—God is helping me." Then they knelt down and prayed, the general, and Mollahs standing near and the crowd looking through the large open window. Then the general said in a kindly tone, "Have you finished, my son?" He was then led into the yard to mount the horse provided by friends, otherwise he would have had to walk to Tabriz in chains. The general then said to the guards, "I swear by Jesus Christ, that if any of you hurt this man, I will cause you to eat your fathers." He then said, "God bless you," to Mirza Ibrahim who in turn thanked him. Mirza kissed Rabi Absalom, and said, "Pray for me that I may be a witness for Christ before the great of my people. I have no fear though I know that I shall die. Good-bye."

Mirza Ibrahim was brought to Tabriz. The guards delivered him to the governor. They then brought a few pieces of clothing and other articles to us to keep for him. The governor questioned Mirza Ibrahim of his faith. "Who oppressed you, that you should want to leave Islam?" He replied, "No one; I became a Christian from conviction, because I was persuaded of its truth." The governor sent him to the city prison where he was chained and put into a dark filthy dungeon along with a number of criminals.

When word was first sent to the British acting consul, Mr. R. M. Paton, of the arrest of Mirza Ibrahim, he expressed willingness to befriend him, and use his friendly offices for his release. The Persian officials in Urumia, advised that no question be raised about him, which would excite the Mollahs and complicate matters, saying that if the affair quieted down they would release him in a short time. This advice was taken in the expectation of his speedy release, because the government officials seemed to show a tolerant spirit and some of them even a sympathy with the prisoner.

Mirza Ibrahim had been arrested in May, 1892. He was brought to Tabriz the first week in June. In the last of June, a placard was posted in the city that it was the command of Mollah Hasan Shirazi (Chief Mujtehid of Kerbela) that all Protestants should leave Tabriz inside of twenty days or they would be expelled. In July the Muharam excitements came around. On the tenth Mirza Ibrahim was not released, though his name was among those handed by the jailer to the governor. Immediately the cholera followed with ten thousand stricken down. Shortly after that, the Protestant church and school were sealed in Tabriz, the reason assigned being that we were converting Mussulmans. After ten weeks, they were opened, January 9, 1893.

Meanwhile Mirza Ibrahim languished in prison. Sometimes he was in the dungeon, a dark, damp cellar full of vermin and filth, chained to vile criminals; at other times, through the indulgence of the jailer, he was in an upper carpeted and heated room. Prisoners are sometimes permitted to have these favors if their friends will pay for them. Christian friends were thus enabled part of the time to ease Mirza Ibrahim's confinement, to send him bedding, clothing, food and writing materials. He was permitted to have his New Testament and to receive letters. Chapters of Meyer's *Shepherd Psalm* were translated and sent to him from time to time. His faith was firm and his confession bold. From the prison he wrote, "Our Lord Jesus has not promised us glory in this world; he has said we shall have tribulation." He witnessed to his fellow-prisoners of Jesus' salvation. One who under torture had refused to declare where certain stolen goods were concealed, was moved under the exhortations of Mirza Ibrahim to send a full statement, so that the property was recovered. Mirza Ibrahim fed upon the word of God and lived by prayer. He might have been released at any time by denying his faith. The same expectation was entertained by the officials as in Acts 24: 26, but like that illustrious "prisoner in bonds," this modern disciple did not desire his release by such means. Sometime after the New Year, Mirza Ibrahim sent a petition to the Shah, confessing himself a Christian, and begging for his release. This was received, but no answer was sent. Through the Evangelical Alliance, the British minister, Sir Frank Lascelles, was asked by Lord Rosebery to intercede on behalf of the poor sufferer. The * American minister, Mr. Watson R. Sperry, interested himself in the case, but before they had yet spoken of the matter a crisis was reached in Tabriz.

For some time the jailer had been treating Mirza Ibrahim more severely, beating him and casting him into the dungeon. His coat and bedding were taken from him. He was compelled to witness the abominable licentiousness of the jailers and prisoners, so that, like Lot, his soul was "vexed from day to day with their unlawful deeds." Christian friends wept when they saw him so pale and sickly, yet withal so true to his faith. One night, when he was in the dungeon with a dozen wicked outlaws, he began to witness to them of Christ. They opposed him, and beat and kicked him. They then took turns in choking him,

---

* From May, 1892, when Mr. Truxton Beale left, until Jan., 1893, there was no American minister in Persia.

saying, "Is Ali true, or Jesus? Say Ali." He said, "Jesus is true. Yes, Jesus; though you kill me." They choked him until his eyes were almost out of their sockets, and he thought he would die. Greatly injured, he was taken from the dungeon. His throat swelled so that he could scarcely swallow or speak. Dr. Vanneman went to see him, but found that the injury had developed into severe œdema of the glottis and that there was no hope for him. Mirza Ibrahim said, "All is well; tell the church to pray for me and commend me to Jesus." He had before said that he knew when he professed Christ he was putting a sword to his throat. To the native Christian who had often gone to him, he said, "I have nothing to pay you back for all your kindness. I was sick and in prison, and you visited me. Jesus will reward you." He showed a loving and forgiving spirit toward those who had treated him so wickedly.

He died Sunday, May 14th, about 1. P. M., having endured with the true spirit of a martyr the horrors and pains of a Persian prison for almost a year. The jailer immediately informed the crown prince of his death. He asked, "How did he die?" The jailer gave word, "He died a Christian." The prince answered simply, "Bury him." As he was borne to his grave in charge of the jailer, the people said, "There goes the Mussulman who became a Christian." His faith and courage were the wonder of all. His martyr-death thrilled our hearts.

> He through fiery trials trod,
>   And from great affliction came;
> Now before the throne of God,
>   Sealed with his almighty name,
> Clad in raiment pure and white,
>   Victor-palms within his hands,
> Through his dear Redeemer's might
>   More than conqueror he stands.

After the death of Mirza Ibrahim, Sir Frank C. Lascelles, H.B.M. minister, had an interview with the sadr azam or prime minister, a report of which from an official source says: "The latter quoted to the British minister the old Persian or Mohammedan law which made Mirza Ibrahim, merely by renouncing Mohammedanism and professing the Christian faith, liable to the death penalty. The sadr azam expressed his surprise that he had been placed in prison instead of being promptly executed. In no respect did he show any lack of sympathy with this old law, or manifest the slightest indication that it was improper or disgraceful to enforce it." To say that this is a great disappointment is expressing oneself mildly; many friends of Persia, who had hoped much from the shah's contact with European nations, would be glad to be assured that the shah, so enlightened and liberal a monarch, will never permit such a thing to happen again. European nations long since abolished the death penalty for heresy. Japan, China, Siam, and Korea give peace and protection to their subjects who become Christians. Even the sultan of Turkey has issued the famous

Hatti Humayoum, declaring that no one shall be liable to death for embracing Christianity. Shall Persia stay behind in the progress of the ages? Let us hope that Mirza Ibrahim may be the last martyr for the faith in Persia, and that in future the sentiment of Shah Abbas II. may be received, viz. " It is for God, not for me, to judge men's consciences, and I will never interfere with what belongs to the tribunal of the great Creator and Lord of the universe."

There is no political reason why the government should object to a Mohammedan Persian becoming a Christian Persian. The situation in Persia somewhat resembles Italy. Church and State are not united, but even at times are antagonistic. As King Humbert is a Catholic, so the shah is a Shiah. As King Humbert puts no obstacles in the way of his Catholic subjects becoming Protestants, and has no subjects more loyal and true than his Protestant subjects, so it is certain the shah of Persia, if he would grant religious liberty, and if some of his Mohammedan subjects should become Christians, would find no more loyal, law-abiding and patriotic subjects than they would be. The conception that they would become English or French or Armenian or something else is prevalent, but utterly erroneous. They would be loyal Persians, paying taxes, serving in the army and doing any other service for their king and fatherland, as the Protestants in Japan have shown.

Moreover the Shiahs of Persia have more theological

affinity to Christianity than the Sunnis have. Not only do all have the doctrines of God, Scriptures, angels, future rewards and punishments, the sinlessness of Jesus, etc., in common, but the Shiahs in their various sects approach more nearly to our doctrine of the incarnation, Trinity, atonement, and mediatorship.

The Sheikhis use almost as high language of Ali as we do of Christ. The divine Light dwelt in him. He voices his power in the thunder, his gleaming sword is seen in the lightning. On him rests the hope of salvation. The twelve imams are the incarnations of twelve qualities of God. A mediator or shafi is necessary. Husain is such preëminently, because he shed his blood at Kerbela. For this God said, according to a tradition, "All mediation and atonement will be by you." Their writings, too, contain the doctrines of the Logos: "God doth speak by an eternal ancient word, subsisting in his essence." "The first manifestation of God was by the Logos, and existence of everything is by it," etc.

Besides these affinities of doctrines, the prevalence of sufeism, or rationalism, numerous sects of Ali Allahis, and Babis, all go to make the people willing and desirous of having religious liberty. If the shah should distinguish his reign by a grant of full religious liberty, it would not only be a cause of great honor to him before the Christian world, but a welcome boon to his own people.

NOTE.—The latest news from Persia informs us of the expulsion of the German Mission, on account of their attempting to do work among Mohammedans. The mission was established in 1894 at Urumia, to evangelize the Jews. Several Mohammedan inquirers presented themselves in Khoi, and Pastor Közle wrote a letter concerning them which was published in the *Nachrichten aus dem Morgenlande*. The Persian minister at Berlin called the attention of the shah's government to it and the withdrawal of the missionaries was demanded of the German government. Pastor Közle was meanwhile stricken down with typhoid fever, and after his death his associate, Dr. Zerwech, withdrew.

CHAPTER III.

URUMIA—THE MISSION TO THE NESTORIANS.

MISSION work by the churches of America was begun in Persia in 1834, by the sending of the Rev. Dr. Perkins to establish the mission to the Nestorians under the American Board. At the reunion of the Presbyterian Churches in 1871, this mission was transferred to the Presbyterian Board. It is not my intention to sketch the history of this mission either before or since the transfer. I will only draw a picture of one or two scenes in detail, and describe its present condition.

Let our first picture be the jubilee of the Nestorian mission. This was in two parts. First a programme was arranged in connection with the annual meeting of the West Persia Mission in 1884, fifty years after Dr. Perkins' arrival. Secondly a popular celebration was held by the Evangelical Church of Urumia in July, 1885; for the founder of the mission spent the first year in Tabriz, and settled in Urumia with Dr. Asahel Grant in 1835.

The first celebration was honored by the presence of Rev. Henry A. Nelson D.D., now editor of "The Church at Home and Abroad," and his son, now a missionary in Syria. Dr. Nelson, came as a delegate from the Synod of New York, bearing fraternal salutations from the Christians of America to the Evangelical Church of Persia. He also came as the semi-official representative of the board at the jubilee. Dr. Nelson is the first and only minister of our Church, not a missionary, who has ever visited the mission in Persia. His visit was a tonic to our souls.

Conducted from Tiflis by the redoubtable Lazaar Beg, the visitors were met at Julfa, the ferry of the Arras River, by two of our number and escorted to Tabriz. After spending some days in observing the work in Tabriz, they, with a large party of us bound for the annual meeting, proceeded to Urumia. During the last day's march the city appeared for a long time in view, with a faint smoke enveloping it, arising from the baths, bakeries and kilns. Noon brought us to the bridge over the Nazlu River, one of the three rivers which water Urumia, the most beautiful, fertile and thickly populated plain of Persia. The bridge is a stone structure, well arched and firmly built, yet in a peculiar Persian style, high and peaked, with steep approaches, so that one prefers to go through the river bed.

Here, about twelve miles from the city, where all new missionaries have been met since the days of Dr. Perkins, an advanced corps of brethren awaited us, and Mr. and Mrs. Oldfather spread a picnic for us on the river bank. As we went forward, one band and then another of the missionaries and brethren met us with their salutations of "Welcome," "Peace be with you," and "God bless your coming." Pastors and teachers, elders and deacons, converging from the city, from the villages of the plains, and from the valleys of mountains, welcomed with hearty handshakings and joyful faces their honored guests. There were Pastor Shimun, the moderator of the Evangelical Synod; Pastor Yacob, soon after elected moderator of the synod; Pastor Yoshana and Deacon Baba, who to their duties in the college added the labor of revising the modern Syriac version; the evangelist Baba, whose voice has been heard proclaiming the word of life throughout the whole field of Persia, as well in the mountains of Kurdistan as in the Elburz, by the Tigris, and by the Caspian Sea. The chief of police, with the soldiers of the Silar-il-Askar, Hasan Ali Khan the governor of Urumia, represented the Persian government and showed its good will to America and American missionaries by honoring this ambassador for Christ. Near the city the students of the high school and college, drawn up in line, saluted us. The whole formed a retinue which, with the fiery horses tossing their heads, the parti-colored and varied costumes of Nestorians, Armenians, Persians and Americans, and the expression of joy and gladness on all faces was a sight long to be remembered.

What a contrast to the reception which Drs. Perkins and Grant, and their wives, met! They arrived in a drizzling rain, took lodging in unfinished and unfurnished rooms, with neither bedding nor change of clothing, because the muleteers were delayed with their baggage and slept on piles of shavings covered with the clothes they had just dried by the fire.

At an early opportunity we called to pay our respects to the governor. As Dr. Nelson bore a letter of introduction from Malcom Khan, the shah's minister to England, his reception was with special honor. Having all put on overshoes, with the purpose of taking them off in imitation of the Persian custom of removing the shoes, we were ushered into a large saloon. The room was adorned with many bits of mirror set in the plaster. The windows excited our admiration. One, which filled the whole side of the room, was of most elaborate workmanship. It was a harmonious combination of minute scroll-work frames, filled with various colored glass. The floor was covered with the finest of carpets; the table with a beautiful piece of Resht embroidery. The governor was one of the most remarkable men in the kingdom, a diplomatist of high rank, a commander of energy, having dealt severe blows to the Kurds. He was dressed in a robe of cashmere shawl lined with fur. He took his seat on a chair and, providing the same for us, conversed freely with many words of welcome and praise of our work and our country. Among his sentiments was this: That a people which had redeemed a country from the wildness of nature and from the hands of savage men and raised it to such a height of prosperity and happiness, could not fail to bring a blessing to whatever country they might come. Our conversation was intermixed with the usual tea, coffee, and candies.

On a subsequent occasion Dr. Nelson addressed a letter to the governor, his reply to which was as follows, omitting titles of the address:

"I am highly pleased with the stay of your country people at Urumia and with the manner of their conduct and good conversation.

Much of my happiness and joy for their stay here arises from this, that every year a great number of the children of our dear subjects receive education from them, and come to partake of the light of knowledge and civilization through them.

One of the desirable results of their stay in our country is this, that it has led to the arrival of an honorable person like yourself in this land, and your visit and the visit of your son to me have given me such joy as to enable me to keep it always in remembrance.

I do assure you that your countrymen here are highly esteemed and honored by us, and, being greatly obliged for your kind intention and good wishes, my prayer to the Most High God is that he may keep you safe and prosperous in your journey, and enable me to have another interview with you.

In order to have something with you that may put you in mind of me, I herewith present you with my likeness and a small rug that has been made in my own native city, begging you will accept this trivial gift."

[The original is duly signed and sealed.]

I cannot dwell on the events of these two weeks, our visit to the French missionaries, feast in the garden-house of the moderator, wedding festivities, church dedication, etc.

The first part of the jubilee was conducted in the English language. After reading of the Scriptures, and prayer by Rev. W. L. Whipple, Agent of the American Bible Society, Rev. Dr. J. H. Shedd delivered an able and intensely interesting address of more than an hour's duration on the mission to the Nestorians.

I followed with a paper on the material progress in Persia during the half-century and the results of mission work among Armenians, Jews and other races in Persia. Dr. Nelson then made an address, commenting on the review of the work. This was followed by remarks by Rev. Messrs. Whipple and Labaree, and the reading of a letter of congratulation from the Eastern Persia Mission. A spirit of thankfulness in view of the past, of deep solemnity in view of the responsibilities devolving upon us as successors of the worthies of the former generation, pervaded the services, so that when Dr. Nelson closed with a fervent prayer, bearing us and our labors, our trials and our cares, all with heartfelt sympathy, before our heavenly Father, some were moved to tears, and we felt like consecrating ourselves anew to the service, that when another fifty years shall have rolled by, and men review our labors, they may see that by God's blessing great advance has been made.

The second part of the jubilee was held in the Syriac language, July, 1885. It was like a feast of tabernacles, full of rejoicing and thanksgiving. I was not there, but insert accounts of it written by those present. Mrs. Van Hook wrote, "A large booth furnished accommodations for the fourteen or fifteen hundred people assembled. Syriac mottoes were put over the platform, 'Jubilee 1835–1885.' 'Praise God, for His mercy endureth forever.' 'And ye shall sanctify the fiftieth year, it shall be a jubilee unto you.' A young Eastern Syrian presided at the organ, and a choir of college boys, under Mr. Oldfather's direction, led the singing. To me the most inspiring moment was when the throng lifted up their voices and sang,

> 'Blow ye the trumpet, blow,
>   The gladly solemn sound;
> Let all the nations know,
>   To earth's remotest bound,
> The year of Jubilee is come;
>   Return, ye ransomed sinners, home.'

"Thursday morning there were sunrise meetings, the principal one being a reunion of the school-girls. After breakfast there were prayer meetings again until the time of the regular exercises. Dinner was served in the garden to six or seven hundred men in every variety of costume, from those 'who had been to the countries' and returned in European dress, to the mountain Nestorian in heavily embroidered clothing of brilliant colors and fantastic shapes. Here a group of Armenians, and there a number of Jews who wished to know if Leviticus 25th would be read, and who asked to come up with the multitude that kept holy day. The white head-dresses and gay apparel of seven hundred women made the scene appear like a moving flower garden. Between rows of trees in the orchard bolts of cloth were spread, at each of which could be seated two hundred people. Posters showed where the delegates from the different villages were to sit, and the dinner was cooked out under the trees in great kettles holding from half a barrel to two barrels."

Dr. Labaree reported: "An invitation was sent out to all who intended to join in commemorating our jubilee occasion to be present on the 15th and 16th of July on our college grounds. Tickets of entertainment were offered for sale at a dime apiece. A programme of papers and religious exercises was arranged and printed. It struck a popular chord, and we became rather alarmed at the demand for tickets, lest we should not be able to manage a crowd of such dimensions. The day came, and we found ourselves thronged by about fifteen hundred people, men and women. But if we were surprised by this outburst of enthusiasm, we were still more so by the quiet and decorum

PERSIA: WESTERN MISSION. 51

that prevailed from beginning to end. I venture to say that no such number of men and women can be brought together between the Euphrates and the Indus, who would conduct themselves with so much propriety at all times, and give such interested attention to long religious services as those fifteen hundred assembled on our college grounds. Supplying them with food was a laborious undertaking, and providing sleeping accommodations, for one night alone, a source of much anxiety. The women had the college buildings at their disposal, and fared tolerably. But many of the men sat up, with only the sky for a covering, the whole night. What the crowd lacked in comforts, however, they made up in good nature. All passed off pleasantly; so much beyond our expectation and that of our wisest native friends that we can but regard it as a fresh token of the divine favor.

"The exercises were opened on Wednesday, at nine o'clock, by a sermon on the intent of the jubilee, by one of our best native preachers. This was followed by a review of the missionary work of the past fifty years, by Dr. Shedd, illustrated with colored diagrams, specially prepared, and in themselves very instructive. Other papers were read, as follows: 'Eminent Nestorians who have Labored in the Gospel,' 'Annals of the Educational Work'—both by native brethren. A paper on 'Female Education,' from Mrs. Grant's time to the present, prepared by three native sisters, each taking a separate period, was next read, closely engaging the interest of all, especially of the women. Papers on the work of the printing press, and on the distribution of the Scriptures, were read by Mr. Labaree, and by Mr. Whipple. The paper on revivals brought the great audience into the very presence, as it were, of the Holy Ghost. The hushed attention was impressive. It seemed as if the windows of heaven were about to open, and a new display of divine power to be witnessed. How deeply those precious histories are interwoven into the spiritual life of the churches was here most affectingly evidenced.

"On Thursday papers were read on 'Medical Work,' 'Trials and Persecutions,' 'Changes, Good and Bad, in the Moral and Social Developments of the Nation during the Fifty Years Past.' The services were closed Thursday afternoon by a sermon from Malik Yonan, an old and always popular preacher. The theme of his discourse was: 'Go Work in my Vineyard.' It was an earnest appeal to all of every class to work for the salvation of souls. At four o'clock the great company dispersed to their homes, as quietly as they had spent the days of service. Dr. Holmes remarked: 'It is the most orderly assembly of the size I have ever seen.'

"The attendance of nearly eight hundred Nestorian women, the most quiet and attentive part of the large audience, was the most impressive feature of the occasion."

A Mohammedan official who was present asked,

"What are those women doing here with books in their hands?" He was told that they were reading and singing. "Impossible!" said he. Then all the women who could read were requested to rise. Fully six hundred of them arose, where fifty years ago not a woman could have responded. "The air was redolent with precious memories of the early missionaries, especially of Miss Fiske and Miss Rice. The presence of some of their first pupils added no little interest to the occasion. One gray-haired woman, one of Miss Fiske's earliest girls, came a distance of two days, half the way on foot over rough mountain roads, to attend the jubilee." "Formerly only the old women could attend the Nestorian church services. The younger women could not attend even those services in an unknown tongue, because it was considered improper."

The question naturally arises, what have been the results of the work and the changes wrought which called for such rejoicings. The narrative so far contains part of the answer. Regarding this, Rabi Sarah, the wife of Professor Yoshana, writes, and in fine English too: "When I compare the past and the present, it appears to me like the early dawn beside the great noonday light. Not that the lives and characters of the Christians are perfect, but there has been great progress in knowledge and light. There is a power more than human, even the power of grace, working in the hearts of men and women. The bright rays of the sun of Christ's kingdom are reaching the dark corners. I do not think there are many Nestorian villages on the plain of Urumia which are not made to hear the sweet echoes of the gospel."

As illustrating the results of the mission work, I will describe the congregation of Geogtapa. This village has about one thousand five hundred inhabitants, one half of whom are adherents of Protestantism. The membership is three hundred and twenty. At the Easter communion of the jubilee year, seventy-six new members were received, and sixty more on probation. This church is self-supporting and contributes to the mission fund; it is well organized with elders, deacons, deaconesses, a Sabbath-school, Bible classes, and a missionary society. Its members are divided into classes under leaders. Of the deaconesses a report says, " Recently they chose six of the best women as deaconesses. Among these the church members are divided, so that each has her own charge. They help the weaker sisters, instruct the ignorant, guide them in their efforts to extend the kingdom of our Lord, and last but not least, they settle all quarrels among the women. A few Sabbaths ago four of the women came to the pastor saying, 'If you approve, we wish to go two and two to Tetrash and other near villages, to teach and help the women on Sabbath.' So they are going to scatter the light which freely they have received. The Kasha told many touching incidents and gave most earnest testimony to the value of these labors of the women. He said, 'Without their help I could not do the work in Geogtapa.'" Morning and evening prayers are conducted in the church. We visited it on Sunday morning. It was well filled— the women on one side, the men on the other, and children between, all sitting on the floor covered with rushmatting. The live, zealous pastor had invited a licentiate who startled us with the text: "It is not the custom in our country to give the younger before the elder." The men and women read from their Bibles and hymn books, scarcely conscious that it was a capability worthy of remark. The worship was orderly without formalism, in spirit and in truth. The old Nestorian responsive chant was retained and was quaint and pleasing. Their fervor in prayer, their enthusiasm in praise, their whole-souled earnestness in exhortation, thrilled the heart even of a stranger to whom the language was not intelligible. It shows us the perfected result of missionary work,—a church holding the pure gospel, and self-supporting, self-governing, self-propagating.

Lately a new church has been erected by the people and the relatives of former missionaries, under the supervision of Rev. F. G. Coan. It is faced with red brick, has a bell tower and bell, and being on a hill of the Fire-worshipers, is conspicuous for a considerable distance. Its erection without molestation shows the advancement of liberty under the present shah. Formerly a Nestorian church was erected in a certain village. It was built of stone, and was quite high. Some Persian ruler thought it looked too large and imposing compared with the mosques, so he ordered the people to tear it down or destroy its beauty. They plastered it over with mud.

At Geogtapa there is an orphanage connected with the Mission which cares for fifty or sixty boys and girls. It was begun after the famine and Kurdish raid of 1880. The department for girls was added after the orphanage at Seir, under charge of the Misses Goode and Morgan from England, was discontinued. The Geogtapa orphanage in charge of Deacon Khnan Eshu is a useful institution and is largely supported by funds from evangelical Christians in England, its special patron being Mr. Henry Tasker of Hants.

The old Nestorian church of Geogtapa, too, is largely permeated by the truth. Its priest is a man educated by the Mission who has church services in the modern tongue. One such village is a stimulus to hope in laboring for the unevangelized. Nor is it alone. Some other churches are not behind it. In many places the gospel light has spread, though others remain in as gross darkness as they were half a century ago. The leaven of righteousness has wrought in and through the plain, raising the Nestorians to a higher level. Ideas of pure and undefiled religion have been widely inculcated, so that the enemies of the truth, without desiring it, have been much enlightened. A spirit of sincere piety is manifested in the lives of not a few. Morals have been improved. Their consciences, deadened through centuries, have been awakened. Habits of truthfulness and faithfulness are being developed. Intemperance has received a check, Sabbath breaking has been restrained. Social purity is on as high a level as in our own land. The houses of the Christians with many additional comforts and a considerable increase in the amenities of life, deserve the name of homes, because there is love and confidence in the family; the wife is the companion, not the slave; the children, girls as well as boys, are educated and nurtured in the fear of God, and the altar of prayer renders up its morning and evening incense. The material, intellectual and spiritual condition of the people is much improved.

The successful organization and development of the Reformed Church is another result of the mission work. The first efforts of the missionaries were directed to the enkindling of new life in the Nestorian Church, to bringing about a reform from within. This purpose was not abandoned until after twenty years of effort. The difficulties were found to be insuperable. The Church Mission Society likewise endeavored to reform the Malabar Syrian Church, but after eighteen years of effort formed a separate organization. The effort to reform the Armenian Church also failed in Turkey. The Church Mission at Ispahan, too, organized separate Protestant churches. In forming a reformed or evangelical church from among the Nestorians no violent shock was given to their ecclesiastical life. The process of reform was gradual. There was no angry schism. Many of the Nestorians entered the reformed movement. Among these were a brother of the former patriarch, three of the bishops, seventy priests and a large number of deacons. Other bishops and priests have been friendly and the present patriarch is not hostile. One of his brothers lately communed with the Reformed Church. The first congregations were formed in 1855 with 158 members; a presbytery was organized in 1862. The system of government adopted is essentially Presbyterian, modified according to the circumstances of the people. A system, which approved itself, as scriptural and efficient, to most of the Reformed churches of the 16th century, need make no apology to ritualism for planting itself in Asia. The Evangelical Church of Persia joined the Pan-Presbyterian Alliance in 1890, at its session in London.

A Confession of Faith, Book of Discipline and Directory of Worship have been adopted and printed in Syriac. The individual church is ministered to by pastor, elders, and deacons. The deacons are ordained with power of preaching, but not of administering ordinances. If they are judged worthy, they are afterwards ordained to the full office of presbyter. The deacon may also represent the church in presbytery. There are four local knushyas or presbyteries, three on the plain and one on the mountains, all of which constitute a General Presbytery. It has under its charge 25 organized churches and 48 other congregations, 36 ordained ministers and 30 licentiates, with a communicant membership of 2300, and 6000 adherents.

Church work is carried on by three Boards. The Evangelistic Board has charge of the churches which are not self-supporting and of new mission work. The Educational Board superintends all schools and appoints the teachers. The Legal Board has supervision of the civil relations of the churches and their members to the Persian authorities and to each other. It aims to adjudicate suits and quarrels of church members that they may not go to law. It also strives to relieve from oppression and unrighteous exactions on the part of the owners and agents of the villages, or of the adherents of opposing faiths. It has a special agent who acts as attorney with the government. On each of these Boards of nine members, two missionaries are placed, and all matters pertaining to the work and its development are considered in their meetings, and by mutual counsel and due regard to the views of all, harmony and unity of action are attained. The chasm between the foreign and native ministry is thus avoided and the brethren led to feel that the work is their work and that they are responsible for its progress.

The yearly contributions in this Presbytery are about two thousand dollars for churches and schools, and three hundred dollars for missions. Four churches are self-supporting. No church is organized until it can bear one-fourth of its expenses. For church erection the congregations furnish one part and the missions two parts of the money. The liberality of individuals, in some instances, shows that they are learning the exercise of Christian benevolence. One man gave two hundred dollars and another three hundred dollars for the Gospel work. A carpenter bequeathed his house and lot as a parsonage and meeting room.

An interesting effort toward self-supporting missions was inaugurated by some brethren under the direction of Dr. Shedd. It was called the Persia Inner Mission. Its object was to send forth consecrated men, two by two, in a humble way, with scanty provision, and if possible on foot. For a few seasons the plan was successful, but later the Inner Mission has prosecuted its work, paying salaries and the expenses of journeys as had been done previously.

A marked characteristic of the work among the Nestorians has been the manifest presence of the Holy Spirit. All who are familiar with the early history of the Mission can recall many instances of the Spirit's presence and power. One of the subjects of the first spiritual awakening thus described it to Dr. Labaree:

"It was in this very room, your study now, that the blessed Stoddard called me to him at the close of that memorable Sabbath. We boys in his school had been unusually reckless in our conduct that day. I was a candidate for bishop's orders and a leader in hilarity. Calling me to him, he said, with a grieved look, and with sadness in his voice, yet in touching kindness,

'Bishop, how long will you thus harden yourself against God?' As he went on, my heart was moved as never before. He prayed with me, and I went out in a state of mind wholly new to me. Others were talked with that same evening. We had no knowledge at that time of what conversion was, or of the power of the Holy Ghost. That night we gave ourselves to prayer, and could not sleep. A conviction of sin we had never before felt filled our souls and drove away sleep. Then it was that we learned of the Holy Spirit's effectual working."

From that time the history of the mission has been one of blessed revivals. These have been specially manifested in connection with the Week of Prayer, called "the spiritual week." This first report after the transfer of this work from the American Board shows a continuation of the previous history. It says: "In Degala a very searching and thorough work of grace has been enjoyed. There are more than twenty conversions. These embrace mostly the aged and middle-aged of the congregation. It was a touching sight when an aged father, his son in middle life, a younger son and two daughters arose, one after another to express their hope of forgiveness. Several husbands, with their wives, were seen presenting their vows to Christ. Reformation from sin, especially from drunkenness, and the duties of giving and working for Christ were strongly enforced." The genuineness of the work was proved by the fact that the church became self-supporting and contributed increasingly year by year to evangelize other villages.

In the same year Mar Yosef, a young bishop, who was pastor at Hassan, in the mountains, gave an account of a spiritual quickening. "The first two days of the Week of Prayer we spent in fasting and special prayer. I believe that God, for the sake of his dear Son, heard our voice, for we are witnessing an awakening beyond our faith and expectation—hard hearts melted, the tears of sinners and the joy of converts. Not only in the place of meeting, but through the village, is heard the voice of prayer and weeping in many houses until the morning. Another surprising thing is the rising of persons in the congregation, confessing their sins, revealing secret faults, acknowledging thefts, and while asking pardon, offering restitution. One young man gave his dagger to the gospel treasury, being unable to discover the owner of an article he had stolen long ago. About twenty persons are beginning a new life. About one hundred and fifty persons assemble every night and the place cannot hold them. Some sit in the doorway and some outside in the cold."

In 1876, Presbytery met in the last of December, at the college, and was closed with the communion. A sunrise prayer meeting was appointed for the next morning. At it the college boys spoke one after another showing that the Holy Spirit was working with them. One said, "I had heard all the discussions but none of them had any effect on my hard heart. Not until I looked upon the broken bread and poured out wine, was my heart touched. Then it appeared that it was my sins that caused the agony of Jesus, and I had no rest last night thinking about it; and I want to confess my sins here; and you, dear friends, when you come to the foot of the cross of Christ to plead for sinners, remember me there, that I may be saved." Many others confessed their sins and asked to be remembered in prayer. They continued the meeting with unabated interest for six hours, forgetting that they had not eaten bread, and so solemn that there was scarcely a dry eye in the house. It was the beginning of a good work in the Week of Prayer that followed, which resulted in the addition of two hundred and forty-one to the church, an increase of thirty per cent.

I cannot tell of all the manifestations of God's blessing in succeeding years. It is better that I give some details of a few, than the outlines of all. In 1886, following the Week of Prayer, there was an awakening in seventeen congregations and the total of inquirers was over five hundred. The reports say,* "The work was conducted almost wholly by native pastors, and a special blessing accompanied the labor of two evangelists. Wherever they went, the Spirit of the Lord seemed present in peculiar power. The churches were too small to accommodate the crowds. The converts

* Letters of Dr. and Mrs. Labaree.

were of all ages, many being men in middle life."

"Two old women were among the candidates in Degala. Their examination was conducted in the presence of the whole church. It is so difficult for aged women to give up their superstitious faith in the fasts which they have rigidly observed from their childhood, that many questions were asked on this point. The replies came heartily and promptly, 'My fasts are of no value (*that is for atonement*). Christ has forgiven my *sins*. *Blessed be his name.*' 'Nothing but Christ; he is my only hope of salvation.' There was a woman in Takka of whom it has been said, 'There is no bad thing that this woman has not done.' Violent, abusive and often drunk, no one dared approach her with an invitation to church. More than once planting herself in the street, she found amusement in reviling, striking, and spitting upon those who were going to meeting. Curiosity brought her to one of the services. Her heart was touched on the spot. She confessed her wicked life and with tears besought the prayers of those present. She seemed to leave the room a changed woman, was constant in her attendance at the place of prayer and active in inviting others to come."

"The scenes in the Dizza Takka church were of peculiar interest. They had recently completed a new church edifice. There were those in the church who fervently desired it should be consecrated by the descent of the Holy Spirit upon its assembled people. A misunderstanding between them and their former pastor, now aged and retired, threatening the alienation of some, was happily removed. The congregation rapidly increased. The daily services of the Week of Prayer were soon crowded, beginning with the early morning prayer meeting before sunrise, until that held late in the evening. The benches, which as a novelty they had introduced at no little expense to themselves, would not hold the audiences, and mats were spread in the aisles and about the pulpit for the children of the schools. The intervals between the services were spent by the church members in visiting from house to house. Backsliders began to be reclaimed. Most humble confessions were heard in the public meetings. One who had wandered farthest (the chief occasion of offense to the former pastor), an unusually intelligent and influential man, made a clean breast of his past misdoings, which called out the son of the old pastor in prompt and hearty response, 'Thank you, Tarriwerdi; that is what we have waited to hear from your lips these several years. We are satisfied. God bless you!' An older brother of one of the officers of the church, who has almost never darkened its doors—a notoriously hard drinker—was, as by accident, brought into the meeting one day. A dream, a few nights after, intensified the impression made upon him by the truth at that service, and he became a regular attendant, gave his heart to the Lord, broke off from his cups and devoted himself to bringing in others to the meetings. As he could not read, he took with him in his visits to his neighbors one of the schoolboys, to read some portion of the Scripture to reinforce his invitations to the house of prayer. Another hard-drinking character, who confessed much habitual dishonesty in his past life, was the means of bringing in several of his former companions in evil. A similar instance occurred in a neighboring village. A young man who had been a scoffer and drunkard was led to surrender himself to the Saviour, and went immediately to work to win his associates to an honest life and to the Lord. His faith was remarkable, and his repeated success proved the blessing of the Lord upon him. So devoted was he to his new work, that his pastor felt constrained to remonstrate with him as neglecting his occupation. His old mother, from other motives, tried to work upon his former superstitious beliefs; but all dissuasions proved of no avail. He replied, in substance: 'The zeal of the Lord's house consumes me.' His case became notorious in the villages around.

"It was a noticeable feature that the children were much interested, and in some places took a part in deepening the religious impression. In Degala a company of children went from house to house singing hymns, reading from the Bible and offering prayer. Many of the old people were much moved to see how God had, out of the mouths of babes and sucklings, ordained praise. Our bookbinder told me that at one of the meetings in this same village, when opportunity was given for voluntary prayers, as all heads were bowed, he was thrilled to hear the voice of his own little son, seven years and three months old, leading off in clear, firm voice, quite moving the hearts of the congregation by his simple, appropriate petition.

"In Gulpashan as in all the villages, extra meetings were continued through several weeks, and, later on, one whole week was set apart for special services, with aid from other pastors. A system of regular visitation among all the families of the village was set on foot, and at the end of the winter all but three of the houses, those of the papal priest and his immediate relatives, had received one or more visits from companies of the brethren. Among the hopeful converts in this village were four or five intelligent young men, who had fallen into habits of convivial drinking. Another case was that of a husband of one of the church members, a sister of great zeal and fidelity, himself a papist and a hard drinker. He has now come out very decidedly on the side of his wife and shows unusually clear views of Christ and his work."

Of the meetings conducted by her in this village Mrs. Shedd writes: "After I dismissed the women not one arose to go. I said, 'If there is any one who wishes to speak or pray we will wait.' Several more with tears confessed their desire to find Christ, and others poured out their full hearts in prayer. They still sat and some said, 'We will stay until midnight if you will talk to us.' An Armenian bride expressed her hope that she had found the Saviour, and her earnest desire to learn to read his word and work for him. Several young girls, with emotion, told how they, too, were happy in a new-found hope in Jesus. The bell for evening service found us still there. An old woman told how she had felt the burden of sin when she was a girl and could not find rest; when she grew older she sought relief by visiting the shrines of the saints, going up into the mountain to a famous church, feeling that if there she found no rest from her burden of guilt she must die. But pilgrimages were all in vain. Then she sought the Roman Catholics and, joining them, hoped to find the rest her spirit craved. In vain; she saw no peace there. One day she heard a deacon of the Evangelical Church talking with some men. He quoted a verse of Scripture which went to her soul like an arrow. She heard of Jesus and peace filled her heart. She has helped many others into the kingdom though she cannot read a word.

"In Ada, their congregations were so large that, although the fifty school children were excluded from the service and sent to another room where a special meeting was held for children, still many went away because there was no room.

"In Abdoolah Kandi the women baked bread a week in advance, to be ready to attend all the meetings when the evangelists should come there.

"In Superghan the congregations numbered four hundred, and *nearly all were women and young people.*

Many men are away in Russia, begging, and wasting what they gather, in riotous living. When invited to remain at inquiry meeting, after the sermon, only one woman went out. They were so anxious to hear that they wanted to sit there all night, and only the weariness of the preachers brought the meeting to a close.

"In Sherabad the whole village collected in the church to listen to the preacher, so that a wedding was left with but four guests to dance to the sound of the fife and drum, an almost irresistible temptation to the people here."

The additions to the churches of Urumia aggregated two hundred and eighty-six, a number greater than in any previous year.

An interesting work began in 1890 among the young laymen. They formed a Young Men's Band for the greater development of Christian zeal and labor. With some tendency to adopt false ideas of perfection and to censoriousness, they yet were earnest and consecrated. The leader of the band was Rabi Oshana, a man remarkable for his zeal and piety. One of their number was chosen evangelist and his salary paid by the band. Several others traveled from village to village preaching the gospel, and were successful in winning souls. "The fact that young men without special education could preach so effectively and would leave lucrative employments and give up the greater part of their time to preaching Christ, attracted much attention, the more so in this land, where the people are so slow to believe one disinterested in Christian labor."

Through the influence of this band and special services conducted by Mr. Coan and Mr. St. Pierre, the winters of 1890 and 1891 witnessed precious revivals. In Ardashai where the church was lifeless and had fallen in membership, it was restored, and sealed its new consecration by raising funds for a new church building. In Gulpashan the power of the Spirit was manifested as never before. One night " it seemed as if we could see the Holy Spirit going from one person to another, pleading for admittance." Many decided to repent, even some who but an hour before had resisted. In all sixty persons professed conversion.

In the following year, as Dr. Labaree reports, " about twenty churches and congregations were blessed with revivals; many of them those that had been visited the winter before. Among these was the large church of Degala. The pastor, in faith that a second blessing was in store for them, had appointed a 'spiritual week.' Much preparation for it had been made in preaching and in house-to-house visitation by the pastor and zealous members of his flock. The young men were especially active, ready volunteers for any service. The attendance increased until the church was full. The preaching deepened in solemnity and impressiveness. Night after night there were new cases of interest. Nearly sixty publicly declared themselves on the Lord's side. . . . "

"The church of Gulpashan is another of our larger self-supporting, thrifty congregations. One of its deacons is probably the wealthiest man in the Nestorian nation; which means that he may be worth, at a guess, from eight to ten thousand dollars. He is a man of sterling integrity, liberal-handed, highly intelligent for his opportunities. And yet he is a man of exceptional modesty for an Oriental. He would be an honor to any church in any land.

"A sad division had occurred in this church. No efforts to reconcile the feud had succeeded. Yet before the season had passed the young pastor had appointed a "spiritual week." His brother ministers were amazed at his audacity, or his faith. The result more than equaled his expectations. The Spirit of the Most High came down upon the congregation, melted their hearts into unity, and brought some fifty or sixty from outside of the church to confess their faith in Jesus. In one of their meetings there came a Catholic Nestorian woman to find an opportunity to pour into the ears of the session her grievances against a church member. As she sat and listened to the word preached she was filled with wholly new views of the Saviour and a new sense of her own sinfulness. She went home rejoicing in Christ, forgetting altogether her grievance against her neighbor. No persuasions of her papal relatives could move her from everywhere publishing what Jesus had done for her soul.

"Ada is another place which has enjoyed a twofold blessing in these successive years. The opposition from the Nestorian bishop and his party has been intense here. Nevertheless, the church was well filled. The interest in the preaching of Bible truth is one of the significant features of these times. A large body of the Old Church women in Ada went to their priests urging them to invite Mr. Coan to preach in the Old Church. Failing of their purpose, they came to the Reformed Church service time after time. It was here that the labors of our Bible woman, Layah, made such an impression that the women took her to their Old Church two successive afternoons to talk to them from the Bible; and the church was filled with eager listeners. Even the Catholic women took her to their church in the hope that she might be allowed to address them there; but they were thwarted by their priest. In several other villages she so won the hearts of the women that they have almost taken her by force to their church. In one instance when a large company were thus assembled, the sexton heard what was going on and came in a towering rage to drive out the heretic woman, declaring it would take the services of several bishops to re-sanctify the profaned building. With curses and revilings, and the free use of his cudgel he attempted to drive out the crowd. But in the darkness of the church and in the blindness of his anger it happened that the Bible woman and a few other women were left behind. When quietly left by themselves the women begged Layah to go on with her talk. First, said she, let us pray for those who oppose the truth. Tenderly she prayed for the old sexton, that he might be forgiven his evil language. When she was through the women broke out, 'We do believe that you are the true Christians. You have prayed for this man who abused you; had it been us he thus cursed, we should have paid him back in his own coin.'"

Educational work among the Nestorians has been highly successful and beneficial. Great progress has been made since the first boys' school was begun in 1836 with seven pupils and the girls' school in 1838 with four. Then only one Nestorian woman, the sister of the patriarch and a few score of men, could read intelligently. Now our mission has among them one hundred village schools, four high schools, Fiske Seminary and a college in all of which there are 2,350 pupils. One-half of the expense of the common schools is from the people. The race and its whole environment has been improved by these schools.

The college was established in 1879 as successor to the male seminary which had been at Seir since 1846. The old institution had among its instructors such honored names as Perkins, Stoddard, Stocking, Rhea, and Cochran. It has had even more prosperous development through the untiring energy and intellectual and spiritual power of Rev. Dr. Shedd, president of the college.

A garden of seventeen acres, two miles west of the

city, was purchased and five acres of it inclosed with a high wall and watch towers. This gave the institution security in the Kurdish raid. Roughs at times have attacked the gates, but have been unable to effect an entrance. The garden is cultivated by the pupils and an income equivalent to the interest of the purchase money is derived from it.

The enclosure is divided into four plots by avenues lined with tall sycamores, along which streams of water flow continuously. Two of these plots are devoted to the Westminster Hospital, including also the woman's annex, the dispensary, and residences for the physicians. The college consists of a main building, a dormitory, industrial workshops, and residences for two missionaries and three professors. The main building, besides recitation, sleeping, and dining rooms, has a chapel, laboratory, a library of 3,500 volumes, chiefly in Syriac and English, with 200 ancient Syriac manuscripts and the beginning of an archaeological museum.

The college in 1893 consisted of 10 teachers and 173 students. These were divided into departments as follows: Preparatory 64, Industrial 10, College regular 65, irregular 10, Theological 18, and Medical 6. They were from Persia and five districts in Turkey, and from both Evangelical and Nestorian communities. The rugged mountaineers with their unique costume give a romantic air to a group of college students. Priests of the Nestorian Church and even members of the patriarchal family have attended the classes. Two hundred and sixty have been graduated from the college of whom one hundred and sixty have been of use in the mission work as teachers, colporteurs and preachers.

The terms of study are arranged so that the students may engage in teaching and evangelizing during the winter months. The degree of self-support is encouraging. An endowment has been started with five thousand dollars from the estate of Henry Marquand of New York. A gentleman in Philadelphia supports the institution with an annual gift of two thousand dollars.

The curriculum consists of Ancient Syriac, Azerbaijan and Osmanli Turkish, Persian, English, essays and elocution, algebra, geometry, history, ethics, psychology, and elements of physics, of astronomy, and of chemistry. The Bible is taught in the entire course. The theological course differs from that in America by omitting Greek and generally Hebrew. Mrs. Bishop criticises the course as higher than is desirable. On the other hand ambitious students after completing it, go to America, "to get an education to fit them for laboring among their people."

The Industrial Department was first started in 1887 with carpentry, hat-making and shoemaking. Because Mohammedans would not so readily purchase hats and shoes manufactured by Christians, blacksmithing was substituted for these. The workshop is not yet fully outfitted. Mr. E. T. Allen, of Canada, a trained mechanic, has charge of it. Its object is to train the boys to self-support, to prevent their dependence on the mission or their becoming beggars in other countries. Eshia, a brother of Mar Shimun, visited it and said, "This is what our people want; this is necessary to raise up our nation."

The religious life of the students is good. Most of them are men of faith and prayer. In the basement is a series of prayer-closets where the students may retire for devotion. An active Young Men's Christian Association is in operation. They were much benefited by the visit of Messrs. L. D. Wishard and Wm. H. Grant, in 1890, on their World Tour of Missions.

Commencements have been attended frequently by governors and other officials and the work highly commended. In 1890, the crown prince and his suite honored it with their presence and inspection. Of the character of its graduates an official remarked, " I say in all honesty that I find no such trustworthy men as those whom you have trained."

The alumni meeting has become a useful and popular institution. It appointed standing committees on the temporal, intellectual, and spiritual condition of the people, and their reports and the addresses and contributions of the alumni are helpful to the advancement of the race. The alumni dinner, with broth and bread, and the toasts drunk with steaming tea, is enjoyed, and the feast of reason and the flow of soul are as abundant as in *more civilized* lands where the champagne or beer flows freely on such occasions.* Institutes are also held for the development of the teachers.

The female seminary has a blessed history, known to the readers of "Woman and her Saviour in Persia," and "Faith working by Love." Founded by Mrs. Dr. Grant, it had for a long period as its principal Miss Fidelia Fiske, whose memory is yet fragrant in the hearts of many. In 1888, a new building was erected, and the name "Fiske Seminary" was given. Up to 1890, twenty classes with one hundred and sixty-six members had been graduated. Of these, one hundred and twenty-seven were then living, and eighty-two were present at the reunion. Miss N. J. Dean, after twenty-four years devoted to the seminary, retired in 1892. Miss Medbery and Miss Russell report an attendance in 1894 of one hundred and ninety-three of whom fifty-seven were in the regular course. The kindergarten, lately opened, is a success. A pastor referring to it said, "I have known the school for twenty-five years; I have seen children hired to go to school and whipped to go; but never before did I see them cry and leave their unfinished breakfast for fear of being late."

---

* The "boys" sometimes tell tales of the old times. The following will be appreciated in both hemispheres. The melons were mysteriously disappearing from the yard. Dr. Perkins laid a scheme to discover the culprit. Soon a boy came to him in great distress, sure that he was about to die. "You have eaten the melons," said Dr. Perkins. He had put tartar-emetic in some of them.

The influence of the seminary has been deep and wide-spread. The homes of its graduates are distinguishable by their neatness and signs of culture. They are centers of gospel influence wherever found. The girls have gone forth as light-bearers into the dark villages and into the mountains. I will cite some instances of this. "Gozel from the mountains was one of the wildest and rudest specimens, who gave as much trouble as an unruly colt, and whom we never credited with much religious feeling. She was found gathering her illiterate neighbors together every afternoon and expounding to them the Scriptures.

"Thirty or forty years ago, a girl from Tiary, named Nazi, was under instruction for a short time. We hear of her holding to her faith in the midst of gross darkness. Through all these years she has braved the ridicule of those who scoff at a woman who can read. Taking her Bible with her to the sheepfolds, she never suffers a day to pass without reading it. All bear witness to her quiet and gentle spirit.

"Men from the vicinity of Van have told of a woman, who is unlike any that they know, a Bible reader of consistent life, enduring the bitter hostility of those about her. This is Nazlu, long lost sight of, who went out from Miss Rice's teaching nearly thirty years ago. She has been the means of converting her husband and a woman in the village. She walked five miles to meet a missionary and though her feet were blistered, she said, 'The tiredness all went out of me when I saw you.' She further said, 'I have forgotten all I knew of geography and arithmetic, but I have not forgotten my Bible.'

"Selby of Marbeshu—now gray-haired and widowed—was one of the three received by Miss Fiske in her first class.* When Selby first went to Marbeshu, she was the only woman reader in the village. Now there are nine readers in her family, besides others, most of whom have been led to learn through her influence. In early years, none of the villagers would listen when she attempted to read the Bible. Now commonly from ten to thirty women assemble to hear her as she goes from house to house, and not infrequently the father and brother will quietly sit among them. Though, unemployed by the mission, and having family cares, she does much for the enlightenment of Marbeshu."—(Mrs. Labaree in "Woman's Work.")

Another of the early graduates, who has had a long and useful life, is Moressa, the wife of Pastor Yacob, an eminent worker. She was converted during the great revival of 1845-7 and after the death of her father, Malek David, was taken by Mrs. Stocking into her family and received a careful Christian training as well as a good English education. She several times visited England and advocated the cause of her people even before the queen. She presented the cause of the famine sufferers in 1878-80 so as to effectually move

---

* Woman and her Saviour in Persia, pp. 51 and 240.

the benevolent sympathies of British Christians. After her death in 1892, Rabi Sarah wrote of her as follows: "Our sister Moressa was noble in person, character, and behavior. Among the fifty girls of our school she was quite unique in respect of natural gifts. She did not care to mix herself up with the affairs of the other girls, so that they thought her somewhat proud and reserved. But she was softened and improved by grace; took on her neck the yoke of Christ; loved her school companions, and sought the salvation of those who might be called her inferiors. Throughout her life she was famous for her great love and care in winning souls to Christ. For twenty-seven years she labored with her husband in Superghan, where his pastoral charge was situated. Of late years they devoted themselves to special evangelistic work, supported by the Turkish Mission Aid Society of England, which has assisted in so many ways the work of evangelization in Bible lands."

The printing press was early established in Urumia as an agency for enlightening the people. Mr. Edward Breath, a printer, arrived in 1839 with a portable press and a font of Syro-Chaldaic type from London. It excited great curiosity among both Nestorians and Mohammedans. In 1841 Mr. Haman Hallock, the missionary printer at Malta and Smyrna had a font of Syriac type cut in America. Three years later, Mr. Breath had cut and prepared two sets of type which were pronounced perfect, and the most beautiful in existence. They have been adopted and reproduced by Oriental publishers in Europe. The Lord's Prayer was the first thing published. During the first year 510,000 pages were printed. Up to 1873, 110,000 volumes, making 21,250,000 pages were printed. From 1883 to 1892 inclusive, 7,732,428 pages were printed. In 1880 a font of Persian type was added.

A newspaper started in 1848, called the Rays of Light, has shed abroad much enlightenment. It is the oldest newspaper in Persia. In 1893, according to reports, the Catholic bishop desired permission to print a newspaper. The shah's government refused. He complained that the Americans were printing one. The government professed ignorance of its existence and ordered its suspension. Representations of its character and purpose procured the royal authorization, after several months' delay, with the command not to refer to Islam or the State.

From 1882 to 1886 Mr. Arthur A. Hargrave had charge of the press, but during most of the last two decades Dr. Labaree has had supervision of it. In 1892 a new building for press and bindery was erected.

The following is a list of its publications: Pilgrim's Progress, Baxter's Saints' Rest and Reformed Pastor, Doddridge's Rise and Progress, The Dairyman's Daughter, The Shepherd of Salisbury Plain, Young Cottager, Church History, Hymn Book (several editions), Westminster Shorter Catechism, Schaff's Catechism, Call to the Unconverted, Annotated New

Testament, Commentary on Matthew, on Daniel, Question Book on the Acts, Confession of Faith, Form of Government, Rules of Synod, Sabbath-School Lesson Helps, Scripture Geography and History, Lectures on Theology, Memorial of Rev. Samuel A. Rhea, Spurgeon's Morning by Morning, John Plowman's Talk, Green Pastures, The Signet Ring, The Night of Toil, The Christian's Secret of a Happy Life, Like Christ (Murray), Best Things and Wonders of Nature (Newton), Wayland's Moral Science, Rollo's Code of Morals, Tracts, Selections from the Rays of Light, Syriac Primer, Speller, Readers, Geography, Arithmetic, Mental Arithmetic, Algebra, Grammars Ancient and Modern, Outlines of History, Simple Science, Physiology, Elements of Physics, and of Astronomy, Persian Hymn Book, and Tracts, Turkish "That Sweet Story of Old."

CHAPTER IV.

MOSUL AND THE MOUNTAINS—THE MISSION TO THE NESTORIANS.

THE evangelization of the Mountain-Nestorians was begun by Dr. Asahel Grant. He lived for a time at Ashitha on the western side of the mountains. In 1839 he visited Mosul. While ministering to the fugitive Nestorians who were suffering from an epidemic of typhus, he was stricken down. Messrs. Hinsdale and Mitchell and their families formally occupied Mosul, June, 1841, and began the Eastern Syria Mission. Five of the seven missionaries died in a short time. The station was interrupted until the arrival in 1850-52 of Messrs. Marsh and Williams, and Dr. Lobdell. A church was organized in 1851. Dr. Lobdell, a man of marked promise as a scientist and physician, lived but a few years. The climate was exceedingly hot. For eighty days the thermometer ranged from 100°, to 114°. In 1853 for a hundred days at 2 p. m. it never fell below 98°. In October in Mosul the mercury was 18° higher than at Seir, Urumia, in August. Owing to this adverse climate, the Eastern Syria Mission was merged into the Eastern Turkey Mission, in 1860, and Mosul was occupied by a mission.

ary from Mardin during the cool part of the year, who directed his efforts chiefly to the Arabic-speaking population.

Meanwhile efforts were made from Urumia to reach the Syriac-speaking people of the mountains. Evangelists and teachers were maintained in the villages, and tours were made by missionaries and colporteurs. Some missionaries took up residence in the mountains. Rev. S. A. Rhea lived in Gawar several winters, and passed a large part of his time in the mountains from 1852 to 1859. Of late years passport restrictions, school-regulations, confiscation of books, interception of mails, expulsion of teachers and preachers, and the disturbed state of the country have made proper superintendence of the work from Urumia more and more difficult. The presence of the Catholic missionaries at Mosul, and of the Anglicans at Kochanes indicated the step necessary for the cause of evangelical truth. Hence Rev. and Mrs. E. W. McDowell were transferred from Urumia, and, with Dr. J. G. Wishard, were appointed to open a station for the mountains. Mosul was decided upon as the place of residence. Rev. and Mrs. J. A. Ainsley, and the Arabic work under charge of Mardin were transferred from the American Board in 1892. Miss Anna Melton from Urumia and Miss Lilian D. Reinhart (1894), began a boarding-school for mountain girls. It is hoped that greater precautions, better residence, and spending the hot season among the Mountain-Nestorians may preserve the health of the missionaries. As a foundation for future work, there are now six churches with two hundred and forty-six communicants and four hundred and seventy-four Sabbath-school scholars, and a native agency of five ordained and nine unordained preachers.

The physical characteristics of these mountains are such as to render evangelization extremely difficult. The roads are very primitive; the rocky ways along precipitous gorges and the arduous passes make travel dangerous. For a number of months during the winter, snow takes possession of the country, so that the evangelist is held a prisoner in a narrow valley, often confined to a single village, and his work checked.

Wild by nature, they are inhabited by wild men. The Kurds are in constant disturbance from tribal feuds and the jealousies and rivalry of Sheikhs and Begs. Among these the free tribes of Nestorians are able partially to maintain their rights by the use of the same weapons. Defended by the natural walls of their deep valleys, and almost equal in wildness to their perpetual enemies the Kurds, they are ready, with equal courage, for robbery, bloodshed, or reprisals on their foes. The Nestorians, who are under Kurdish control, suffer many oppressions and their condition is such as to call forth sympathy. Sometimes their flocks are all stolen and they are driven out homeless and destitute. In 1893, twenty-five families came down in a body to the plain of Urumia. They were described as having all their possessions on their backs, clothed in dirty rags, the original color of which could not be distinguished, their hair matted and disheveled, as if it had never been combed.

The ignorance of these Mountain-Nestorians is extreme. A woman entered a teacher's house and said, "I have suffered much this night in a dream, and must kiss your clock." She kissed it repeatedly and said, to it, "I am your sacrifice." She was asked, "Why have you faith in that thing?" She replied, "Why should I not have? It goes of itself." After much explanation she said, "Don't remember it against me, I am as ignorant as a brute." Yet they have a thirst for knowledge. Some of the girls walk fifty or a hundred miles to enter the school. Their opportunities are very limited. A boy was reading his book upside down. Dr. Wishard asked him why he did so. He replied: "There was only one book in our village and when placed on the floor, the son of the melek had the best place in front, those of lesser rank at the sides, and I had to read from the top." Having learned in that way he wished to continue to do so.

The lawlessness of the region brings the missionaries into considerable personal danger. Sometimes attacks are made upon them by the Nestorians. Mr. McDowell gives a graphic account of an attack on him and Dr. Wishard in 1889. "While passing through Tkhom we were robbed by some Nestorians. It was done in daylight and in the very streets of Gundikta, all the people looking on. Our lives were threatened and all our goods taken except some effects. We went on to Muzrai, a village in which we have a church and quite a strong following and which is only fifteen minutes from Gundikta. They were rushing after their guns and reinforcements to make war. We quieted them and returned to the robbers, endeavoring to recover Dr. Wishard's papers, which were very valuable. One of the men promised to return what he had taken, and did so when a gift was made. This was the doctor's trunk containing his papers. Marcus, who had been our scholar in Urumia, had taken some things to keep them out of the hands of others. He restored them without pay, and rendered us valuable service, probably saving our lives. But the rest would listen to no threats or compromise. We returned to Muzrai, and summoned the chiefs of the valley from a lower village, and laid upon them the work of receiving our goods. Late in the afternoon, hearing they were accomplishing nothing, we went up and found them and our robbers and the village priests, all drunk. We could accomplish nothing with them, but recovered a few insignificant things from individuals. That night we sent all our remaining valuables over the mountains to Boz, and concluded to proceed empty, believing there was no danger to our lives.

"We were scarcely in the village when we were seized. One boy rushed at us furiously with drawn dagger, but was held back by Marcus. We were taken to the churchyard and were finally led along the road by a few men who were anxious to divide all the spoils among themselves. There were two parties which we were able to play off against each other. For two hours they followed us or carried us along, alternately fighting among themselves or demanding money of us. Finally the minority party, which the others had been endeavoring to drive back, began to stone us, whereupon our self-constituted protectors turned upon us, knocked Dr. Wishard down and tore off some of his clothes and searched him for money. I was subjected to the same process, only more gently. They found nothing. One of the party acted like a madman, and, no doubt, had he not been restrained, would have killed us. They were still unsatisfied and followed us, their number being increased by the way. At each fresh increase a new suggestion would be made as to the whereabouts of our money, and again they would search us, finally partially stripping us. However, at my suggestion, they returned our clothes excepting half of the doctor's vest.

"We finally got away. We had rather a cool ride over the snow of the high mountain pass, as it was raining; but by using old carpet or horse-blankets belonging to our muleteers, we kept tolerably dry and warm. In Boz we secured the valuables sent by us and the things brought through by the Muzrai men, which had been returned. They had to fight their way through, the young fellow who had tried to kill us receiving a severe cut in the head in the fray."

More frequently the dangers come from the Kurds. Dr. Wishard writes: "It is not unusual for our preachers to be attacked by robbers. One from Tkhoma was attacked and stabbed in a number of places. He would have died, I doubt not, except for the skillful attention of Dr. Cochran and the benefits of the hospital. In 1890 Mr. Coan and I were stopping in Hassan. Pastor Yohannan, hearing that we were there, joined a party of three or four Nestorians and came over to see us. On the way a band of Kurds suddenly came down upon them, took their animals, stripped them of their clothing, gave them a dreadful beating, gagged them, threw them into a dense thicket of underbrush, and went off and left them. One succeeded in freeing himself (all were bound hand and foot), and after a time was able to find his companions, the robbers having carried them in different directions before leaving them. The day was very hot; the remainder of the journey (fifteen miles) had to be made with bare feet, and they reached our tent late in the night in a sad plight. They never succeeded in getting any of their property returned nor the men punished, although I think the government would gladly have punished them, had they been able to capture them.

"Last summer (1891), Mr. McDowell with his family and Miss Melton and myself, were out at Hassan (one hundred miles northwest from Mosul) for the summer. The village is some distance from any Turkish government center, and is under the control of a powerful

Kurdish sheikh, who oppressed the people dreadfully, often requiring them to give up their clothing and bedding.

"The chief had been, previous to this time, an excellent friend of ours, but he soon saw that our being there would be in the way of several of his wicked schemes; so he sent us notice that unless we left within three days he would come down upon us with four hundred armed horsemen, destroy our property and put us out of the region. We paid no attention to his threats until he sent his messenger to us the "third and last time," when we wrote him a letter telling him we had legal rights in the country and since he had made the threats, he would be held responsible by our government for any harm that came to us, and that under no consideration would we leave until we were ready.

"The chief lived in a castle high up in the mountain, about eight hours from Hassan, in a village of twenty chiefs, he being the leader of them all.

"We sent a messenger to him with the letter and awaited anxiously the reply, feeling it was a crisis in our work, and that unless we were able to assert our rights and hold the ground, our work in all the region must suffer; for, in all probability, if we were expelled our helpers would soon follow. When our messenger gave him the letter, he read it and with an oath stamped it on the ground, saying that in three days we would be out of there; that he had four hundred men ready to come down upon us, etc., etc. Our messenger returned late in the evening and gave his report (he was so frightened he was confined to his bed for two days), and after a 'council of war' it was decided that Mr. McDowell, with the ladies and children, should spend the night inside the village, and I with some trusty men should look after the tents. We placed men on all roads leading into the village to give the alarm in case they heard the chief coming. This was on Saturday night, and the same precaution was taken by us on the two following nights. They were days and nights of great suspense to us, for we well knew the chief to be a man of almost unlimited resources and cruel enough to do anything. By Tuesday morning, the fourth day, matters had reached a point where we almost wished he would make his attack—anything to relieve the dreadful suspense—and you can imagine the pleasure we took in a letter that arrived from him that morning, saying that he had misjudged us; that he wanted our friendship to continue;—in fact, his 'love for us had never ceased!' Later he sent word that he would pay us a formal visit, that the people of the region might know he was our 'friend and protector.' We heard that the reason of this sudden change of attitude toward us was due to his belief that we had some great power behind us that he knew not of, or we would have run away when his messenger first came to us. It is wonderful how God's promises uphold one at such times, and in this respect we did have a Power 'that he knew not of.' There is no doubt that he intended to come down upon us; that his warriors were anxious to come; and yet, by an unseen hand, we were safely kept. It was wonderful, too, what courage was shown by the ladies during the summer, for the country was filled with robbers and highwaymen that often came into the village."

In 1893 Mr. and Mrs. McDowell and Miss Melton took up their summer work at Amadia, a famous old Kurdish fortress, five days north of Mosul. Miss Melton accompanied by Pastor Zachariah, and his sister went to the village of Daree. Her tent was pitched on a roof. On the same and neighboring roofs, a number of families and two men with guns were sleeping on the night of June 14th. Miss Melton writes: "I was awakened by what I thought was some one hammering on the shackles on the mule's feet. I rose up and listened, but hearing some one walking in the direction of where the guard should be, concluded it was he and lay down without suspicion. I was again awakened by some one fumbling at the saddle-bags. Supposing it to be the girl, I said, 'Is that you, Baharee?' Then the figure rose up and I saw it was a man, but, from general appearance as I saw him in the dim light, I thought it was the guard, and I said, 'Mar Yacob, what are you doing here? what do you want?' He started toward the bed. I cried out, 'Mar Yacob, don't come here!' He had a large walking-stick, such as are in common use here, and began striking at me. The blows were warded off by a frame I have over my bed for supporting a mosquito-net. At the first attack I began screaming and calling for Kasha, the pastor. The man broke the frame from the bed, and with one of the sticks, one and a quarter inches square, with beveled corners, commenced beating me over the head. I was tangled in the net and helpless, but freed myself, and, I don't know how it was, but grabbing the stick I wrenched it from him with ease. He immediately took hold of me with his hands and it seemed to me he was Satan himself, and, with more than natural force, I loosened his grasp and held his hands so that he could do nothing. It was only for a moment, for, with an oath, he flung me across the tent. In the meantime guns had been fired on the mountain above the village. The first man was picking up things to carry out, and striking me at long range.

"I went outside the tent where I found Baharee beating her head and wailing, 'O, why have they poured ashes on our heads?' She had been waked by some one choking her and telling her to keep still. I asked 'Where is the pastor?' 'O, when you first cried, he threw himself over the wall and fled; and Mar Yacob has fled; and the whole village has fled; and we are alone.' I had before this felt terrified as if in some horrible nightmare, in which, if I could only hold on till some one could hear and come, I would be saved; but now to know that I, with this girl, was left alone in the hands of these men gave me such a feeling of despair as I can never describe. Baharee began begging for mercy of the man, in Koordish. The first man, carrying out my bedding, stepped toward me and gave me a terrible stroke across the abdomen with the head of his cane. In doing this he slipped and fell off the roof, and then for some reason, we knew not why, they went away. They seem to have taken only those things they had in hand at the time, viz.: a bed-quilt, a native lantern in box, a tin box of candles, and an empty *hourj*. The contents of the tent had been carried outside. Why they did not take them is a mystery.

"As soon as they had gone, Baharee began beating her head and wailing, 'O, you are killed; you are killed!' I looked and saw I was covered with blood and felt it running down from my head. She then called out, 'Come back, the robbers have gone, they have killed Khanum, O, come back.' The charm words 'the robbers have gone' brought the household back. I bound up my head in tannic acid, wrote a note to Mr. McDowell, and then, with the men in and around the tent with their guns, waited for the morning. As I looked around on the villagers and their guns, I felt there was no one among them but, if the robbers came back, would take to his heels."

Miss Melton returned to Amadia and her wounds were dressed. It became evident that the attack was not an ordinary one for robbery, but to intimidate the missionaries and bring about their withdrawal. Knowing this, Mr. McDowell continued his work in the villages, while he took vigorous measures to discover and bring to justice the culprits. The kaimakam, and the vali of Mosul were informed. The U. S. minister at Constantinople, Judge Terrell, made vigorous representations which were backed by the secretary of State, Mr. Gresham, demanding the punishment of the assailants. They were shown to be leading Kurds of Amadia. Their arrest was ordered by the vali, but interminable delays were interposed by the officials. For two weeks Mr. McDowell had almost daily contests with them, and many were the subterfuges. Finally the kaimakam, being pressed from Mosul, demanded of the Turks that the guilty ones be produced, or he would arrest thirty of the chief men. They parleyed; two were thrown into prison; the city was excited; the gates were held by the friends of the prisoners, and supplies, especially water, kept out. Finally six more were thrown into prison. There seemed a possibility that the Kurds would rise and rescue them. They were ordered to Mosul under guard. Here vexatious delays occurred. On this account, according to a telegram of Minister Terrell, the vali at Mosul was removed and the grand vizier "duly instructed the new governor to punish the guilty." The United States Government pressed the matter with considerable persistence. President Cleveland in his message to Congress, Dec., 1894, gives the final state of the case as follows: "Three of the assailants of Miss Melton have been convicted by the

Ottoman courts, and I am advised that an appeal against the acquittal of the remaining five has been taken by the Turkish prosecuting officers."

Besides the wildness of the people, evangelistic work has to encounter, in the Mosul field, the organized and powerful opposition of Roman Catholicism. For two centuries it has been entrenched at Mosul, having gained over by reason of internal dissensions, large sections of the Jacobite and Nestorian churches which are now called United Syrian and Chaldean Catholics. They have a large property in the heart of the city and a strong force of French monks and native priests, educated in the College of the Propaganda. Their converts were received *en masse*, simply changing their ecclesiastical relation, and remain in the same ignorance and superstition as before. They too need to have the gospel preached unto them. Our mission is to them as well as their Nestorian neighbors. Mr. McDowell gives the following narrative of work in a village which was Catholic, and its people very ignorant and bigoted. There lived here two men, K—— and T——, no better, no worse perhaps, than their neighbors. Being muleteers their business took them occasionally to a neighboring city where, in some way, they came into contact with a native evangelist. This man not only preached to them, he took them by the hand and talked with them of Christ. At first they set themselves against his words, but finally, for the truth had taken hold of their consciences, they promised him that they would search the Scriptures for themselves. This promise, however, involved their learning to read. They bought primers and Testaments, and on their return home secured a teacher, then one of the worst characters in the village. He afterwards became a consistent Christian.

The New Testament was a new book to them. They had never heard such truths before. Fear, sorrow, surprise, joy, were intermingled in their hearts day after day. As they read their interest deepened. K. would read far into the night though the mother scolded about the waste of oil. As they read they marked the most precious truths, and when they had finished, almost every leaf of the Testament was turned down. These truths they used among their friends, innocently supposing that, like themselves, they would be glad to have their eyes opened to the great errors in which they had been living. But they were first ridiculed, then threatened, finally were persecuted, and, worst of all, their chief enemies were those of their own household—mother, wife, sister, and brother. This led to their meeting to read in secret in a secluded spot among the hills, where, under the impulse of the Spirit, they learned to pray aloud before each other.

The change in their character could not long be seen without bearing fruit. The first convert was K.'s sister; then his wife, who, once habitually abused and beaten, now finding herself treated with consideration and love, could not but appreciate the change in her husband. Next, the old mother, who had been so devoted to her church as to mourn for her son as dead, was united to him again in a common faith.

T. now fell sick and soon died, but not without first giving evidence of the power of the gospel to give peace and support in death. His last request was that the usual mourning, heathenish in its nature, be omitted at his burial. His calmness and peace in death impressed those who witnessed it. Two young men especially were so moved by what they had seen and heard that when K. went to the hills to pray, mourning that, as he supposed, he must hereafter at such times be alone, he found these young men following him and beseeching him to receive them into his company. From that time they became his fellow-disciples, and are in the church to-day. A few others also were gathered, chiefly from among K.'s kinsmen.

At this juncture it was reported that the Catholic bishop of Mosul was soon to pass through their village. Great was the rejoicing among the people. "Now," they said, "the *Pruts* (Protestants) will get their deserts." The bishop was, as he now is, a very powerful man, able to fine, to beat or to imprison any who might incur his displeasure, and very naturally his coming excited fear in the hearts of those who had left the church. Some of them went back to the church, although still clinging to the new doctrine, but K. with his own house and a few others stood firm. The bishop came, and K., having a gun, was called to stand guard before his tent, and while there was summoned before him to answer to the charge of heresy.

As he laid aside his gun and dagger, his knees trembled, but on entering the tent, he recovered somewhat. It is the custom here for a layman on entering before a bishop, to get down upon his hands and knees at the door and so crawling up, to kiss the magnate's outstretched hand. K., without being taught by man, had, through the truth which makes free and gives manhood, received a different spirit. Without meditating it beforehand, and though really fearing the man, he somehow could not get down on his knees, but walked upright into the bishop's presence and gave him the ordinary respectful salutation made to men of rank.

The bishop was angered by his boldness. His first question was: "Are you a teacher in Israel?" "Thou sayest it," replied K., all fear going with the first answer. Then followed badgering, coaxing, threatening on the part of the bishop, all of which were met by Scripture or by such answers as are prompted by the Spirit in fulfillment of Christ's promise. Some of these of which I have learned, were remarkably apt, logic boiled down—unanswerable; an illustration of what the incessant study of the Bible does for the intellect.

The entrance of a good Catholic who had tarried too long at the wine, and who could go no better on four feet than on two, interrupted the interview, and in the disastrous failure of his attempt to kiss the bishop's hand, furnished K. with such a good illustration of orthodoxy that the bishop's anger was turned toward the new offender, and our friend made his escape.

The bishop had come and gone; had examined K. and had done nothing. People began to conclude that the Pruts could not be so bad after all, and many of them accordingly attended the meetings which the muleteer now began to hold. Those who had fallen back were restored and others added, among them the rais of the village. This caused an uproar; the heretics were mobbed, the rais was wounded, and he and K. thrown into prison. A heavy fine was inflicted upon them. K. was released on bail and went to Mardin to seek the help of the missionaries. Through their influence with the government the fine was remitted and the men were set at liberty.

The little band were now for the first time organized into a church and were given a pastor.

But most of them having been brought into the fold by K., would recognize no other shepherd. K. was therefore asked to go to our school in Urumia and pursue a course of study to fit himself for this responsible office.

He returned to his village, and under his care the church is steadily growing and is exerting such an influence that even the Catholics openly declare that the entire village must before long become Protestant.

In 1889, an evangelist was stationed at Elkosh, the

reputed tomb of Nahum, to tour among the Yezidees, from there as a center. Elkosh is a stronghold of the Catholics. Near by is one of their important monasteries. After a while the people of the village showed a curiosity and desire to hear what the Protestant preacher had to say. This could not be allowed by the ecclesiastics. One Sunday morning, they gathered at his house and ordered him to leave the village. He replied that he intended to begin another journey on the morrow. They insisted that he should leave immediately, and suiting their action to their words, they put a rope around his neck and dragged him out of the village, beating him, destroying his books, and taking away his property. The assailants were four priests and about four hundred of their flock.*

Mar Shimun, the patriarch of the Nestorians, resides at Kochanes, a village on a precipice in the lofty mountains, difficult of access. Surrounded by the free tribes, he has considerable power both civil and religious, with a limited income from his people and a stipend of a thousand dollars a year from the Turkish Government. The patriarch has in the main been very friendly to our mission. Occasionally under Catholic or Anglican influences he has been hostile. During one winter, the preachers and teachers in the mountains were arrested by his order, subjected to great indignity and finally expelled. A large number of Bibles and other books were returned to Urumia.

* Mr. Ainsley, in The Missionary Herald.

Mar Shimun declared that by the terms of his agreement with the archbishop of Canterbury, through his agent who had recently visited him, he could allow none but their teachers in his diocese. Mr. Brown, of the Anglican mission, has since taken up his residence at Kochanes, leading the life of a monk and in close contact with the patriarch. The Anglican mission has opened up schools in many villages, using the old priests as teachers. Mar Shimun in 1890 enjoined all parents to send their children to these schools. As a consequence, some of our schools closed. But the instruction was so much inferior that the parents soon desired their children to return to the Protestant schools.

After a while the patriarch, disappointed in his hope of political and material assistance from the Anglicans, was more ready to turn an ear to the Catholics. The Catholic patriarch, at Mosul, began negotiations with him to unite the Nestorians with the Roman Church. Negotiations went so far that a day was appointed for conference in Ashitha, and the delegation from Mosul came at the time appointed. The news was published far and wide in Europe and America that the Nestorian Church was about to submit to the pope. Mar Shimun was inclined to these overtures because of sharp and active dissensions in his own family, the rival party having made his position very uncomfortable, cutting off his revenue and driving him to desperation. When, however, the people were informed of the negotiations, delegations daily arrived to protest; one band even threatened to kill the patriarch. A relative drew his sword and at its point dared him to proceed. The metropolitan of Nochia, Mar Khnan Eshu, whose prerogative it is to consecrate a new patriarch, was prepared to excommunicate him. The patriarch-designate vigorously opposed the negotiations. This opposition convinced Mar Shimun that his course was unwise and fraught with danger. About this time Mr. Coan visited Kochanes and was instrumental in strengthening the new resolution of the patriarch to refuse the inducements of the papal representatives.

It is evident that the old Nestorian Church is in an unstable condition. It behooves those who desire to see it incline to evangelical truth to make efforts earnestly and quickly to sow the gospel seed. It is like an old ship, too worm-eaten to sail the open sea, which, when they would drag it to shore for repairs, falls to pieces of its own weight. Not only its spiritual, but also its ecclesiastical and material life is almost gone, and the time does not seem far distant when it shall be absorbed in other folds.

CHAPTER V.

THE ARMENIANS AND THE GREGORIAN CHURCH.

THE Armenians, one of the oldest races of Western Asia, are Aryan with a mixture of Semitic blood. They were the first race to embrace Christianity, being converted under the influence of Gregory the Illuminator, in A. D. 268–276. The Scriptures were translated in the Armenian by Mesrob in 411. They have retained their race unity, language and religion to a remarkable degree through centuries of subjection, and justly claim that they came out of the dark ages with a purer form of faith than the Greek or Roman Churches. They number about four millions, one-fourth of whom live in Russia, three-fourths in Turkey and remnants in Persia, India, Europe, and America.

Their number in Persia has varied much, being greatest perhaps at the time they reckoned the province of Azerbaijan as Pers-Armenia, and Tabriz as one of their cities; the least in 1830, when there was a wholesale exodus to Russia. At that time their unconcealed sympathy with the enemy brought popular fury upon their heads and led to a plot for a general massacre of them and the appointment of a day for that purpose. It was only through the active and energetic protection of the English residents that they were saved from destruction. Guards were placed at the avenues of the Armenian quarter and many taken temporarily into English households. At that time thousands left Persia. After the war was ended by the peace of Turkomanchai, Prince Abbas Mirza recognizing their value as citizens and elements of the State, encouraged their return and is even said to have secured the Armenian priests in his service by liberal donations. Dr. Eli Smith in his tour of research, prior to the establishment of the Nestorian mission, found but sixty families in Tabriz. Now, however, they have increased more than tenfold. There are twenty-nine thousand in Azerbaijan.

The Persian settlements may be said to be on the eastern circumference of the family circle which has its center in the mountains of Ararat. Small communities are now scattered through Persia, in the fertile plains of Salmas and Urumia, under the shadow of Ararat, on the northern slopes of the Elburz in Karadagh, in the cities of Tabriz, Teheran, Hamadan and Ispahan and their surrounding districts, on the shores of the Caspian and in the valleys of the Bakhtiaris. These communities * are preserved in the midst of thousands of Mohammedans. Who can doubt that Providence has preserved them as well as the

* See article written by the author in the Missionary Encyclopedia.

Nestorians, for a grand purpose, to be a leaven among the Mohammedans, when their Christian life shall be revived? They are like a metallic mirror, rusted and needing repolishing, that it may again reflect the light of Christ.

The Armenians are a fine race. They are typical Caucasians. They have a good physique, their complexion is slightly dark, their eyes black and piercing, hair dark and straight. Many of their women are beautiful, and the Armenian gentleman in his broadcloth suit, made after the Paris fashion, is handsome and urbane. The villagers dress according to the style of the Persian or Kurdish community around them. They have bright active minds, displaying good mental capacity in many lines of activity. As farmers, artisans and tradesmen, they apply themselves with industry, energy and success. They are skillful in the mechanical arts. The women are busy at home in household work and sewing and knitting. They have large financial ability. As money-makers, they equal the Jews. In Persia and the Caucasus their average wealth is much above that of any other race. There are not a few multi-millionaires among them in Russia. Large importing and exporting trade, and a fair share of the oil refining, are in their hands. Many of them are said to be unscrupulous in business. The sharp watch they keep shows that they have no confidence in each other's honesty. Many of them say plainly that deceit is necessary in business. In managing large enterprises they have shown ability. Among them have been famous generals like Lazaroff, Count Malikoff, Nubar Pasha, and skilled diplomatists representing both Turkey and Persia at the courts of Europe. In the postal and telegraph offices of Persia and the civil service in general they hold many positions. Their linguistic ability is high and is specially cultivated by the circumstances in which they are thrown. Many of their children learn to speak three or four languages. Rev. A. Amirkhamañtz, who was leader of the Armenian Protestants of the Caucasus, is master of four oriental, four European, and four ancient languages. Their capacity at oratory could not be better seen than in the Protestant preacher Rev. Gregor Guergian, a thrilling, impassioned orator, though as a rule their oratory is not of such a high order. In literature they have developed very greatly in the last half century and bid fair to surpass their ancient literature. They are prolific as poets, novelists and historians. The number of text-books, magazines and newspapers published by them is surprising in a race just awakening from a sleep of centuries. The most prominent novelist among the Ararat Armenians was Raffe, a native of Salmas, a voluminous writer, who pictured the condition of his race, and did much to excite its aspirations intellectually and politically. The Armenians show an intense desire for education, and an independent spirit in providing themselves with educational facilities. In Etchmiadzin and Tiflis are seminaries supported by the Church, in Moscow, Erzroom and Calcutta are schools founded and endowed by wealthy men, affording a fairly high education. Mukadasi Simon Tomaniantz, the leading merchant of Tabriz, has built two schools in the different wards of the city. One of this family lately married, and instead of having the customary feast, gave five hundred dollars to the schools. The spirit of liberality in their efforts for their advancement is most commendable, and a matter of rejoicing, even when called out by fear of the missions.

They are progressive, ready to accept new methods in education and business, and all the amenities of civilization. In their dress, house-furniture and social customs they are following close upon their foreign models. They have their clubs, Dorcas societies, patriotic Sunday-schools, reading-rooms, theatricals, and benefit-lotteries. In truth the young men seem sometimes entirely too apt disciples of advanced thoughtlessness. They have heard or read of French infidelity and are tinctured with it. They dress handsomely, swing canes, puff cigarettes, ride fast horses, play cards, toast with champagne at dinners, attend the theaters and are as complacent as a modern dude. The conservatives who continue to kiss the hand of St. Sargis and reverence the relics of the saints are left in the rear. It seems natural that the first awakening should bring with it excess. But it is a matter of congratulation that the old lethargy has passed away, and the age of progress is fully entered upon.

Another characteristic of the Armenians is their intense patriotism. Next to their desire for education and the acquisition of wealth, this is most remarkable. The feeling is intense, fervid, overpowering. Their watchword is "Our Race." They have a passionate, burning longing for independence; with it has come a revival of the study of national history, a dwelling on the days of glory of the ancient kings, a setting apart of days, as Vardan's day, to the commemoration of their deeds, and to exhortation to emulate their heroism. With it has come increased love for, and use of, the mother tongue, and its cultivation as a literary language. The new spirit says, "Let that woman be considered a traitor who talks any other language than the Armenian to her children." This spirit has created for itself, and fans its fires with, patriotic songs embodying the ardent longings of the race and the intensest hatred of its enemies. It voices itself in books and newspapers, and in every assembly of the people, where police permit. It entwines itself around the Gregorian Church as the only visible embodiment of national unity, the bond of the race, its representative. The skeptic joins the devotee, the enlightened scholar joins the superstitious and ignorant in supporting, though not approving of, priest and bishop and their formal rites, not from love to religion or care for its ceremonies (which are despised), but because the

Church is the recognized and only organization of the race.

Three or four patriotic societies are engaged in political propaganda, some on principles of proper agitation for relief from oppression, and for the enforcement of the sixty-first article of the treaty of Berlin, by educating public sentiment in the race and creating sympathy in other nationalities. Others with terroristic and nihilistic principles, believing that the end justifies any means, and that no principles of law or gospel should be allowed to stand in the way of attaining the object.* This patriotism specially directs itself to relieving the Armenians in Turkey from their oppressions. It aims to see created around the headwaters of the Euphrates an independent Armenia after the manner of the Balkan principalities. If trustful in Providence, this spirit cries out, "How long, O Lord! how long?" If skeptical, it exclaims, "Away

---

* The spirit of this class may be seen in the following paraphrase of the Lord's prayer made by one of their poets.

"Our Father, which art in Heaven, hallowed be thy name,
Give an earthly kingdom to the Armenians.
Let thy will be done in all things,
Only leave not the Armenians under the yoke.
We wish neither dry nor fresh bread,
Only give a weapon to each Armenian hand.
We ask not forgiveness for personal debts,
But take away the abominable tax of the Turk.
Turn us, O God, to the temptation (trial) of war,
That quickly thy Armenian race may be freed."
                                    GAMAR KATIBAYI.

with a gospel that teaches us to love our enemies, or says that when smitten on the one cheek we should turn the other."

Regarding the moral character of the Armenians, I have only a few words. They are "Orientals," with whatever of good or bad is embraced in that term. Those of Turkey, Russia, and Persia differ considerably according to their environment. Those in Persia have many of the qualities of their Persian neighbors. We must except those that pertain to polygamy and its accompanying evils. Family life is purer than among the Mohammedans, and woman holds a higher place. Desertion and unfaithfulness on the part of the men come largely from their long absences in Russia and other places of business. Husbands go off, sometimes immediately after the honeymoon, do not return for years, after a while neglect to send support, and may never return. Divorce is rare. The sale by parents of their daughters into concubinage and prostitution exists, as is well pictured by Raffe in his *Innocent Merchandise*. It is not condemned by public sentiment as severely as it should be.

The independence of spirit of the Armenians frequently manifests itself in difference of opinion, divisions and quarrels among themselves. They say that their downfall as a nation was due to envy and internal strife. Their passion against each other is one of their greatest weaknesses. Naturally with this fact is a corollary that they are not as polite to each other as the Persians are. One of their besetting sins is drinking intoxicants, one disgrace is their being so largely the liquor sellers of Persia. Like most races of the world they have an abundance of pride and self-conceit.

The Armenian or Gregorian Church is called by them Lusavorchagan (Illuminatorian), from Gregory the Illuminator. In doctrine it agrees closely with the Greek and Roman churches. It rejects the Council of Chalcedon and subsequent councils, and is classed as Monophysite. It rejects the "filioque." It holds to apostolic succession, transubstantiation, the confessional, priestly absolution, intercession of the saints, Mariolatry, extreme unction, and prayers for the dead. It seems to reject purgatory. It practices triune immersion of infants, at the same time anointing them with holy oil (merun).

The clergy are a regular hierarchy. The head of the Church is the catholicos, who resides at Etchmiadzin, the center of their religious life. An inferior catholicos resides at Cis, in Cilicia, and another at Aghtamar on Lake Van. They must receive the *merun* from Etchmiadzin. The patriarch of Constantinople ranks after the catholicos in dignity. The diocesan bishops are appointed from the vartabeds or doctors, the highest order of monks. The higher orders of the clergy must be celibate, the priests and lower orders must be married, and only a single time. If the priest's wife die, he can retire to a monastery and rise

AN ARMENIAN PATRIARCH

in the ranks of the higher clergy or he can engage in secular pursuits. The first catholicoses, Gregory, Ishak, and Nersis were married, and son succeeded father in the office.* The election of a catholicos is an interesting occasion, especially because the whole Church has a voice in his selection. Not only is the bishop of each diocese a member of the Synod, but the laity are allowed to select one delegate from each diocese. The selection of the lay delegate is an exciting time. Two such occasions have happened in late years, one in 1884, another in 1892. I shall describe the former. There were two assemblies, one at Constantinople for the Armenians of Turkey, the other at Etchmiadzin for those of Russia and Persia. The latter was composed of thirty-three members, eight being representatives of the Council of Etchmiadzin, seven appointed by them, nine diocesan bishops and nine lay delegates. Though the people have a voice they are largely overpowered by ecclesiastics. The delegates assembled on the 8th of May, O. S., at the palace, and marched in procession to the Mother Church in which place the only-begotten Son is said to have descended, giving the name to the city *ëtch* or *ëj* meaning "descend," and *miadzin* the "only-begotten." An immense concourse of people thronged

---

* The same was true in the Syrian Church. The bishops of Seleucia were married. The eighth in succession, Achadebues, was son of the seventh. No less than five patriarchs of the Nestorians in the 5th and 6th centuries were lawfully married. Patriarch Elisha married the daughter of his predecessor.

about. The mass was then celebrated and prayers offered, after which the lay delegates took a formal and solemn oath, standing up and placing their hands on the Gospel. Then kissing the book and the cross, they all subscribed to the oath. At this point the representative of the czar took the floor and gave them, in Armenian, the imperial salutations and praises, which were responded to with diplomatic cordiality. The archbishop, Margar, then eloquently and briefly rehearsed the history of the last four catholicoses, and ended by nominating Nersis, patriarch of Constantinople, Kremian ex-patriarch, and Melchizedek, bishop of Smyrna. Isaiah, patriarch of Jerusalem, was also nominated. First Nersis was chosen, but afterwards Melchizedek, and after approval by the czar, he took his seat. The people of Tiflis watched for the bulletins in regard to the election with much the same eagerness and excitement as are displayed in regard to political elections in other lands, and the successful candidate was flooded with telegrams from all directions.

After his death, Mugherdich Kremian surnamed Hairig or "dear little father" was elected May 1892. He had been a priest, but after the death of his wife and daughter, he entered a monastery at the age of thirty-four, became superior of the monastery of Varok, near Van, afterwards patriarch of Constantinople, and representative of the Armenians at the Berlin Congress. For his part in that he was banished to Jerusalem by the sultan. After his election, a delay of a year and a half occurred while he was arranging with the czar and sultan. The latter to the last refused to let him pass through Constantinople *en route*, so he went by way of Austria and Russia. His progress was with great honor and enthusiasm in the different Armenian communities until he reached Etchmiadzin. He is regarded as a spiritual and enlightened man, of marked ability and progressive spirit, a patron of education and an author of eminence. Later, the sultan refused to allow his first encyclical to be distributed or read in the churches of Turkey because there was no prayer for him in it.

A visit to Etchmiadzin well repays the traveler. Here antiquity and modern life are strangely mingled. Here are churches, parts of which are said to be 1,500 years old, a monastery with cells, and a quaint old refectory with long stone tables and stone seats, a collection of manuscripts of various ages, a treasure-house with the antiques and rich ornaments of the hierarchy, along with a flourishing seminary and press and library of modern days—all set in groves of fine old trees.

The government of the Armenian Church in Persia is by two bishops, one located at Ispahan, the other at Tabriz. They are appointed by the catholicos. Tabriz is a hard diocese to fill. During fifteen years two bishops have withdrawn, three have died and a new incumbent lately arrived. Very often the feeling between bishop and people is one of dissatisfaction.

The bishop's position is one of great power. When Bishop Sukeas Barzian entered Tabriz in 1894 he was received with great honor. The crown prince, governor, foreign agent and consuls sent representatives to welcome him, and many of the Armenians with carriages, horsemen and banners in long procession (all being idle because it was Sunday) with school children, joined in escorting him to the episcopal residence.

When his predecessor, Khachadur Vartabed died, his funeral was with great pomp and ceremony. After many hours of services and mass with the anointing of his body with holy oil, it was borne through the street with martial music. Every few squares the procession would halt, a carpet be spread in the street and further prayers and chanting engaged in. Representatives of different departments of the government and of foreign governments attended.

The power of a bishop in Persia, as well as in Turkey, is not religious only. He has the civil powers of a judge in many cases between Armenians. He is the advocate and protector of his followers before the Persian government, presenting and urging their pleas in case of oppression or wrong, appealing from lower to higher officials. He is *ex-officio* manager of the schools and chairman of their popular assemblies and even sometimes executive of the patriotic propaganda. He manages the church property, has oversight of the endowments, and altogether has such an amount of worldly occupation that he pays no attention to spiritual work. He rarely preaches and takes no time for oversight and correction of the morals of his flock. He never seems seriously to inquire how he may lessen lying, dishonesty, drunkenness, fornication or skepticism. According to oriental custom, he takes fees for his trouble in litigations and often amasses considerable wealth.

The laity have considerable voice in the Gregorian Church. Not only, as mentioned, in the election of the catholicos, but in the election of their priests and in other things. Generally the people designate the man whom they wish to be made priest in a congregational meeting, send notice to the bishop and he ordains him. The installation of a priest in Tabriz against the will of the people raised a loud protest. The people even exercise a right of protest against the appointment of unacceptable bishops. One of the people also acts as elder or vice-elder (the priest being called *the elder* or presbyter) and helps the priest to administer the church funds and have oversight of the worship. The congregation often votes regarding church building, repairs and other affairs.

The rites and ceremonies of the Gregorian Church resemble those of other ritualistic churches. Their manner of worship will best be brought out by concrete cases. Let me take the reader with me to their church at Christmas or Epiphany, both of which are celebrated on January 6 (O. S.). They suppose an interval of exactly thirty years to have passed between Christ's birth and his public appearance at baptism. We arrived about 8 o'clock. The service of prayer had begun in the early morning and mass was being celebrated. Many Europeans and some Mohammedans were present, the latter simply to see the sights. The bishop or khalifa was dressed in robes of gorgeous splendor, which reminded one of those exhibited in Catholic churches. He was attended by a full company of acolytes, priests and deacons, and there were sliding curtains enough to satisfy actors in a different sphere. The usual pictures adorned the church, receiving the incense of a thousand tapers. The service represented the baptism of Jesus. After the ritual in the rarely understood ancient Armenian, a vessel of water was placed on the platform. In this a silver cross was immersed. Then another priest came bearing a silver dove filled with holy oil or *meron* which was poured out upon the water to symbolize the descent of the Spirit. This sacred oil is believed to boil, in a golden bowl, miraculously through the influence of a piece of the true cross or of St. Gregory's hand at Etchmiadzin. It is made of flowers. It is indispensable to confirmation, ordination, and all the important ceremonies of the church. It is sent out by the catholicos through his agents and becomes a chief and never-failing source of revenue. After this outpouring of the Spirit's grace upon the baptized symbol, the dove was borne in procession through the church as an object of adoration. A child took the cross from the water and placed it upon its breast before the people and for this sanctifying privilege a good sum of money is willingly given by the parents. When the ceremonies were through, the people rushed up with bottles and vessels to obtain some of the precious and holy water as a panacea for many ills.

This festival is called *jour orhnek* by the Armenians, i. e., the blessing of the water. The Persians call it *Hach Bayram* or Cross Festival and are accustomed to ask, " What sign did the cross give?" regarding it as an indication of the kind of weather there will be. After the church service, the people go to each other's houses and salute with, " Blessed be the birth and baptism of Christ." They continue for two or three days visiting, eating, and drinking tea and coffee, wine and arak.

We called on the bishop, Guerg Mushegian in his residence. He was pleasant, and cordial, his reception robes were black and flowing full to the floor, with a black cowl of stiff shining silk, coming to a point above his head and falling down on his back. On his breast was a large silver cross pendant, and an enamel picture of Christ, on silver. The bishop in the midst of other conversation, inquired about America, and asked whether we were descended from Columbus or from the Indians; if we were of the red men and our language the Indian language. During these rounds of visits generous collations are served in the houses of the merchants. This is especially so at the Russian-Armenian chief-merchant's. In the center of his table was a roast calf entire; then different kinds of meats, with fowls, tongue, sturgeon, herring, sardines, caviar, pickles, sweets, cakes, and a variety of wines and liquors. A poor man generally has several kinds of candies, some *nazuki* (delicate (?) cake) and colored boiled eggs. The poor man wishes to receive visitors even though his house has only one room, with oiled paper for window glass, a pan of coals for fire and pillows for seats. He has the utmost cordiality and a hearty welcome. Custom requires one to drink something, and even by limiting oneself to tea or coffee, thirty cups, though small ones, are more than one's head can comfortably stand.

On our way to America, Easter Sunday found us at Nakhejevan, (Russia). The bells rang out cheerily, the first we had heard for eight years. In Tabriz, on account of the Mohammedans, the beadle knocks at each gate with a maul to announce the hour for service. In villages of Persia a sounding board is struck with loud raps ending with three taps for the Trinity. We went to the Armenian Church. It is a fine new structure anointed or, as we would say, dedicated in 1874. The main building and arches are of red, and the dome of gray, sandstone. Four large pillars of stone in the body of the church help to sustain the arched roof. The back part of the church is for the women, the central part for the men, the two separated by a railing about a yard high. Carpet was spread for the people to stand on. An innovation was that there was one bench on which some occasionally sat down. Another innovation was that some came in with their shoes on, and even muddy.

The other third of the church, separated from the men by another screen, was devoted to the priests, with the altar and holy of holies in the center and dressing-rooms at the corners. The altar curtain was of purple velvet, its screen a scroll frame work ornamented with figures of doves, all in gilt. The central picture was of the crucifixion, with Mary clinging to the cross. Below was a tapestry of Mary with the child Jesus in her arms. The altar doors were life-sized pictures of apostles, the one holding a handkerchief with Christ's face on it, according to the tradition relating to King Abgar, the other holding a similar picture of the "Mother of God." The panels had pictures of the visit of the Magi, the embalming of the body of Jesus, the resurrection and the ascension. The panels of the front of the pulpit were the twelve apostles. On the walls were pictures of Gregory the Illuminator (life size) and Mesrob, the inventor of the Armenian alphabet, seated with pen and paper in hand looking up at the dove which is bearing in its mouth a paper inscribed with the seven vowels, the shape of which was so important as to need a special revelation from heaven. On the pillars are the martyr, Stephen, and St. George with a shield in one hand and a lily in the other. Before each picture were lighted candles.

It was interesting to observe the individual worshiper. Entering the church, he would face the altar, cross himself, put a copper on the table before a candle-seller, that his little flame of devotion might be started before some picture. Then taking his stand with the other men, he would kneel, place the palms of his hands on the floor and finally his forehead. After repeating this several times, he stood and listened to the service, understanding very little of the ancient Armenian liturgy except the holy names and at each mention of these he would cross himself. Out of a population of three thousand or more Armenians, there were only eighty persons present. All usually attend twice a year, but the rain was pouring and the thunder pealing in the dome. "A rainy Sunday" is an excuse in Asia also.

The bishop was consecrating the *badarag*, or sacrifice. He was dressed in long flowing robes, with gold embroidered cloak, and a very large miter, covered with enameled pictures, and with gold and precious stones. To the eye the spectacle was pleasing, but it was grievous as a perversion of the simplicity of the gospel. The bishops, priests and deacons read alternately, and the choir of boys joined in the chants. Two boys stood beside the altar and shook the cymbals. Once a procession of all marched around the church bearing aloft a banner with a picture of Christ's baptism, the bishop bringing up the rear with a collection plate in one hand and a cross which the people kissed in the other. Usually the bishop stood before the altar. Now and then he would turn and pour his peace upon the people and they would bow in response. At a certain stage the priest came to the railing, and announced to the nearest man, "Christ is risen from the dead," with a bow first to one side and then to the other as if embracing him. He responded, "Blessed be the resurrection of Christ." Then this man announced the glad news to those nearest to him, with the same bows, and they to others. One man passed the greeting to an aged sister and she to the other women, the bowing and greeting thus going through the whole standing congregation.

Finally the host was prepared, the cover of the golden vessel was removed at the time of its second elevation and the congregation bowed prostrate before it. It was placed on the altar and an offering again taken up. This was a curious sight. Seven or eight officers, each with a collection plate,—the sexton, doorkeeper, warden, deacon, priest, etc.,—followed each other closely, passing the rows of men. Each man threw in a five or ten cent piece, and took out change in coppers, in order to be ready for the following plates.

Then communion was administered. Very few participated. They were chiefly boys, the people having generally confessed and communed since "Great Friday." One child was held up in his father's arms and received the wafer. A small piece of the white light wafer, previously dipped in wine, was placed in the mouth of the recipient. After the bishop had left the altar a sickly babe in arms was brought into the holy place. A priest seeing it was late, took from his pocket a small silver case, in which the wafer is always kept ready for emergencies in sickness, and put a morsel in the child's mouth.

Then a man passed around the church with a basket from which he distributed to each one a small roll of bread. These contained pieces of meat from the sacrifice of a sheep or an ox made by some prosperous man. They were to be eaten as the breaking of their fifty days' fast. This distribution is ostensibly a giving to the poor. After this, the bishop came and stood by the railing between the holy place and the men's quarter, holding the Gospels in one hand. The cover was ornamented with silver and large precious stones. Beside him stood the assistant holding a waiter with the wafer broken into small pieces. The men passed in succession, kissing the book and taking a small bit of the wafer to share with those who had remained at home. Afterwards the women and girls did the same thing.

When all had left the church, the coffin of an aged woman was brought from the inner room and placed in the center of the church, her funeral being postponed until the morrow on account of the feast. The people all went home to the post-lental feast, and to great rejoicing and visiting.*

Other feasts which specially attract attention are two in honor of the Virgin Mary or the Mother of God as she is generally called. One is the feast of purification or the presentation in the temple. In the villages its old style celebration is still retained. Beginning at sundown, they usher in the day with a bonfire of thorn bushes in the churchyard. When the fire is burning, young men and maidens, old men and matrons, merchants and priests leap over it. Their sins are supposed to remain behind them in the fire. Afterwards the ashes are taken home and poured on the branches of trees to make them fruitful and rubbed on the foreheads of the women for the same purpose. Returning from the church they light fires on the roofs, and shoot off guns. The day succeeding is more holy than a Sunday. In Tabriz the custom is different, the church is lighted with candles. These are taken home to illuminate the houses. Some of the brides still light some thorn bushes on the roof and jump over them. Mussulmans close their windows to prevent the smoke from entering and defiling their houses.

The other festival celebrates the assumption of Mary, bodily to heaven. It is preceded by a week of

---

* Easter is sometimes called the Feast of Fresh Eggs. Every house has its red eggs, rich families preparing as many as a thousand. The visitors take them. The boys gamble with them in the streets. The egg which breaks is forfeited.

fasting. The celebration was described in an essay by a scholar in our Tabriz school in the following manner:

"There is a church of the Mother of God in a village called Sayidabad, near Khoi. On September 25th at an hour after noon the pilgrims follow the road toward the shrine that they may present their thanks for their preservation in the past year or deliverance from any special trouble that may have befallen them.

"If the one who has vowed is rich, he takes with him a sheep to sacrifice, but if poor he must at least take twenty or thirty candles to burn before the picture of Mary the Mother of God. The Turks seeing the Armenians gathering from the villages, load their donkeys with watermelons and take them to sell to the pilgrims who will remain over night in the churchyard. For those who are paying a vow must remain all night and engage in prayer. They buy and eat of the watermelons and so pass the night.

"When morning arrives the Dĕr-Dĕr or priest of the village comes to the church to sacrifice the offering. The animal must be killed with its head toward the East, to which they look in prayer. The skin and one quarter must be given to the priest, but the head, feet, liver and tallow to the sexton. Then they rub the sacrifice with salt, cut it in pieces, and put it in a kettle to boil while the people enter the church for prayers. There is a confused multitude. The brides and girls are praying, the men are burning candles, some are praying earnestly, but the women are talking so incessantly that they neither hear anything nor allow anybody else to hear.

"Meanwhile the pots are boiling and they begin to steam. When mass is finished, the priest goes out, blesses the sacrifice, and says to the people, 'Those who love God may sit down and partake.' The priest and all the people sit down to feast. Then the priest says a *Hyer Mir* (Pater Noster) and afterwards says: 'Eat in peace, and God accept your sacrifice.'

"After eating they enter the church, kneel several times before the pictures of the Mother of God, burn a candle and in the cool of the evening return home."

On the following days sacrifices of sheep are often made at home. The poor should be invited, but more often the friends partake. Charity-feasts, for the rest of the soul of a departed one, are considered very efficacious. Sunday following the feast of the Assumption is the day for the blessing of the fruits. Many Armenians will not eat grapes until that day. Then a quantity is brought to the church, and prayer is made for a blessing not only on the grapes, but on all the fruits of the year. These are then distributed, and they go and enjoy their vineyards. This feast accomplishes one good thing in that it keeps some Armenians from eating unripe grapes as the Mussulmans commonly do. But in some seasons and places, the grapes have ripened several weeks before the festival.

One of the most ever-present ordinances of the Gregorian Church is fasting. Lent lasts fifty days preceded by the time of *baregendan* or good living. There are six other fasts of six days' duration, and every Wednesday and Friday are fast days. The total number is 165 days during a year. I was curious to know why they supposed every Wednesday and Friday had been ordained fasts. I was informed that it was because the child Jesus always refused to suckle on these days. Its origin others dated from the garden of Eden, for did not Eve eat the forbidden fruit on Wednesday and Adam on Friday? A story is told of a Mohammedan and a Karadagh Armenian who were disputing as to who had the most fast days. The Armenian maintained that the Mohammedans had the most and *vice versa*. Finally he said, "Give me one stroke for every day of ours, and I will do the same to you." The Armenian smote for the Mohammedan month of Ramazan and the few others. The Mohammedan said, "I will not give you your due, but only smite for the Wednesdays and Fridays."

The rule of the fast is strict abstention from all animal products including milk and eggs. The result in mountain regions is practically to reduce the people almost to bread and water, during nearly one half of their lives; for vegetables and fruits in mountain villages are few, and many of the former cooked without butter or milk are not very palatable. The children begin to keep these fasts when they are seven years old. Until lately they were strictly kept. This is not so now in cities; and besides, the culinary art being much more highly developed and the supply of fruit and vegetables superabundant, it is no great self-denial in the cities and plains, but in the mountains it is one of the greatest hardships of life. The people are laden with burdens grievous to be borne, being commanded to abstain from meats. The secret of their willingness to bear them lies in the fact that they regard such self-denials as expiatory and as a meritorious ground for the remission of their sins.

In some churches the pictures are veiled during Lent, the congregation not being allowed during that time to look upon the holy faces. The altar, too, has its curtain before it. On a certain day, the priest goes before the curtain and one of the lectors as representative of the people comes and asks admittance. The priest replies, "You are not worthy." He pleads for admittance. The priest says, "If you repent and put away your sins, you can enter." He professes repentance, the curtain and veils are withdrawn and the worshipers look upon the Presence as represented by the pictures and crucifix.

CHAPTER VI.

ARMENIAN WEDDING CUSTOMS.

OLD style proposals and wooings among the Armenians were always done through a third party, generally through the mothers or some old women friends. The young couple had considerable opportunity of acquaintance, seeing each other and knowing much about each other. This is becoming more and more the case, customs having now been modified so that they can converse and correspond with each other. When the match has been arranged, a public betrothal takes place at the house of the bride. The invited friends assemble. Tea and liquors are served; platters of cakes and sweets are placed on the floor with a large loaf of sugar in the middle of each. On another platter the engagement pledges are brought in. The priest stands before the couple, asks them of their desire to become engaged, and the pledges, consisting of a ring, a necklace of beads and gold or silver coins, a silver belt, a set of earrings and such things, are presented. Then the priest sits down, breaks into pieces the head of sugar, serves it with candies on saucers to the guests, reserving a large end of the loaf for himself. The guests are supposed to take a good deal of their sweets home with them.

These betrothals are considered very sacred, and are rarely broken off. If this is done all the pledges must be given back and the expense of the betrothal service paid by the girl. I know of a girl who being in doubt as to the wisdom of her engagement, began a forty days' fast eating nothing each day until evening, and asking God to direct her. After twenty days she became sick and broke off the fast and the engagement, too.

The age at which Armenian girls marry varies much. In villages and towns they are not seldom married at ten or twelve. In Tabriz, seventeen or somewhat more is a fair average. A nephew of a Nestorian bishop was married to a girl ten years of age. The length of the engagement varies. There is a saying that if a widow is not married within a month of her engagement, it falls through. The favorite time for weddings is just before Lent, as they cannot be celebrated during its continuance nor, I believe, until after Pentecost. The law of the church prohibits marriages between persons related within the seventh degree of either consanguinity or affinity. In small communities almost all are within these limits. The bishop can give a dispensation for a proper consideration.

The old marriage customs are seen best away from the large cities. The old-time weddings last eight days. The first day the friends are invited to the houses of the bride and bridegroom. The rich go taking a loaf of sugar, the poor a bouquet, a quince or an apple. On the second day the boys come together and have wrestling matches. On the third day the girls collect, put on red veils, take sieves and sift the flour. The saying is, "Let those sift to whom God has given the kismat," i. e. the fate to get married.

The fourth day the bride collects her companions and puts *henna* (red dye) on their hands and afterwards on her hands, and they all sew at the outfit. On the fifth day prominent guests are invited, and the musicians sent for, whose playing is a sign that it is time to gather together. This band is composed of players of the viol, drum, and tambourine. They are generally Persians. The tambourine player sings, in loud falsetto songs not very choice in sentiment, and can be heard by all the neighbors. With them frequently is a dancing boy, with long hair, dyed with *henna*, dressed in an embroidered black velvet coat and red silk skirt, with little cymbals or bells on his fingers and bells on his toes, whirling round in the dance accompanying the music. Sometimes he whirls on his heel and his skirt stands out like an umbrella, then suddenly sitting down, it spreads out in a perfect circle around him. Sometimes he acts the pantomime, making motion as if greeting the company, or drinking out of his cap, or chasing off the flies. Again he throws over himself the *chadar* and appears like a girl, or puts it on as the headdress of a dervish, or again he lies down and covers himself with it as if dead. Again a fantastically dressed man comes on the scene and dances around keeping time with loud snaps of his fingers. Relatives and friends, too, especially when the wine, which flows freely, has excited them, jump up and act their antics around the room, waving the handkerchief and perhaps joining in the Turkish songs. The sixth day is that of the marriage ceremony. Let this day be described from the standpoint of the bride's house by Mrs. Wilson:

"No daintily engraved cards, but an old woman with a red apple brings the invitation. The gentlemen of the mission are not invited to the bride's house, nor indeed any men, so the ladies must escort each other, and, as it is my first invitation to such a festivity, I join the party with a good deal of curiosity. We were invited for four o'clock P. M., and as we didn't get home till midnight, we saw the whole performance.

"As we enter the courtyard we see a big chest on one side, a Persian Saratoga, ready to carry away all the young bride's possessions from her childhood home. We have heard the music from afar, and find the musicians sitting in the hall, piping away at full blast. The room we enter is crowded with women, girls and babies, a company of ninety, I should say, seated compactly on the floor, and able to sit thus comfortably for hours without moving, an accomplishment we have not yet mastered. Waiters of steaming, sweet tea in little glasses are being passed, and there is a perfect babel of gabble, but just now there is one subject of common interest for the trousseau is being exhibited. Bundles after bundles pinned up in silk covers are laid before the show-woman, an old relative, who unfolds and exhibits each article for public inspection. It is not only a satisfaction of curiosity, but in this way many witnesses could testify to the bride's property, if occasion required. Sometimes the outfit is very elaborate, from half a dozen silk dresses down to the furnishing of the work-basket and all the fancy-work the girl has ever done; but there are articles included that seem ridiculous for public exhibition—a bed, which means comfort, pillows and quilt, tied up in a big cotton cover; an outfit for going to the bath, from the large, round, copper tub down to soap and towels; and lastly every precious toy, even the doll or childish ornaments that have been carefully laid away till this grand occasion.*

"Meanwhile the bride is being dressed, and we are allowed to get a peep at her. Her name is Tagoohe, which means queen, and she has a calm, quiet beauty not unqueenly. Her dress is pink silk, and over it she wears a black sacque, which looks rather inappropriate, though comfortable. Her hair hangs in long braids down her back, but now she lays aside the girl's round, saucer-like cap and is crowned, which in

* Clothing the bride is an elaborate ceremony. Each garment has to be carried around her three times to keep off the evil eye.

Armenian is the idiom for "to be married." Her crown is a band of embroidered velvet, and on it is pinned a dainty white gauze veil which delicately frames her face. The white silk head-kerchief over all completes her head-gear. It adds a romantic interest to know that every article, even down to her little white slippers, were sent yesterday as a present from the bridegroom, brought on a man's head in a great wooden tray adorned with apples and candies. The same tray went back carrying his suit, shirt, paper-collar and all, in exchange.

"We return to the company and notice how gay they look. Dark, dresses are not fashionable, but purple, green, blue, and red are favorite colors. The girls are dressed just like their mothers, and act like sedate little women, many of them tending baby sisters, who look like small mummies in their swaddling clothes. Dancing is now in order, and it is certainly in the mildest form imaginable. Two girls face each other and make little courtesies all around before beginning. Then, perfectly independent of each other, they move up and down the room with a graceful, gliding step, moving their arms alternately. Meantime an old woman goes about collecting coins, which are her reward for various services. When the bride herself dances, a silver coin is expected. The approach of dinner is indicated by the entrance of a young man with basin, ewer, soap and towel, who pours water over each guest's hands. Long, white cloths are spread on the floor, and we sit picnic fashion at each side. Salt and pepper-cellars, sheets of bread and plates of cheese, onions, herbs and sliced turnips are brought in as an opening relish. Four courses follow, chicken and fried potatoes, a stew of meat and quinces, a stew of mutton and peas, and lastly a dish of pilav. Two share a plate, and fingers do duty as forks and spoons for most of the guests. The sons of the family act as waiters, stepping over the cloth and around the dishes in stockinged feet, and accomplish the task of feeding the multitude deftly and efficiently. After dinner, basin and ewer are in requisition again and hands are washed vigorously. Then there is a long, wearisome time of waiting in momentary expectation of the bridegroom's coming, relieved only by the monotonous music and dancing which have now begun to pall on us. After brides, girls and children have all taken their turn, two old women take the floor and are applauded as they renew their youthful pastime.

"At last there is a cry—'the bridegroom cometh'—and all is animation. The bride, covered with a red gauze veil, stands in one end of the room with relatives on either side. The music waxes louder and her brothers dance up and down the room in front of her. There is a glare of torches in the yard and the bridegroom enters arm-in-arm with his 'best man,' wearing festive white cotton gloves and large buttonhole bouquets of artificial flowers. An old priest precedes him and advances to bless the bride. The young man, though beaming with pleasure, affects reluctance and is encouraged to go forward by pulls and pushes till within arm's length of his bride.* The priest joins their right hands, laying his own on top, and repeats rapidly the benedictions, calling them king and queen. Then bridegroom and best man, with the bride between, head the procession for the church. The bride's friends remain behind, for the idea is that she is taken from them. The guests from the other house, each with a little taper, go out into the dark, deserted streets, only illumined by the torches' glare. Night is preferred as the time for weddings, as the procession will then be unobserved, though the music draws some spectators, who peer down into the darkness from the housetops, and at the guardhouse the soldiers bar the passage with their guns till they receive the expected present.

"It is a weird scene to be in, as we wind about the streets, taking the longest route so as to avoid the ill omen of retracing our steps as we return. The little church is lighted with candles and looks pretty in the subdued light with its arches and altar and pictures. Confession is the first ceremony. Two old priests lead the young couple separately aside and kneel with them as they confess, in the sight of all. They then go

* When joining hands they sometimes endeavor to step on each other's toes. The one stepping hardest has the other in subjection through life.

hand in hand up in front of the altar, and a priest in rich robe and miter, with two assistants, chants the service."

The Armenian marriage ceremony is an interesting mixture of beauty, triviality, devotion and superstition. First there is a long ceremony of blessing the clothes of the bride before the bridegroom sends them to her. The priest and deacon enter the house scattering the incense. After invocations to the Trinity, this prayer follows: " Unwedded Mary! Mother of light! Blessed among women! Mother of the Immortal Bridegroom! Cease not to intercede for our salvation. Eternal Bridegroom! By the intercession of thy heavenly mother, Mother of God, thou hast invited us; make us worthy of thy marriage feast. Only begotten! Bless these wedding garments." The priest then makes the sign of a cross over the garments and blesses them in the name of the Trinity, praying: "O Christ! Bless these wedding garments with spiritual blessings that the wearer may not be ruled by the bad influences of devils and sorcerers." He then clothes the groom and continues prayer for the bride's clothes in great detail as, "Bless the clothes and ornaments, namely, the braids of the hair and the ribbons, the crown, the face ornaments, ruffles, necklace, bracelets, earrings, finger-rings, armlets; the brocades, feathers, cloak, morning dress, the muslin red and blue, the gauze embroidery and decorations; the cameo, agate and topaz; the shoes, all woolen articles, the very beautiful white garments and smaller embellishments." After this unique petition follows a beautiful one that their "invisible spirits may be adorned with chastity, Godlike virtue, and clothed with divine light as with a garment."

They then proceed with torches and tapers, accompanied by the shrill airs of the Persian drum and fife to the house of the bride. The priest joins their right hands and after other unexceptionable prayers says the following: "Mother of Christ! O Virgin! who art always the intercessor for the world, called blessed by all nations! Pure Dove and Bride of Heaven! Mary, the temple and throne of the Word of God! By thee the angels became pleased with us who are dust, and by thee we draw near to the tree of life. In thee all nations rejoice."

They then go to the church. At the vestibule the couple thrice bow the knee and the priest confesses them. He then twists silk cords and puts one over the neck of the groom and the other on the bride. While winding the groom's cord he says a prayer, beginning, "Lord, in thy strength let them be strong." While winding the bride's, he says, "The King's daughters." The priest joins their hands and gives them an appropriate exhortation, after which they enter into covenant. The priest says, "My child, are you master until death?" The groom answers, "Yes, holy father, by God's command I am master." The priest to the bride says, "My child, are you obedient until death?" The bride answers, "Yes, holy father, by God's command I am obedient." These questions and answers are repeated three times. Then the priest says, "God, who is invisible, but sitteth upon his holy altar, is witness of this thing; so also are our holy guardian angels, this holy Church, holy cross and holy Gospel, the company of priests and the congregation. Are they all witnesses?" They answer, "Yes, holy father, let them be witnesses." The priest then says, "God is in these things, and let them not be shaken. Help, Lord." They then approach the altar, and in the midst of a chant the priest takes the Bible around the altar, the bride and groom kiss it, or the cross upon it, and sometimes they are placed forehead against forehead and the Bible on their heads. After several passages of Scripture and long prayers, opportunity is given to partake of the communion, the wafer being dipped in the cup. Owing to certain regulations the sacrament is rarely taken at this time.

To resume Mrs. Wilson's description: "Congratulations are now in order and they turn to face the company, the bridegroom holding the Bible in front of him. The priest stands near the collection-plate and the coins the friends drop in are the marriage fee. If a gold piece gets in, the name of the generous donor is in every one's mouth as a prince of liberality. The sleepy children, who have been standing about through the long service with their dripping tapers, are ready to go home by this time, as we all are, and at midnight the procession reaches the bridegroom's home."

In some places a lamb is sacrificed before the party who walk over its blood, and the "friend of the bridegroom" cuts a cross over the door with his sword to make good luck. The following day the priest again comes, puts the bride and groom head to head, takes the sword of the groom and puts it on their heads with the sign of a cross. After prayers and Scripture reading, he takes a cup of wine, and having prayed gives it to them to drink. Having thus pledged themselves, and been blessed in the name of the Trinity, the marriage is completed. Then the bridegroom's mother makes a feast, and the trousseau is again exhibited with many a joke. If she sees that the bride has brought a large dowry she says, "May the khanum's (lady's) house be always prosperous." The same day the groom and his companions go to the house of the bride's parents and the groom says, "May the bride's place not remain empty." The bride's mother brings bread and wine and the groom and his companions eat and drink to their heart's content.

The bride, her mouth bound with a kerchief, has begun a period of subjection to her mother-in-law. She must not speak nor sit down in her presence without permission until the birth of her firstborn. I visited a graduate of the girl's school, who had been a bride for three months. She had not yet addressed a remark to her father-in-law. When a child is born it must not be kissed by anyone, nor even looked upon by a stranger before it is baptized. If it gapes, the names of the Trinity are said over its mouth, that the devil may not enter. When the mother leaves the house, a piece of iron is put at the child's head to ward off the evil eye.

Persian law is that no Mohammedan woman can marry an Armenian or Nestorian or other Christian unless he becomes a Mohammedan, and no Mohammedan can take a Christian wife unless she accepts Islam. Hence there is no intermarriage except when a girl elopes with a Mussulman or is abducted. Some of these cases are due to the foolish whim of the girl. At other times they are decoyed or deceived. Some years ago in Tabriz while the mother and grandmother of the house were absent, a girl of twelve was enticed away and taken to a Mussulman harem. The family were poor, and the promises of ease in the house of a wealthy Mussulman attracted her. For two days it was supposed she was visiting with some friends. When the truth was known, the distress of the mother and the Armenians knew no bounds. Consular influence was exerted to have the girl examined to know whether her going was voluntary. But they compelled her to speak Turkish and dictated her answer so that she remained in the harem. Formerly abductions were common but now they are rare, and the Persian government shows a readiness to deal fairly with such cases, not caring to offend Christian people by injustice about a few girls. It is one of the threats perverse children hold over their parents; "If you don't, I'll go and become a Mussulman."

CHAPTER VII.

TABRIZ AND SALMAS.—THE MISSION TO THE ARMENIANS.

AT the time of the transfer of the "Mission to the Nestorians," in 1871, it was decided to enlarge its scope. Its name was changed to the "Mission to Persia." A station was opened in Teheran in 1872, and in Tabriz in 1873. Previous to this some efforts had been made to enlighten the Armenians, by means of evangelists and colporteurs. For ten years previously a Bible depot had been kept open in Tabriz. Rev. Mr. and Mrs. Peter Z. Easton and Miss Mary Jewett, arrived in Tabriz, Oct. 1873, and established the station.* Rev. Mr. and Mrs. S. Lawrence Ward and Mrs. L. C. Van Hook, arrived in 1876, and Rev.

---

* Rev. Mr. and Mrs. Perkins remained in Tabriz a year and three months, until Dr. Grant and Mr. Merrick arrived. Mr. Merrick remained in Tabriz from 1835 to 1837, and in other parts of Persia till 1842. He published in Persian, Keith's "Evidence from Prophecy," which to this day is useful. "A treatise on the Christian Religion" and one on astronomy were left in manuscript. He published in English a translation of Shiah traditions, "The Life and Religion of Mohammed."

Mr. and Mrs. John N. Wright, in 1878. At first there was a friendly spirit on the part of many of the people, which gave opportunity to reach them in their homes. Curiosity drew many of them to the services. But soon opposition arose. The Armenian bishop tried to impress upon the government that the mission had political motives. Slanderous reports were circulated; such as that the Protestants spat on the picture of the Virgin, and that they gave money to every attendant at the meetings. The work was enlarged by stationing evangelists from Urumia in Maragha, Khor and Ardebil, important cities of Azerbaijan. Among the first communicants was Mr. Mateos Nazarian, who had first professed his faith, in Teheran. He has been for years an honored elder and Sabbath-school superintendent in the Tabriz church. He was a wealthy merchant and an ardent devotee of the Gregorian Church. He habitually attended church and went through the forms of prayer before the pictures, burning the candles and crossing himself in all devoutness. He would go to Muzhumbar and offer many sacrifices at the shrines. He read his prayer-book in the ancient tongue every day. One of the pictures now hanging in the Gregorian church was a votive offering from him. He then knew little of true spiritual religion. But misfortunes came upon him. A ship on the Caspian with a large amount of his goods was wrecked. The family property fell into the courts in litigation, and has remained there since. These reverses of fortune drove Agha Mateos, as he was called, to read his Bible with new earnestness. He went to the missionaries and learned the truth more perfectly. He embraced it with ardor, becoming a thorough and consistent evangelical, completely breaking away from the lifeless rites and traditions. For many years he has been the faithful custodian of the depot of the American Bible Society.

Another one influenced to accept the truth was Wascon, a son of a priest at Sheverine, near Hamadan. Mrs. Hawkes has recorded his story from his own lips. "At the age of eighteen I, who had never been farther than two miles from home, went to Tabriz for the purpose of learning to read and write. There, by the help of an aunt, I attended school. Five years served to collect money to take me to the sepulchre of John, which was eight hundred miles from Tabriz. While tarrying at the sepulchre an earthquake occurred, which cracked the walls of the building. Then doubt crept into my mind, and the question arose, 'How can the saint help others if he can't keep his own house from earthquakes?' I came away in grief. Returning to Tabriz, I was met by a crowd of Armenians and ushered into the city with honor, and there I lived a life of strictness, keeping the fasts and being constant in prayer. I had a companion, Stephen, the son of a priest; and one day we heard that a man had come from Urumia who had been known to say that Mary was not the mother of God. We made a compact that, if this proved to be true, we would kill him, and for this purpose went to his house. When the question was put to Shamasha Ishu, he said, 'This name is not in the Bible.' I said, 'If I find it, I will kill you;' and his reply was, 'My blood shall not be upon you.' I told him I would see him again in regard to this matter, and, going to the priest, asked him to show me where the statement was made, that I might give an answer to the Protestants. His reply was, 'Oh, cursed man! do you too blaspheme?' And he drove me from his house. Going home, I took up my Bible with grief; and returning to the Protestant, asked him to teach me. Three months I went to him, and he read and explained the Bible to me. My friends hearing this, some chided me, and some with soft words tried to bring me back to the old Church. But, searching more and more, I saw the truth to be on the side of the Protestants, and the word of God had power on my heart and drew me to God like the attraction of the magnet, and from that time I have been going toward God."

He was for a time a colporteur in Tabriz, and then returned to Hamadan and continued to live in the truth. At some time during his life he lost the use of one eye, and a few years ago, while at Hamadan on a visit, the sight of the other was destroyed by the accidental discharge of a gun; but his mind is well stored with Scripture truth, and in the same village, where his father was priest, he is teaching a purer faith.

To further the work among the Armenians, an evangelist, Mr. Gregor Guergian, was called from Van in Turkey. He was a man with a remarkable experience and history. At our request he wrote his story, which I have translated as follows: "As an apprentice in Malatia, Turkey, I had no thought other than to clothe my body. At last in my mind thoughts arose concerning my soul. My conscience was very uneasy. I sought a way that I might be saved. Whatever I heard from those around me, I immediately did. I had no acquaintance with the Scriptures. I did not understand what I read. Before men I was not objectionable, but my chief thought was of my stomach. I lived as a worm in selfishness. Because of the smitings of conscience, I listened much to the superstitions of old women. I wished much to go to a monastery, that by an ascetic life I might be saved. I began to pray unceasingly, day and night, in the wilderness and stony places. I shed many tears that my sins might be washed away. I fasted for weeks and months. I went continually to church and remained there so long that people were angry with me. Whatever money fell into my hands I distributed to the poor. I knelt before the pictures, I burnt candles, I read religious books, but without peace of conscience. I was more hungry and thirsty for salvation than for meat and drink. In my agony I cried out, 'What shall I do to be saved?'

"When I was ready to go to the monastery to become an ascetic, by God's great mercy an evangelical preacher came and lodged opposite the house of my master, as Peter was sent to Cornelius. But I was filled with horrible thoughts against the evangelicals. If it had been possible, I would have done great injury to the Protestants. I was one day praying, weeping and reading a religious book that my sins might be forgiven, when the preacher, hearing my voice, came up and said to me in a quiet voice, 'What do you read?' I replied roughly, 'It is none of your business.' He said, 'I would simply say, "Read the gospel."' I replied, 'Ah! would you have me read the Bible that I may turn to your religion? Your gospel is corrupted.' He said, 'Let us compare them.' Then we compared several places, and I saw there was no difference. Though I had nothing to say, yet in heart I was antagonistic. I was striving by wrong means to reach the fountain of life, but, alas! I found myself in a burning desert. I had wept for a long time, but I thought one said to me, 'Prayers in an unknown tongue have no value.' One day I went to the preacher's house, I know not with what purpose. By good fortune it was the time of worship. The preacher was praying. I dumbly listened and drank in the words of the prayer as a dry tree. In my mind a voice said, 'This is the prayer acceptable to God and profitable.' I said, 'Is it possible for prayer to be in such plain, intelligible language, as man speaks to man?' After this, by God's grace, I had a spirit of prayer.

Though before men I prayed according to custom, yet privately I made known to God the thoughts of my heart and the needs of my soul. After a little while I had so much love for the preacher, his worship, reading and companionship, that I thought, 'Would that manna would fall from heaven; I would eat and continually stay with him.' But being a hungry apprentice, I could not. In my heart I threw away my old religion and became in love with evangelical truth. Whenever I found a pretext, I quickly ran over to the evangelist, though others observed it and began to prohibit and persecute; but it was impossible to keep me back. On Sunday they took great care that I should not go to the preaching, and that I should go to the old church, and they went with me, that I might not run away on the road. But often I fled by distant gardens, and through thorny hedges, that I might reach the evangelical brethren. I was more willing to remain hungry and to hear the words of the gospel than full to remain away.

"After much wandering about I was received by Rev. Mr. Richardson, of Arabkir, as a student. Day and night I studied hard. An old blind man helped me in arithmetic. I lived in my aunt's house, who took care of me. Her husband, Sergis, was a gunsmith, who for three-fourths of the year was away among the Kurds, and while at home was making preparations to leave. His disposition was somewhat like a Kurd's. In my aunt's family were three daughters, two sons

and a blind sister. By God's grace they all became
enlightened and became an evangelical family. I
taught my oldest cousin to read, and explained to her
the word of God. She accepted the gospel from the
heart. I specially charged her not to marry till she
found a believing husband, though there was no such
an one in our city. The blind sister embraced the
gospel with great zeal. The neighbors and friends
became angry and threatened us, saying, 'Wait till
Sergis comes, and we will show you what it is to be
Protestants.' I had another aunt who came and saw
me pray and heard me read and talk. She complained
of her oldest son, saying, 'My boy is living with evil
companions. It is impossible to talk with him. We
are all afraid of him. He strikes us with the first thing
he can seize. We can keep nothing in the house. He
opens all the locks, steals and spends everything for
drink and with evil companions. I will send him to
you. Perhaps if you exhort him he will become
better.' He came to me, and in a little while the wolf
became a lamb and joined himself to the brethren.
Then his mother began to accuse herself that she had
allowed her son to become a Protestant, and the
people threatened that they would not give their
daughters to him in marriage. His parents, hearing
these threats, were enraged at me. My aunt came
and said, 'You have torn down our house; by deceit
you have made my son a Protestant.' And the boy's
father said, 'I would kill Gregor if I was able to pay

his blood-money to the government.' The boy fled from their house, and they never received him again.

"When Uncle Sergis returned home and heard the thousand slanders he became enraged, and I was compelled to flee from the house. My aunt said, 'Never return. My husband says he will kill you, because my daughter has promised to marry a Protestant. He says, "My house is destroyed; I will go away that I may never hear this name."' Nothing remained for me but to pray. In my mind I said, 'My whole success is destroyed.'

"At this time I became a member of the church, and went to Harpoot Theological Seminary to take a course in theology. There I continually prayed for my uncle Sergis, but I said to myself, 'Miracles are possible, but what will God do? how can he persuade him?' At last God heard my prayer, praise to his name! They brought me news that my uncle had accepted the truth in the following manner: When my uncle returned home and was working, there was in his house a poor family. The mother was a good evangelical. By God's wise ordering she became sick, and the evangelicals, with their pastor, came every day with much burning love to the sick one, and served her in many ways until she became well. For many days my uncle observed this and was amazed. Through this God's Spirit worked on his heart. One day he said to my aunt: 'Wife, the Evangelicals are true. All I have heard of them is false. I have never seen such a thing among our people. I will certainly go to church next Sunday.' Wonder of wonders! That which is impossible with man is possible with God. 'Love one another' is the mark.

"I forgot to tell that when my uncle was enraged he married my cousin to an open profligate, but by great grace the girl caused the prodigal to return. Praise! God's ways are wonderful!"

His theological course was interrupted by a disease of the eyes. He became almost blind, but by the partial use of one eye, finished his studies, and after laboring at several places in Turkey, came to Tabriz. He remained four years in Tabriz, reaching many with the gospel message.

Mr. Easton, shortly after his arrival in Tabriz, wrote: "Judging from all I can see and learn, such is the thirst for knowledge among the Armenians, and such is also their dissatisfaction with their own schools, as now carried on, that we should find no difficulty in establishing two schools, one for boys, and one for girls. The drawback is teachers." Two small schools for girls were shortly opened in charge of Miss Jewett, in the two Armenian quarters. The teacher of the Lelawa school was a woman named Mariam, of meagre education, but one who had received the truth in sincerity, and though now many years dead, she is yet remembered for her true Christian character.

When it was proposed to enlarge and emphasize the

educational work, a difference of opinion developed among the missionaries. Mr. Easton held that Christ's commission forbade the missionary to teach as a means of reaching the people, that the missionary's business was to herald the gospel, and after a community of believers was gathered, they should establish their own schools. The majority of the station and mission, and finally the Board, held that schools might be used among the diversity of operations. Mr. Easton had also certain different theological views, so he tendered his resignation to the Board, and has since resided in Tabriz, carrying on an independent work with his own means.

It was to fill the vacancy occasioned by this resignation that the writer was appointed to Tabriz in 1880. Miss Jewett, returning, and Miss Mary A. Clarke went out at the same time. Dr. G. W. Holmes, who had previously been at Urumia, opened the medical department in 1881. (See chapter on Medical Work.) Miss Gretty Y. Holliday arrived in 1883. Let me briefly indicate the work of each during the following years, that I may quickly resume the more general subject. Mr. Ward had charge of the church and evangelistic work. In 1887 he was transferred to Teheran. Mr. Wright had charge of translation and the station treasury. He began in 1884 and continued through some years a revision of Rev. A. Amirkhaniantz's version of the Bible in Azerbaijan Turkish. In 1885, Mr. Wright was transferred to Salmas to open a new station. I had charge of the boys' school, book department and mission treasury, while itinerating, superintending the out-stations and teaching the training class were engaged in conjointly. Miss Jewett had charge of the work for women. Mrs. Van Hook, Miss Clarke (who later went to Teheran) and Miss Holliday had in succession and sometimes conjointly charge of the girls' school.

In 1885, Rev. J. M. Oldfather and family were transferred from Urumia to Tabriz, remaining until 1890. The frequent transfer and changing of missionaries is unusual and has been a great detriment to the work. The missionaries had gained many friends in Tabriz, and their departure was a loss and regret. Mrs. Annie Rhea Wilson joined the mission, Dec. 1886.* Dr. Mary E. Bradford started medical work for women in 1888. Dr. and Mrs. W. S. Vanneman and Rev. and Mrs. T. G. Brashear arrived in 1890, the former taking up the general medical work, the latter evangelistic work.

It is unnecessary to give a detailed account of these years, or of each missionary's earnest efforts. Glance

---

* On her departure from America the following lines were addressed to her with reference to her father, Rev. Samuel Audley Rhea, who died at Ali Shah and was buried at Urumia :

> " From out the grave of one
> Who laid his weary body down to rest
> In Persian soil, methinks I see a spirit rise,
> Who like the Macedonian angel stands and cries,
> ' Dear child, we need thee, come !'

at the worker among the women and fill in the details by imagination. See her as, Bible in hand, she goes day after day from house to house of the poor and ignorant, sits on the floor of the low room or, may be, cellar, covered with a simple carpet, with bare, mud walls, and with windows where the light comes in through paper, and endeavors to impress a few plain truths of the gospel upon their minds. See her when she is called to the home of a rich woman, who, though the walls of her house are frescoed, its floor covered with khallis, and its divans with rich embroideries, finds no consolation, but whose mourning for her husband causes her to pull her hair from its roots and tear great gashes in her breast, and there, by request, reads and prays with her, and points her to the Burden Bearer. Follow her when she goes to the house of a

> " A vision then I see
> Of those who gather round the great white throne,
> With songs of praise, ' With joy exultant now I raise
> My song to thee,' says one. ' to thee be praise.'
> ' Glory and honor be.'
>
> " ' Thy promises how true
> At home with thee, I from my labors rest
> In joy and peace ! The precious child thou gavest me
> Returns to bless the land of her nativity.
> Through her I work anew.'
>
> " So now we send thee forth,
> Rejoicing that the Master fills thy heart
> With love for Persia. As patient teacher, Christian wife,
> Christ's faithful lover, may thy earnest busy life
> Reflect thy parent's worth."

sister of the church whose child has died of the smallpox; and, having previously endured this disease, she fumigates the house, assists the stricken family in preparing the dead, and comforts the mother. Or again, see her, as she distributes tracts which she herself has translated, first reading them to the women, and then leaving them for the husband to read; or as she gathers the women together for regular instruction and prayer, or organizes them into a missionary society. Go with her to the annual meeting, and though making stages of nine hours on horseback in the hot sun, yet letting no evening pass without gathering the women together and delivering the message. See her as she goes to the neighboring plain for a tour, and fifty miles from any other missionary, itinerates through the villages sustained by the companionship of Jesus. In the heat of summer and the severe cold of winter, in the midst of slander, opposition and sickness, her one desire is to reach the women with the truth. Such is the character of the labor of the workers among the women of Persia.

No part of the work is more enjoyable than touring in the outfield. Missionaries and evangelists have done much of this. I will narrate a few experiences among the mountain Armenians of Karadagh. How the ignorance of the people about spiritual matters surprises one. At different times when I put the question, "What must one do to be saved?" they would answer, with a blank look, "How do we know?" Some of them

A PERSIAN VILLAGE.

knew not why Christ came into the world, how he was put to death, or why he suffered death. Some would exhaust their thought on the subject by saying, "The Jews killed him." Some were surprised to know that Christ's death had any relation to us. Even a priest said that Christ died for the heathen, but Christians must save themselves by good works. The little religious knowledge of these mountaineers comes more perhaps from Mussulman traditions which they hear than from the gospel. They will tell you that Christ was born out of the side of Mary, and talked when a new-born babe. About the Holy Spirit they seem to know nothing but the name, which they repeat in the formula of the Trinity. The sign of the cross is of great importance; even the coats of the boys have a bright colored cross on the back.

To these ignorant lost sheep of the new covenant it was our privilege to speak day by day of the truth. Immediately on entering a village curiosity drew a crowd around us, whom we found ready listeners to the gospel, which we read and explained in an informal way. During the day, at the threshing floors, in the blacksmiths' shops, under the mulberry trees, at the mill race, in the street, now here and now there, we reached the few or the many. A setting forth of sin and an appeal to their consciences received startling response. One man replied, "We are steeped in sin. We steal, lie, cheat, slander, extort and what not. No one goes truly in the way." I told him that the doers of such things could not inherit heaven. He said, "None of us will; we sin and know not how to do otherwise. No one has taught us." At another place the thought of sin moved the householder to deep conviction, and he exclaimed, " If my sins were put into this deep valley before the village, they would fill it so that you could walk over on the level." We heard many such confessions of sin.

But prejudice and misrepresentation are so strong that it is hard for them to receive the truth from us. They have heard that Protestants have no baptism, no Lord's Supper, no wedlock, no sacrifices, that they spit on the picture of the Virgin, in short, that in the last analysis, we are atheists. They say, "Those missionaries are a good people, but they have a very bad religion." They have strong belief in their own way. A member of the Protestant church wished to take one of these poor, ragged mountain girls to Tabriz as her maid-servant. As an inducement she said, " I will give you nice clothes." She replied, "No! you want to make me a Protestant. I am willing to wear poor clothes, but I am not willing to deny my faith." The bishop had sent orders that they should not receive us, so that some were ready to say, " Exhort yourselves; " but even a priest welcomed us cordially to his house and said to objectors, " We should not put obstacles in the way of these men, they preach the gospel as it should be." We see prejudice melting away and the conviction forced upon them, as a man expressed it in a word when we were saying farewell, "In the end this doctrine will conquer." Some interesting experiences happened to us at Khoi. In the suburbs we have a school and an evangelist. We appointed preaching services every night in the week, and a good attendance aroused the priest to oppose. He preached against us in the church, saying, "By going to the Protestants you will become contaminated in two months and become lepers." (They nickname us "*Prots*" and the word for leper is "*Barod*.") "They are wolves in sheep's clothing. They will steal your hearts. I will have to shut up the church." He stood in the street before our door and said, "Those that love me, pass by." The priest's two sons afterwards became Protestants or Evangelicals, as they prefer to be called. The priest in the other ward cursed us strongly and threatened the people that he would not marry, nor bury them, baptize their children, nor give them the sacrament if they came to us, and his daughter came and turned back the women from our meeting. In a village on the Khoi plain, opposition was severe because an Armenian inclined to Protestantism, had "eaten" his fast. Most indignant about this breach of ceremony was the man who kept two concubines without evident pangs of conscience. A monk perambulating with a relic or arm-bone of St. Stephen, encased in gold, was collecting money to build a church on the saint's tomb. The text on which he founded his plea was, "Ministering to the necessity of the saints." When this vartabed or another like him had finished his discourse, some of the people said, "We have a preacher here, who can beat you, but he is a Protestant." The vartabed said, "Where is he? Let him be accursed! Strike him!" The people began to fisticuff the preacher, but some took his part and a free fight arose in the church, in the midst of which the priest not only received some blows, but lost his chance to pass the hat, for the congregation dispersed in the uproar.

In the village, one place of meeting was the stables. The *sakki* or platform of the stable is a great winter place of congregating. We took an earthen castor-oil lamp by which to read. The heat from the oxen, donkeys and buffaloes supplied the place of a stove. (From forty to one hundred would crowd around.) The air soon became steamy and stifling, so that one was compelled to break through the conventionalities, and take off his coat. The people, from forty to one hundred, crowded around so that they had not sitting room. Generally the service ended in a free discussion. Thus the opportunity for seed-sowing is abundant, but success arouses opposition. A man may be a drunkard, impure or profane, and no one has a word to say; but if he become evangelical, he has denied the faith and is subject to ostracism. A merchant told me, "I believe Protestantism is the best form of Christianity, but if my brother becomes a Protestant, I will beat him." Under such difficulties, work grows slowly, but the people are surely becoming enlightened.

It was first thought that the work of Tabriz station could be carried on by means of the Turkish language, as all the races of Azerbaijan speak that as a vernacular. The first training class was taught in Turkish. In 1884 it was decided that the school and training class should be in the Armenian language, and that all missionaries, except the physician, should learn Armenian. In 1880 a meeting house was built. About the same time a Protestant cemetery was purchased and a wall erected around it. Some years later by subscription among Protestants, native and foreign, a reservoir for irrigation was made and trees planted and grass sown. This project stirred up the Armenians to beautify their cemetery, which until then had been a desolate waste. In 1885 Mr. Nicoghos Guleserian, an Armenian preacher, was called from Van, Mr. Shmuel, who had been three years in Tabriz, going to reopen the work in Soujbulak.

About this time the attention of the mission was specially drawn toward the need of evangelizing Salmas. Preachers and teachers from Urumia had been in several villages for a number of years. The Armenians seemed friendly. When I was itinerating there, many of them requested us to come and open up schools among them. In some of their schools the Bible in the modern version was being used. At one place the school room was thrown open to us for a meeting. The priest sent out and invited his flock and they listened with approval to the truth. The priest himself specially requested me to exhort the people on the observance of the Sabbath. After dinner they said farewell with many kind words. At another village they confessed with sorrow their utter ignorance of spiritual things and lack of true Christian experience. The need was evident, and the people seemed accessible.

It was decided to establish a new station, including in its field Salmas, Kotur, Khoi and Maku, with a population of over one hundred thousand, ten thousand of them being Armenians. Dr. and Mrs. Shedd, from Urumia, temporarily occupied the field in May, 1884. A house was rented in Haftdewan, the largest and most central Armenian town on the plain of Salmas. It has a population of two thousand. Its streets, though crooked, are of good width and have water courses running through them lined with large willows. The walls of the yards are unusually high and betoken the prosperity of the inhabitants.

The governor of the crown villages, of which Haftdewan is one, determined to prevent our occupying the house unless he received a large fee. Some of the villagers were opposed to our coming. The master took a security-paper of one thousand tomans from the villagers that they would prevent our occupying the house. A prolonged contest arose. Dr. Shedd and others made many efforts to arrange the affair. While I was in Khoi, I interviewed the khan, endeavoring to have him withdraw his opposition.

He refused, saying that even if the shah ordered it, we must arrange with him, and informed us indirectly that the sum he desired was £100. I told him we must then refer the matter to Teheran.

After I left the house, he called his diviner and asked him, "Will the missionaries locate in Haftdewan?" Holding up the brass plate containing the Zodiacal and many cabalistic signs, and counting the mysterious numbers on his beads, he rested his finger on the plate, and declared that they would. The khan's face clouded up and he said, "Perhaps after Noruz, I will be superseded, and they will succeed." Telegraphic word was sent to U. S. Minister Benjamin, who had already been made acquainted with the situation. He brought the matter to the attention of his majesty, and orders were at once telegraphed to the silar-il-askar, governor of Urumia, to investigate the case. Later a telegram came, "Government orders house to be given, and khan to report in person to Teheran." The silar, soon afterwards made Amir-i-Nizam, in passing through Salmas to become governor-general of Azerbaijan, severely reprimanded the khan, who made profuse apologies and requested a paper from Dr. Shedd that he had withdrawn all opposition. He enjoined the people to honor us, informing them that such orders had come from the shah. Shortly afterwards Rev. J. N. Wright was transferred from Tabriz, and took up his residence in Haftdewan (1884). Active opposition ceased, but the Armenian bishop wrote, enjoining the priest to prevent any one from coming to us. Some bound themselves with an oath not to have anything to do with the missionaries. But the common people heard us gladly, and teachers and preachers were requested by them in some of the villages. Miss C. O. Van Duzee of Erzrum, came and opened a school in Haftdewan. Rev. Mr. and Mrs. J. C. Mechlin joined the station in 1887; Miss Emma Roberts in 1887, and, after her return to America, Miss J. F. McLean, in 1892.

In 1890 a sad and shocking event happened in Salmas which cast a gloom over the mission and for a time greatly interrupted the work. This was the murder of Mrs. Wright. In 1885 Mr. Wright was married to Miss Shushan Oshana, a Syrian by race, an educated and refined woman, daughter of Pastor Oshana, professor of ancient Syriac in the college at Urumia. In 1888 they visited America, and Mrs. Wright won the esteem of all who came to know her. Owing to the gross misrepresentations that were made, it is well to give a correct account of her murder. There was in the employ of the missions in the village of Ula, where Mr. Wright was then residing, a teacher named Menas. By race he was Armenian on his father's side and Syrian on his mother's, a Protestant by profession, and a graduate of Urumia College. He had a good reputation, but it was discovered that he had improper relations with a widow on the premises. Mrs. Wright discovered his crime, informed Mr. Wright, and Menas was dismissed. Blaming Mrs. Wright for being the cause of his dismissal, Menas deliberately planned to murder her, prepared his weapons, and coming to the house, settled his accounts with Mr. Wright, attacked Mrs. Wright with a dagger, wounding her in five places in the back. Dr. Bradford hastened from Tabriz to her side, and she and Dr. Samuel did all that medical skill could do. While Mrs. Wright lingered she showed a wonderful degree of fortitude and patience, and at the same time a most sweet and forgiving spirit in regard to her assailant. "If I die," she remarked one day, "I shall go to heaven; but if he dies his soul is lost forever." Her Christian character shone out brightly to the last. She said to Mrs. Shedd, "All is light about me."

The murderer fled to Turkey and would certainly have escaped had not Col. C. E. Stewart, H. B. M. consul-general, been providentially in Salmas. Through his personal and energetic efforts Menas was captured on the road to Van. United States minister Mr. Pratt and Col. Stewart demanded his proper punishment. And now, most strangely, many of the Gregorian Armenians, headed by Bishop Stephanos, took the side of the murderer, and blinding their eyes to the positive proof of his guilt, set themselves to free him by the circulation of slanders, the use of political influence and of money. Though some were persuaded by these means, the shah was not deceived, and sentenced him to imprisonment in Teheran for life. During the cholera scare of 1892, when everything was in confusion and there was no American minister in Persia, the jailer was bribed to release Menas.

The sequel showed that it would have been a public benefit had severer punishment been inflicted, for others were encouraged to commit crime in the hope of exemption from punishment. This excitement had scarcely cooled down when another startling crime was reported from Salmas. This time an Armenian Catholic monk, Serapeon, was the victim of assassination. An Armenian Gregorian, under pretext of receiving alms or religious instruction with a view to embracing Catholicism, procured the opportunity to assassinate the monk. The crime was laid by the Catholics at the door of the Armenian Nationalists, and they hesitated not to charge Bishop Stephanos with being the instigator of the crime. The Nationalists practically admitted their complicity by replying that the monk had betrayed their national secrets to the Turkish government. A long and bitter contest arose, in which many innocent people of Salmas were arrested and fined, and the Persian officials fattened by sucking the golden blood of the Christians. In the midst of these troubles the startling news came that a Gregorian monk, while returning to Van and stopping over night in the Gregorian churchyard at Haftdewan, had been murdered. He was an inoffensive man and had no personal enemies. The Gregorians immediately raised the cry that the Catholics had committed the murder in retaliation. The Catholics replied that the Gregorians had done it with the purpose of casting the blame on them. One of the murderers was wounded and captured, from whom it appeared probable that the murderers were a band of young Gregorians, probably intoxicated. The Catholics apparently cleared themselves of all participation in the crime. There were suspicions, counter-accusations, arrests and imprisonments of various parties; some fled, and their fathers suffered much loss on their account. The Mohammedan officials more and more lined their pockets with fines and bribes, laughing in their sleeves at the spectacle of how Christians love one another, and saying, "Let the dogs fight." The final upshot seemed to be a victory for the Catholics and the accession to their ranks in Salmas of a number of Gregorians to escape further annoyance.

The work among the Armenians of Azerbaijan has been a difficult and trying one. One great difficulty which indeed manifests itself among all the races of Persia, is the mercenary idea of religion. The idea seems deep-rooted that religion is a matter of worldly policy, and is to be valued in proportion to its temporal benefits. In Islam it is the established custom to render the convert financial aid. The Koran says, Surah IX. 60: "Alms are to be given . . . . to those whose hearts are won to Islam." Omar said: "This alms was given to incline your hearts to Islam."

A Christian or Jew, turning Mussulman, is presented, it may be, with a wife and a full purse—two essential requisites in their eyes. Formerly he was permitted to confiscate all the property of his Christian relatives. If he be under sentence of death or condemned to pay a large fine, profession of allegiance to Islam secures instant pardon. A missionary was preaching to some villagers, and his words meeting with their approbation, they said: "You seem intelligent; if you will become a Mussulman, you may be our mollah, and we will give you a wife, a farm and three yoke of oxen." So imbedded is this principle in their minds, that they cannot but think that we are working on the same plan. If they hear that so many thousands are raised by the Christians of America for missions, they think it is to buy converts. They think we get so much a head. A not uncommon question is: "Sahib, what do you give such a one for being a Christian? what will you give me if I become one?" This inquiry is made not with shamefacedness, but in the full expectation that we will hold out some pecuniary inducements to them to become converts. A woman listened to the gospel for a few hours, and then said: "Lady, I believe in Christ; won't you give me a new skirt?" A young man came to the meetings for a few Sundays, and when I gave him a cordial shake of the hand and invited him to come again, he replied: "I will if you will give me something for my living."

An Armenian came before the church session seeking admission. The pastor asked him why he came. He replied, "I have a debt which troubles me." Another, when asked why he wished to be a Protestant, replied, "It is a *mudakhil*." In other words, "There is gain in it."

Not only to obtain money and work, but for various other objects, men become attentive listeners to, and pretended believers of, the truth. There was an Armenian village which professed a willingness to become Protestant in a body. They had a grievance concerning their taxes, which they thought might be redressed through our influence with the government. They made the same offer to the Catholics, and were accepted. Much of the papal influence in Urumia was upon the foundation of pecuniary and political influence; and since the death of Archbishop Clozel and a partial change of policy, many have deserted the Roman fold. A short time ago a pervert Nestorian Mussulman made a confession to me. He had been under sentence to pay a fine of two hundred tomans for extortion and violence, and wished influence with the government. He said: "I went to your gentlemen; they would do nothing. Then I went to the archbishop; he spurned me. So I went before the mujtehid and accepted Mohammed, and was pardoned. But," he continued, "I am tormented unutterably; waking or sleeping, walking or eating, in company or alone, my conscience burns me as fire, because I have denied my Saviour. I long to escape from the dark pit into which I have cast myself." Yet, even in his remorse, he wanted me to send him to Russia and recommend him to friends for support, not being willing to return to Christ unless his life and a living were assured to him.

At first I thought this impression, that faith and finance are indissolubly connected, and that godliness is gain commercially, had arisen from some error in mission policy or in the distribution of the famine funds, or from imperfect conceptions of the communism of the primitive church of Jerusalem, of the example of Christ in feeding the hungry and of his instructions on alms-giving, but more accurate observation shows that it is a deep-seated error of religious thought.

In every station there is need of Christian servants, colporteurs and teachers. Fallow fields lie ready for the sowers. Every instrumentality must be utilized, and those who labor in the gospel must live by the gospel. In some stations many church members are employed in various ways, and are, for the most part, doing good work and thoroughly earning their salaries. For church and school building, carpenters, masons and contractors are necessary; for the necessities of life we must patronize tradesmen; and they reason rightly that we will more likely employ and patronize them if they are brothers in the Lord. And, indeed, it seems contrary to brotherly love to employ an unbeliever, when a church member can do the work. But in this lies the temptation to unworthy men to make a pretense of conversion; and so there springs up a lot of "loaves and fishes" or "rice" Christians who put on the livery of heaven to serve their own selfish ends. We have had a number of such who, while in employment, were good Christians, but when they went into other occupations threw off their allegiance to their Saviour. A dismissed colporteur exhibited signs of repentance for eighteen months, but when convinced that he would not be again employed, said: "Well, then, you may take my name off the roll." A carpenter, because jobs were given to an outsider—a more capable workman—determined to withdraw from the communion, bitterly complaining that Christ commands, "Feed my sheep;" while we were taking the children's bread and casting it to the dogs. If this mercenary spirit is gratified, such converts continue bringing nominal strength, but positive weakness to the Church. If it is not gratified an offer of aid, from the other side, is accepted and the man returns to the Gregorian Church or becomes a Catholic, his last state being worse than his original one, because he played the hypocrite and seared his conscience. I could fill pages with narratives of how we have been deceived, though trying to discern between the true and the false and even keeping catechumens on a long probation to test them. Of too many the squib is true which was said of a woman, "Her religion is very much like her dress, she can put it on or off just as she pleases." "Yes," was the reply, "and like her ball dress too, there isn't much of it." That this is not true of all is abundantly evident from incidents in other parts of this book.

Another difficulty has been the power and persecuting spirit of the Gregorian hierarchy. One of the first troubles after my arrival was concerning the validity of Protestant marriage and the right of our pastor to preform the rite. Early in the spring of 1882, one of the Protestant Armenians in Maragha, named Hacob, a gunsmith, was married to a woman of the Old Church. Pastor Moshi performed the ceremony. The woman entered the compact of her own free will and desire. But the affair was offensive to the Armenian priests. The hope of their gains was gone if marriage fees were withdrawn. Their indignation, from words and threats grew to action. Mob violence was resorted to, the pastor's house was stormed by a crowd headed by the drunken priests. Through fear the friends of the woman separated her from her husband. Appeal was made by the Armenian party to the Mussulman authorities to enjoin the repetition of the marriage ceremony by the priest. In addition charges of personal indignity, etc., were trumped up. An imaginary pulling of the priest's beard gave, for the fourth time, a ground of complaint. Laying aside all minor issues we felt that the right of Protestant marriage must be maintained. The first decision of the case by the governor of Maragha was in our favor. This only aroused the fury of the opposition. The case was appealed to the amir Nizam, governor of the province, and all the power of money and the personal influence of the khalifa or bishop and of the wealthy merchants were exerted upon the officials. With no official influences we had to rely entirely on the justice of our cause. The foreign agent even refused to hear our counter petitions. All our efforts in Tabriz seemed in vain. The appointment of a new governor in Maragha made uncertainty more uncertain. Mr. Wright, afterwards reinforced by Dr. Holmes, succeeded, however, in impressing him with the justice of our cause, his previous inclination being strengthened by what he regarded as interference with his authority by superior officials. He refused to reverse the decision already made, so, finally, after months of waiting the bride was restored to her husband.

But the contest was not yet over. The bishop announced his intention of going in person to the scene of conflict, and great fear fell upon all our friends. Indeed, his words were so full of violence, and he was reported to have such strong orders from the governor and crown prince, that we ourselves looked for vigorous action, and perhaps the temporary overthrow of our work. But his efforts proved wholly futile. The husband and wife remained undisturbed. Threats of violence and of burning the house rented by us, failed to cower the owner. The bishop's anathemas fell flat. His prohibiting attendance filled our meetings. His denunciations of us to the authorities met with reply from the Mussulmans themselves. One of prominence whose acquaintance with the Bible and with the Koran are equally remarkable, maintained to him from the Scriptures the truth of Protestantism. The bishop's excessive wine drinking brought his cause into reproach. His requiring largesses for decisions in ecclesiastical disputes aroused indignation even among his own people, and his yearly stipends were given with reluctance.

During Bishop Jermakian's administration, 1884-86, a more Christian method of opposition was adopted by him. Our scholars were often drawn away and our schools depleted, but it was not done by violent and persecuting methods. This bishop not only visited our schools but corresponded with us in regard to difficulties. He was a man of learning, knowing many languages and able to correspond with us in English. His liberal views and tolerant spirit were made a ground of complaint against him, and he resigned a position now made uncomfortable for him.

His successor, Bishop Stephanos Mekhetarian 1887-1892, was a different kind of man. He had not much learning, but had untiring energy and indomitable will. He loved discord and agitation and had a persecuting spirit. He kept the Christians of Azerbaijan in a turmoil the like of which has not been known. Before coming to Tabriz he was reported to have got into a quarrel with fifteen of the bishops at Etchmiadzin,

and to have put aside his episcopal robes and taken a
club to attack the venerable body. At Tabriz he first
got his own flock under control. A merchant, who
opposed his views in a public meeting, was summarily
ejected with blows. The directors were taught that
he would run the school according to his own will.
The teachers must do his bidding. Once the teachers
came to me in a body and offered, if I would employ
them, to bring their scholars along with them. He
installed a priest over the people, against their will,
contrary to custom.

One method of his work with Protestants was as
follows: He would tell a man, "Believe what you
please, be an infidel, or Evangelical, only don't break
away from the mother Church; if you do, you cease to
be an Armenian, you become a traitor." Their greatest objection to us seemed to be: "Protestantism is
unpatriotic; one who leaves the Church leaves the
race." We would reply, and I have spent hours and
days trying to convince men, that a convert only
ceased to be a Gregorian, and became an Evangelical
Christian. He is and continues to be an Armenian;
that is his race, his blood, his type. His change of
religious belief does not affect that. The confusing of
race and religion is so fixed in the Oriental mind that
one despairs of eradicating it. An Armenian wishing
to know my religion asked, "Of what race are you?"
I replied, "An American." He repeated the question.
Knowing what he wished to know, I still replied "An

American." Finally he said, "What is your religious profession," and received the answer he was wishing for, "I am a Protestant." They insist that one who ceases to receive their creed and to obey their bishop, abandons their race. This misunderstanding is used with great effect to turn young men away from us and even to draw some of our number away.

The bishop's first definite attack on us was by sending a copy of the Mezan-al-Hak to the mujtehid, falsely alleging that we were distributing that prohibited work. The result was the arrest of several colporteurs and the prohibition for a year of the sale of the Scriptures by colporteurs in the province.

He chose as his agent in Maragha a man who some years before professed himself a Protestant while in danger of imprisonment for slandering a former bishop, and who is now a Catholic and acting as their agent. At that time he was teaching in Maragha. The bishop sent an order for the people to oust pastor Moshi. They replied, "You send the missionaries away from Tabriz and the pastor will leave of his own accord." He then ordered that none of his people should rent the pastor a house. He was compelled to vacate a house we had occupied for eight years, because the owner was frightened from renting it. In the emergency one man was persuaded to sell us his house. Then the fire of the bishop descended upon his head, and for two months he had no peace. The agent frightened the seller into giving him money and threatened the brethren with imprisonment. One evening a mob of several hundred Mussulmans and Armenians collected around the house in which the pastor was alone with his family, determined to expel him by fright or violence. The lieutenant-governor refused to hearken to his pleas for protection. It was not until he had sent the third time, and accompanied the request by a present, that the officer sent a force of police to his relief, fortunately in time to prevent any violence. On account of a standing order of the government the house in Maragha was bought in the name of the pastor, a Persian subject. The bishop, bent on compelling us to withdraw, raised a furor about its being so near the Armenian church. The street doors are near, though there are two houses and seventy-five feet between the buildings; so that it is not likely much pollution would reach the church from our unhallowed services. This pretext was especially hollow, as the church is surrounded by wine shops, whose best patrons are the priests; but on this pretext he based a plea to the government to compel the pastor to return the house. This was strengthened by other petitions, signed by the ignorant people, many of whom are unable to read, the signatures in some cases being procured by beating and other forms of violence. These petitions demanded that the preacher be expelled from the city as a disturber of the peace. In fact, he was beloved by a majority of the people, and respected by all. Dr. Holmes was much occupied by this case, and exerted the influence acquired by his practice to bring about a successful issue. The foreign agent and governor were urgently appealed to. The latter sent a telegram to Maragha that the inhabitants be put under bonds to keep the peace, and that representatives of each party should be sent to Tabriz. Here several attempts have been made at compromise. We expressed willingness to take, either by rent or exchange, any other suitable house, provided they would take the present house off our hands, and in no way injure the man who had dared to sell to us in spite of the bishop's prohibition. The latter threatened to make his life not worth living. After vexing negotiations, the government finally decreed that, owing to the proximity of the purchased property to the Armenian church, it should be returned, but that the Armenians should rent us the house which had been withheld from us on account of the bishop's threats. The Armenians claimed the victory, but we had all we wanted at first—secure residence in the city, with no restrictions on our work.

The result afterwards showed that we made a great mistake in not contesting the case, even presenting it to the shah; for the impression universally prevailed that we were weak, and would be unable to protect Protestants and save them from persecution. The bishop's power for harm was tenfold augmented.

Shortly after this Dr. I. Casparian, a physician, educated in America and England, settled in Tabriz. Because he was a Protestant, though an ardent patriot, the bishop attacked his interests, tried to forbid any Armenians from renting him a house, or employing him as a physician. These and similar events were frequent. Sometimes a teacher would be drawn away by specious promises; a Protestant would be offered lucrative employment, if he would forsake his faith; temporary discontent of a brother would be fanned by flattery and lies that he might withdraw himself. By flattery and intimidation twenty-five boys were taken out of the school in a week. A young man attending preaching services was threatened at the dagger's point with violence if he did not cease. Others would say to us, "I would like to go to your meetings, but I am afraid." Yet, in spite of all, scholars and church members were more at the end than at the beginning of his administration.

The boys' boarding school had increased beyond the capacity of our premises. We had three or four houses rented for its accommodation. The church building was considered unsafe, and its appearance and condition were such as to render it unsuitable in such a city as Tabriz. About this time Mr. John I. Covington, of New York, wrote to his classmate, Mr. Oldfather, that his daughter Ruth, a member of the Acorn Mission Band, of Brooklyn, had died, and they wished to build a memorial of her. Building a church in Tabriz was suggested and cordially accepted.

We applied to Teheran for permission to build. The

American minister, Mr. Pratt, sent us in 1889 a copy of an order to the amir-i-Nizam, "directing that no impediment should be put in the way of the American missionaries purchasing a site and erecting a church." The original was not forthcoming, and the amir refused to take cognizance of the copy. He also observed that the order directed us to sell the present place before purchasing another. We appealed again to Teheran, after the return of our minister, and received a favorable reply. Meanwhile the foreign agent said that by the payment of a building license-fee permission would be given without any further decree from the capital. Permission was thus granted and the church erected in the summer of 1891. The work proceeded without interference of any kind. During Muháram, a chain-band marched into the churchyard, around the building and out again, saying to the workmen, "May it be blessed," "May God give you strength." Our quiet in building is remarked upon, on account of subsequent events. The city was in commotion over the tobacco monopoly. Excitement ran high, and it seemed that riot and revolution might be the next thing. In the autumn the governor and foreign agent were both removed.

The church is a handsome building, of moderate size, capable of seating two hundred and fifty, with a session room at one end. It is sufficiently beautiful to be a fitting representation of our faith before the people. Ruins of old walls and wells were found far below the surface, and tons of lime and stone had to be poured in to make a solid foundation. The expense ran over the amount of Mr. Covington's generous gift, and a subscription of four hundred and thirty tomans from the native and foreign Protestants completed the amount necessary. The dedication was held on December 20, 1891. The audience of two hundred and fifty was the largest ever assembled for Protestant worship in the city. The services were of the usual character for such occasions, in the morning in Turkish, in the afternoon in Armenian and English. During the summer the buildings of the Memorial Training and Theological School for Boys were also completed, and occupied September 10. The superintendence of these buildings was one of the most difficult tasks I ever undertook.

With these additions to our working power, we felt like planning a special campaign of spiritual work. Mr. Gregor Guergian, whose story was given above, returned to Tabriz, after ten years as preacher for a Lutheran congregation of Armenians at Shamokhi, Russia. Special meetings for prayer and consultation as to ways of reaching the people were held week by week by the workers. Visiting in the homes, distribution of Bibles and tracts and earnest personal labor were emphasized. In the use of these means, Mr. Guergian was above all active and efficient. In preaching, his originality and clearness of thought, fertility in illustration, wonderful command of language—impetuous as a torrent and aglow with fervor,—thrilled and carried along his audience. Night and day he was busy exhorting men to repentance, and presenting Christ as the Saviour. His marvelous fund of anecdotes, apt and telling, made his conversation highly entertaining as well as instructive. He might have said with Paul, "This one thing I do." His energy and power excited the fear and enmity of the opposers of the truth. Threats were made to beat and kill him. A young man struck him a severe blow on the head from behind in the street. Snow was thrown on him from the roof. Two young men came to his house at dusk and threatened him. Another, a special confidant of the bishop, came to his house, and told him that if he did not quit his preaching the bishop would have him killed. He was alarmed in view of the number of murders that had taken place in Salmas. Finally, at Noruz, the Armenian bishop made charges to the kala Begi against the preacher, desiring to have him silenced. The kala Begi made formal complaint to the Turkish consul-general, who called Mr. Gnergian and informed him of the charges. Then and not till then he told the consul how he had been beaten and threatened. The consul, unwisely, took vigorous action against the young assailants, a formal trial was held before the foreign agent, they were imprisoned, fined and made to give security for their good behavior. This turn of affairs aroused the Gregorians to a white heat. The chief men made strong protest against Mr. Guergian, demanding his expulsion. They even offered to buy up all the mission property if the government would send out the missionaries. The complaint against the preacher was forwarded to Teheran and approved, and an order for his expulsion was sent, but the Turkish consul refused to accept it and maintained that he was not worthy of expulsion. He, however, said it was simply his business to protect his person; as for his work, he would better cease it, publicly. Meanwhile complaint was sent by the foreign agent to Mr. R. M. Paton, acting English consul. It stated as follows: " Whereas the English consul has been established as the one who attends to the affairs of the Protestants in Azerbaijan, I give you trouble concerning one Gregor, who, by faulty conduct, gives the gospel and other papers in the streets and bazaars to the Armenians, and invites them to the religion of the Protestants. He refrains not from entering the houses of the Armenians without leave, enjoins them to works and prayer in the Protestant way, and casts tracts and books into the yards of the Armenians. He also says to Mussulmans: 'Your religion is empty and nothing.' Dear friend, you must know that this Gregor and the other preachers and teachers *have no right* under any consideration *to invite Armenians to their religion.* They must be reproved, and if this evil continues, it will become the duty of the officers to prohibit Gregor from these unworthy acts."

The part of this accusation referring to the

preacher's zeal and devotion was true, but I know of no houses he entered without leave, though some doubtless preferred he would have stayed away. In several cases he prayed with people who did not wish it, his partial blindness preventing him from seeing their unwillingness expressed in their faces. One man voiced his objection in this way: "Why, he talked to me as if I was a common sinner." However the effort to expel the preacher was unsuccessful, the partial prohibition of his work was removed by the Osmanli consul being replaced, but the Gregorians socially ostracized him, and a year afterwards he accepted a call to Erzrum.

In the midst of these excitements a curious incident occurred. The Gregorians of Kuhna Shahr, Salmas, wishing a new priest, selected a blacksmith, prepared a fee for the bishop of twenty tomans, and sent him with the elders to Tabriz for ordination. Here he must undergo for forty days in the church certain penances and fastings as a purification, and learn certain liturgies. Delay occurred owing to the bishop saying the fee was too small. They must make it thirty tomans. One night the candidate took fright and fled to the protection of the French consul, stating that he had received word that the Gregorians were going to kill him and lay the crime to the Protestants. The man made affidavit to that effect, which was sealed and certified and shown to me by the French and Turkish consuls. The information given the candidate was probably a hoax. I imagine neither Gregorian nor Protestant Armenians knew anything of any such plot. The man was sent off to Tiflis.

Several excitements of those times were about marriages, for there must needs be a woman in every trouble. One beautiful and accomplished girl, a Protestant graduate of our girls' school and teacher in it, became engaged to a Gregorian. It is not uncommon for them to intermarry. In this case the objection was to the character of the man. He belonged to a band of terrorists, some of whom were socialists, others free-lovers, many skeptical and dissipated. Afterwards the girl came to me with tears and supplications, pleading that she might be released from the engagement. I told her she had entered into it of herself; if she broke it she must do it of herself, adding if she did, we would see that she was not *forced* to marry him. There seems to have occurred a contest in her between conscience and natural affection. She wavered and acted with duplicity, pretending to us and deceiving us; at times driving him away and again accepting his attentions. The result simply was that the people became convinced that we were trying to *force* her to break away from him, and an exceeding bitterness of feeling arose. The man threatened to kill her, her grandfather and others if he was disappointed. The windows of the Armenian preacher's house were broken with stones. The miserable affair hung fire for a year, before we were convinced of her duplicity. Then we sent her away from the school to settle it or not return. She wrote to us from her home that "she was lost, she was going to hell, she did not love him, she was forced to marry him," and yet the next day she married him openly and of her own free will.

Another love affair gave us some lively incidents. Vartan, a theological student, was the accepted suitor of Satenig, a pupil in the girls' school. Both were Protestants. Her father was dead. Her relatives were agreed to the match on condition that the Gregorian priest should perform the ceremony. This the couple refused to concede. The relatives then threatened and beat the girl to make her give up Vardan. But she drew her finger across her throat and said: "You may kill me, but alive I am his, and dead I am his." Then the mother consented and took the girl's side. After some time two uncles were going to Tiflis, so the girl came from school to say farewell. That night they beat her and tried to change her mind. They refused to let her go back to school, even at the demand of her mother. It was rumored that they intended to carry her away to Russia. The mother finally made petition through Mr. Easton to the English consul, who kindly secured a hearing of the case before the foreign agent, at which he himself took the trouble to be present. Mr. Easton and I were present with the mother and Vardan. The police were sent and brought one of the uncles. *En route* a mob, headed by a priest, tried to release the uncle. They were beaten back by the police, severe blows were dealt, and the uncle was brought before the court with his face and clothes bespattered with blood.

The girl was not given to her mother, but taken to the bishop's house, and there kept by force, and all arts, persuasions and threats used to make her change her mind. She wrote to Vardan from the bishop's, "Pray for me that God may give me wisdom and memory and the Holy Ghost to stand in trial before my proud relatives. I said to them, 'Be assured all of you, until the world passes away, it is impossible that I receive the Gregorian ceremony.'" Several days passed; the mother went day by day to the office of the Mustashar-i-Doulah, thowing dust on her head and with other Oriental signs of grief, and, pleading that her daughter be restored to her, sat until evening. Every day the officers went to bring the girl, but the bishop refused to give her up. Finally the mother declared she must telegraph her petition to the shah. The Mustashar-i-Doulah replied: "If the bishop does not release her to-night, I will get soldiers from the crown prince and break his doors and fetch her." The bishop yielded to the inevitable and sent Satenig to her mother. The betrothal service and in due time the wedding were celebrated with Protestant ceremony, and the young couple, united in faith as well as love, received many congratulations.

Our excitements were not yet ended. Shortly after this happened the imprisonment of Mirza Ibrahim, the placards for the expulsion of the Protestants, and the dire plague of the cholera (August, 1892), as related in other chapters.

In the cholera Bishop Stephanos died, manifesting the same courage and determination in facing cholera, as he had shown in attacking Catholic and Protestant missions. Even after his death, an egg which he had laid, was hatched and a serpent, live with venom, came forth to sting us. This was a scheme against our church and school. They had been in use about a year. The Mustashar-i-Doulah, foreign agent of the government, had visited our school the winter previous and approved of it. On October 27, while I was away at Hamadan, and Mr. Brashear and Mr. Whipple at Urumia, and Dr. Vanneman busy at his medical work, without official or personal notification to the mission, the mirza of the Mustashar-i-Doulah and the chief of police of the kala Begi entered the yards of the church and the school, locked the doors, and putting red sealing-wax over the key-holes, sealed them, saying that they did so by order of the government. The history of the case was never exactly understood. But it seemed that some hostilely disposed persons presented an accusation against us to the crown prince, exaggerating and distorting facts and misleading his imperial highness. This was most unfortunate, for the prince's friendly and gracious conduct on many occasions had given us every reason to be grateful.

Many of our scholars, shut out from our schools, went to the Gregorian schools, where they took papers from them that they would not return to us. Dr. Vanneman, after some futile efforts in Tabriz, referred the matter to Teheran. The U. S. legation was then in charge of Mr. John Tyler, vice consul, who took hold of the affair with such efficiency and helpfulness as to merit our most cordial thanks. Slowness of the mails, and the absence of the shah on a hunting expedition made much delay. It was some weeks before we definitely knew the reasons assigned for the sealing. These were finally stated as lack of proper permission to build the church, having the ten commandments written in the interior of the church in a Mohammedan language and in the sacred blue color, having a water-tank under the church in which to baptize converts, having a tower in which we intended to put a bell, baptizing Mussulmans, of whom Mirza Ibrahim was now in prison, receiving Mussulman boys into our school and women to the church, having Dr. Bradford's dispensary near the church, etc. Two or three pictures of Mohammedan women were specially emphasized as objectionable, one in particular where an old soap peddler had intruded herself into a family group. Everything that had happened in twenty years past, and some things entirely without foundation, were made grounds of accusations. These charges were answered, the authorities at Teheran satisfied, and orders given to remove the seals. When this was not done, the congregation of Armenian and Eastern Syrian Protestants sent a petition to the shah with about sixty signatures, begging that they might be allowed to resume their prayers for his majesty in their church and to continue the education of their children. This was answered favorably, but some officials were angered by it. On the following Sunday three Armenians were arrested while going out of prayers, then being held in the girls' school, and one of the signers of the petition was arrested on a false charge.

The authorities now declared that they would open the doors provided we would agree in writing to certain conditions. This we refused. Some of the conditions were,—that no religious lessons should be given to Armenian scholars, that we should not preach to non-Mussulmans except in the presence of an officer of the law, that the ten commandments should be erased, that the doctors should not treat either men or women, that missionaries should not go to any Armenian house except when specially invited, should not give their religious books to any one, that when they assembled they should only pray in Turkish but must not preach in that language, that if a Protestant should take a photograph of another Mussulman woman and it be proved, they should all go out of Azerbaijan. It seemed almost as if the scribes of the foreign office must have written these conditions as a joke to show to Armenians who had petitioned against us.

But at that time it seemed quite serious and we were perplexed as to what the outcome would be. Six or seven strong telegraphic orders had already been disregarded. We had used every means at our command except the one the officials wished us to use. The prospect seemed indefinitely delayed. In our extremity God taught us a lesson of faith. We were holding our meetings of the week of prayer. Friday afternoon we were much cast down. We determined to appoint Saturday as a day of fasting and prayer for the opening of the doors. It was done with earnest supplication. How marvelous that on Saturday at ten o'clock both the buildings were opened and we met for communion preparatory-service in the church with deep thanksgiving to God.

But there was nothing miraculous. Our answer had come by natural but to us unknown means. The arrival of U. S. minister Mr. Watson R. Sperry fell on Friday, and in order that his first word with the shah might not be one of complaint, a peremptory order was sent that the seals be removed immediately and word sent that it was done. Saturday morning the officers came to my house and read the following order, "That we must not receive Mussulman women and children to our schools or church, that we must not take photographs of Mussulman women, that we must not conduct ourselves contrary to custom." Then the officers removed the seals as quietly as they had put them on ten weeks before.

The conditions had one element of toleration which was gratifying. It will be noticed that the attendance of Mussulman men at church is not prohibited. Heretofore the police had claimed the right to arrest, fine and beat a Mussulman who might be found at our church worship.

Since the opening of the seals, we have had two years of most remarkable quiet and have pursued our work undisturbed. Church services continue to be held in Turkish, Armenian and English. The attendance at the English service has varied greatly. It was largest during the time Col. C. E. Stewart, C.B., C.I.E., C.M.G. was consul-general. He and Mrs. Stewart, not content with encouraging all to come to the Sabbath service, organized a Friday Bible reading at the consulate, which was well attended by Europeans. His heart was strongly enlisted in Christian work, and he who had won high decorations for bravery in the service of his queen, was also a faithful soldier of Jesus Christ. He wrote, "It is also a great pleasure to be able to assist the missionary cause in any way. It is my earnest desire and daily prayer that I may be able to help the missionary cause and the advance of God's kingdom."

Worship in the Protestant congregation is conducted in the usual non-ritualistic style. In the mosque, Mohammedans sit on the floor, standing or kneeling or prostrating themselves during prayer; in the Armenian churches the congregation stands, occasionally prostrating their faces to the floor. We have introduced pews, and that the people might not pile their shoes up at the door, have left the church uncarpeted. In a carpeted meeting-room people have been known to take off their shoes at the door and carry them to their pews. Singing is generally with the foreign tunes, though Mrs. Wilson has learned and introduced some of the tunes of the Gregorian Church which are very popular. The chants of the Nestorian Church are used in the Evangelical churches in Urumia. Persian native airs would be very acceptable, were they not associated with vulgar words. The introduction of the organ in worship was an innovation in Persia. Mohammedans have frequently asked, "Why do you have an organ? What prophet authorized it?" Our reply, "David," satisfies them. The separation of men and women is continued in our Protestant churches as in Oriental churches, only they are given an equal chance to hear and see. Formerly a screen was passed down the center to separate them. This has not been continued, but the women keep their *chadus* or head-covers closely over them.

Candidates are examined with care and kept on probation to test them. About one hundred and forty have been received into the Tabriz church, one half of whom are at present enrolled. In January and March, before my departure, twelve were received. The contributions through the church treasury are about one hundred and twenty dollars a year. The week of prayer has often been a precious season to us. The Sabbath-school at Tabriz has about one hundred and ten, with lessons in three or four languages.

The missionaries, preachers, teachers and colporteurs of Tabriz and Salmas fields have several times met in conference. The first of these conferences was in 1887. It continued for two weeks, and was attended by a score of the native workers, besides the older scholars of the schools. It is the first time in the history of these stations that such a convention has been held, and it proved to be a valuable opportunity for instruction and counsel. Three sessions were held daily. The morning and evening sessions were occupied by lectures from missionaries on the following topics: The kingdom of God, the divinity of Christ, the typology of the Old Testament, the methods and success of missions, methods of instruction and hygiene. The lively interest manifested in these themes, and the intelligent and earnest questions concerning them, displayed at the same time the knowledge and the mental activity of the brethren; their own papers and conferences in the afternoons showed their high spiritual aims and practical acquaintance with the work in its various aspects. Such topics as work for Armenians, Jews, and others, medical work, colportage, schools, Sabbath-schools, self-support, temperance, the Sabbath, were introduced by two of the brethren in addresses of thirty and twenty minutes in length. High grounds were taken in regard to almost every question.

Loyalty to the Sabbath was emphasized, especially in view of the customs of the Armenians, making it in Tabriz a day for sociability, in Salmas a market day.

It was declared inexpedient to attend their Sunday feasts, even for the purpose of doing them good. One related how two church members had been disciplined for buying a couple of dimes' worth of tobacco on Sunday. Another recalled how the Protestants of Turkey had refused to work for the government on the roads on Sunday, and bakers had closed their shops, and how after suffering imprisonment for the truth, an order was issued by the government that Protestants should not be compelled to labor on Sunday.

The varied character of the opposition to our work was brought out in many ways in our conferences. Sometimes it is the curses of the priests, sometimes the oppression of the rich. In one place the teacher has been driven out by the farmer of the taxes; in another a paper was taken from the parents, making them liable to a fine should they send their children to our school; in another the man who rented us a house was driven from the village, and the helper abused and plundered. Not infrequently the attendants at schools and congregations are reduced from a score or two to almost nothing by persecution or the fear of it. Religious intolerance often takes the form of civil annoyance.

Another of these conferences was held in 1892. It was decided to form a regular presbytery composed of the missionaries, ordained preachers and churches of Tabriz and Salmas fields, to be connected in a synod with the native presbytery of Urumia. Pastor Moshi, of Maragha, was chosen moderator. After organization, four students lately graduated in theology, at the Memorial School, were examined and licensed.

If the direct results of this work are not as large as we wish, we must remember the truth contained in the words of ex-U. S. minister Benjamin: "The laws of progress followed by the Great Ruler, indicate that great reforms, when wide and permanent, come gradually and by the sowing of the seed for ages by husbandmen, who, perhaps, see the harvest only with the eye of faith."

In a published article he says of the mission work: "Among these races (Nestorians, Armenians and Jews), the American missionaries are laboring with a most encouraging success, a success which at present arouses at once the respect and the apprehension of the Mohammedans, and will ultimately command their assent as well."

CHAPTER VIII.

MISSION SCHOOLS IN TABRIZ AND SALMAS.

THE old time Armenian school has been admirably described in Raffe's novel, "Gaidser," "Sparks." A glimpse of it is obtained in the following essay by a boy in our Tabriz School.

"Formerly Armenian children went to the priest's yard from seven in the morning until noon. Each boy was supposed to bring a carpet to spread under him.

"It was necessary to go to school without breakfast, because the *Der-Der* (priest) said, 'Whoever eats bread before coming to his lessons, I will pull out his ears.' But how did the *Der-Der* know? When the boys came in he would call them and say to one of them :

"'You silly brute! Hah! Have you eaten bread to-day, that you came so late?'

"'Oh! no! Father Priest, I have not eaten.'

"'Put out your tongue.' The *Der-Der* looked at it. If his tongue was red the poor boy's day was black, for the *Der-Der* would give him such a terrible slap that he would feel it for hours and hours, but if his tongue was white the boy would escape by God's blessing.

"If it happened that a pupil did not know his lesson, there were two heavy books ready for his punishment. These great church-service books were placed on his hands and he was obliged to stand on one foot and hold them up until the *Der-Der* permitted him to sit down.

"The boys would often run away from these severe punishments, but alas! in vain, for the *Der-Der* would go and bring them from their houses by force. When the father first brought his son to school he would say, 'Priest, the flesh of the boy is yours, the bone is mine; only teach him good science.'

"And did the *Der-Der* teach him good science? If at the end of the year you asked a pupil the letters of the alphabet he would not know them.

"But now there is a change in Khoi; which is by the favor of the Protestants. When they opened a school, the Armenian boys all went to it, but the priests saw this and sent and brought a teacher from Van. Now there are two schools, but the greater part send to the Protestants, who receive the girls also."

The Armenians have made great progress in education in Persia in the last twenty years. Incited by a desire for education and spurred on by our mission schools, they have opened schools in cities and villages. In Tabriz they have now two schools for boys and two for girls, with reading-rooms and circulating libraries attached. Russian-Armenian teachers familiar with German methods give good instruction. For the impartation of purely secular instruction, mission schools are not necessary, but as a means of instilling gospel truth into the minds of the young, for the educating of the children of Protestants and the preparation of teachers and preachers they are a necessity and a success.

Reference has previously been made to the beginnings of educational work among Armenians in Tabriz. The girls' boarding-school was opened November, 1879, with three boarders, which number was increased to seven by January. Of it Mrs. Van Hook gives a picture:

"A low, native house with long, narrow school-room on one side, the entry and miniature sitting-room on the other; a tiny chamber on the roof and a dark cellar-kitchen reached by a flight of stairs from the end of the hall. A missionary lady a mile distant from any associate, in a quarter of the city where no English-speaking people reside. Three little Armenian girls, Eve, Margaret, and Jawahir.

"Many wishes for a girls' school had been expressed, many assurances of patronage given, but when the time came not one of those who had professed desire to give better opportunities to their daughters was willing to brave the derision of friends and opprobrium of the community to place a child in a missionary school."

Then female education was little valued. Parents would say, "What good will education do my daughter? Will it get her a man?" or "Will you make priests out of our girls?" A member of the training class was astonished when a missionary lady wished to translate an arithmetic and said, "Why! have you studied arithmetic?" The Armenians had at that time a small girls' school in which plain reading and needle work were taught. The bastinado stood in one corner of the room to scare the children.

A girls' school building was erected in 1882 near the Kalla, and on the same lot a residence for Mr. Ward, who superintended the building operations. In digging for the foundations, a pot of old coins was found and divided among the workmen. Rumor spread through the city that a treasure had been unearthed. The workmen were called by the government, which claims all treasure-trove. It was then declared that no permission had been given to build a school. Concerning this, word was sent to Teheran. After a month's delay and negotiations, permission was granted by the foreign office on payment of a building fee. Mrs. Van Hook draws a picture of the building thus: "A large, handsome, red brick 'Vienna house,' as it is styled by the Persians, with a handsome suite of rooms for women's meetings, entertainment of visitors and family life; sunny and commodious apartments for a group of missionary ladies; school rooms, dormitories and all else needful for the comfort and instruction of a family of thirty girls, counting the day scholars who assemble with them." This school was built by the

Second Presbyterian Church of Chicago, which supports the school. It has done a good work in the intervening years. A kindergarten first taught by Mrs. Dr. Holmes in her own house, grew into a very important department of the school. The good development of the school is seen in the following report on June, 1885, written by Mrs. Van Hook:

"'Honorable Lady: The teachers of the American missionary girls' school have the honor to invite you to bring your excellent grace on the 10th, 12th and 14th of the present month to the newly-opened (school) building, and to be a partaker in the examination of the young lady pupils, in the morning from 8 to 12¼ o'clock.'

"The above invitation, and a similar one for gentlemen, brought a good audience of those most interested in the school to its closing exercises. These were largely the parents and family friends of the girls, but the teachers and pupils of the Armenian schools and of our own boys' school slipped in and out as they could take time from their duties. The most conspicuous guest during two days was the Armenian bishop Jermakian, a fine-looking old man, with snow-white hair and beard, intellectual face and dark eyes, whose smoldering fires indicate great spirit and will. Gentle and polished manners, added to his ecclesiastical dress, completed a striking picture, and his interest in the cause of education led him to take an active part in the exercises.

"The pleasant upper rooms used for the kindergarten and main schools were thrown together by means of folding-doors, and all the available space filled with seats. The walls were hung with useful and ornamental articles made by the busy fingers of the girls—patchwork quilts, crocheted and knitted edgings, gloves and mittens in plain and fancy stitches, one nicely-made calico dress, mottoes, etc., in perforated cardboard, sofa pillows, table covers, tidies, work-baskets in various styles of material and stitch, with the work on paper and cardboard of the kindergarten pupils."

Let me interrupt the report to tell the appearance

of the girls. They are bright and pretty, with rosy cheeks, sparkling black eyes, and a modest mien. A class of six are about sweet sixteen. They attract much attention. Their dresses, as well as those of the small girls, reach to the floor. This is considered proper. They have blue and green and drab and wine-colored delaines, trimmed with a row of black lace or braid. Each one has a belt largely covered with silver, her mother's bridal pledge, and worn by the daughter until she gets one of her own. Ribbons, or coral or amber beads, adorn their necks. Their hair hangs in many small braids down their backs, sometimes with silver ornaments at the ends. On their heads are pretty skull-caps, embroidered in gilt or colors and over them various colored kerchiefs. No wonder that after such public examinations there is always considerable hubbub among the boys' school boarders and several proposals within the next few days. The report continues:

"The classes were called, and, after some general questions by the teachers, all were invited to take part in the examination. The guests made good use of this privilege. We were especially proud of the intermediate class, composed of girls about ten years of age. Miss Holliday has been teaching them English, and their examination in this was especially satisfactory. Hatoon had taught them arithmetic orally, but with the aid of the blackboard, and the ease with which they could read, write, add and subtract numbers up to a billion surprised some of the men and boys present. As I was giving one of the older girls some examples to read, up in the millions, a man exclaimed, 'What is the use of her learning so much? There are not so many stars as that.' Miss Holliday won as many laurels from her music class as from her English. The examination of the older girls in Armenian history was well sustained, and was supplemented by the reading of a translation of Patrick Henry's famous speech, 'Give me liberty or give me death,' and the recitation by one of the girls of an original poem written by their teacher. Their recitation in Bible history was not what I hope it will be another year, when I expect to teach the class myself. The catechism class gave a perfect recitation, six receiving a prize for having completed the book.

"After my long absence in America, 1881-1884, I was very much struck with the contrast which this examination presented with one I held four years ago, at the close of the first year of the school. Then the institution was all elementary; now it is up to the grade of an intermediate department at home. Then our accommodations were a small, rude native house; now we have a handsome, convenient building. Then I had almost no help in teaching; now we have native teachers able to carry on their classes with but little supervision, one of them, educated in the school.

"Our oldest pupil is a church member, and a girl of lovely Christian character. Her principle was shown recently in refusing an offer of marriage because her suitor was not a converted man. To a sister who attempted to urge the matter, she said: 'I have come into the light myself, and wish to draw my family after me, instead of going back to an unchristian home and life.' Philomena, also, who is the daughter of Christian parents, trusts that she is a child of God, and her life justifies her hope; but she has not yet been received into the Church. During the winter these two girls, with the matron and teachers, who are church members, have organized a prayer band, each one choosing a certain girl as a special object of prayer and personal effort. I select such subjects for evening prayer as will arouse a sense of sin, and show the plan of salvation, and have had personal conversation with nearly every girl in school. One girl, who had shown a very bad spirit early in the year, was put on a diet of bread and water for some misdemeanor. A relative, hearing of it in some way, came to take her out of school; but she refused to go, saying: 'I have done wrong, and it is right I should be punished; I will bear it to the end.' After a missionary meeting upon China, one of the girls requested the privilege of working a month, and giving what she could earn to China. In imitation of what they have seen in the missionary ladies, the older girls have organized a mission band, which holds a prayer and conference meeting, at which they contribute of their own earnings."

A report in 1889 gives another view of the school and of its widening influence.

"There are classes in language, literature, science, history and music, besides daily, diligent study of God's word by every member of the school in memorizing, narration, exegesis and map-drawing. Besides the American lady in charge, there are masters in the Persian and Armenian languages, a competent resident teacher trained in the school and a teacher of needle-work under whose supervision the skillful fingers of the girls bring in a revenue of about one hundred dollars per annum. Twenty-four little ones chatter merrily over their kindergarten occupations. Two bands of King's Daughters one by one take a little brother, a mother, one of the servants or some one else in whom they have become interested and instruct them in the Bible or teach them to read, and, in turn, to go out with one of the missionary ladies to learn practical missionary work; for all but one or two of the older girls have a hope in Christ and some are church members.

"But the picture would be incomplete without some side views. One gives a glimpse of the pastor's home at Resht, on the Caspian Sea. The wife, who had much private instruction before the Tabriz school was opened, entered its third year, and, after two years of study and two more of teaching, married, and now to her home duties adds a school for girls and meetings for women; she is one to whom those in perplexity or sorrow come for help and comfort. On the borders of Turkey, at Khoi, is one who, against constant opposition of friends, remained six years in the school as pupil and two as a faithful teacher, and is now devoting herself to the women and girls among whom God has placed her, her greatest joy being her Christian home and the opportunities it gives of filling her hands with work for Christ.

"At Mianduab, over on the edge of Kurdistan, is another home-scene, another little school, another gathering place for women, and another light shining in a dark place, as the following extract from a letter shows: 'Because there is much work here, I implore you to always pray for me, that God may pour out his spirit upon me and upon the village.'

"The assistant teacher at Salmas is another busy worker from the graduates."

Mrs. Van Hook and Miss Holliday, who have done such efficient work in this school, are remembered with great affection by many pupils and friends.

The first training class of Tabriz station resulted in the preparation of three men for the work. One of these, Stephen Haritunian, was licensed and sent as an evangelist and teacher to Sayidabad in the Khoi plain; another, Haritun Boghosian, became a teacher in Mianduab. Later they both settled in Salmas. In 1882 another set of boys was gathered from different parts of Azerbijan. They had to start with primary branches, some of them not even knowing how to speak their race-language. Few of them were from evangelical families. They were in bondage to old church traditions and addicted to old superstitions, knowing little of the gospel in its simplicity. The school had twenty-five Armenian scholars, seven of whom were boarders. It soon increased to seventy.

Most of the teaching since 1883 has been done by Mr. Vohan Tamzarian, an alumnus of Harpoot College, Turkey. He has recently been graduated from Lane Seminary and returned to resume his work. Beginning with primary lessons, he took the classes as high as algebra, geometry, astronomy, physiology and physics, besides teaching them some English. I have taught the undergraduates history, physics, geology, physiology, algebra, evidences of Christianity, and Bible and Catechism. Mrs. Wilson has taught much, from the kindergarten to the theological class. Six languages have been taught. For these we have had a Persian mirza and Armenians from the Caucasus. Our constant aim has been toward the spiritual improvement of the scholars. Their course of religious instruction included the Child's and Shorter Catechism with proof-texts, Bible history, life of Christ, Acts, interpretation, evidences of Christianity and Bible hand-book. and School prayer-meetings, young people's societies church services, with personal oversight, have surrounded them with religious influences. This moral and religious training has been most difficult and trying.

STUDENTS AT BOYS' SCHOOL, TABRIZ

With inherited prejudices, public opinion, home training and influence, and the active efforts of opponents working against the truth, our labor was often discouraging. We watched with anxiety the gradual development, trusting that God would work upon their hearts and prepare them for his service. He has not disappointed our faith. The Holy Spirit has wrought with us. All but one of those who finished the course have professed the truth and united with the Evangelical Church, though some have since fallen away. The change of character and conduct in some of them has been marked.

After seven years of labor and patience we reached, in June 1889, our first commencement and sent out our first graduates. These were seven bright, handsome young men of fine physique, and well equipped intellectually, averaging twenty-two years of age. We took just pride in them. The commencement exercises included, first, four days of public examinations. Two hundred invitations, hectographed in Armenian, English and Persian, were sent out, and the attendance was good. A special day was arranged for all races with examinations in English, Turkish, Russian, Persian, Arabic, book-keeping, geometry, and physics with many experiments, and with songs in English, Armenian, and Turkish; and Persian instrumental music of which they say: "One of our tunes is sweeter to us than are a thousand of yours." Among those present were the English consul-general and his wife, the Osmanli secretary, the Austrian general of the shah's troops, several princes, khans, officials and chief citizens. All were highly gratified. The commencement itself was a novelty in Tabriz. For young men to stand up before an audience and deliver orations on such subjects as "Man's Object in Life," and "The Progress of Knowledge," was something to draw forth hearty applause, and was a thing worthy of note. Five of the graduates spoke in Armenian, one in Persian, and one in English. I followed with an address in Armenian. After the conferring of diplomas, one of the class responded in an address of thanks. The diplomas were printed at Shusha after the style prevalent in Russia of naming and grading in each study. Besides the studies mentioned above there were sciences, etc., making in all twenty-six studies. The commencement was concluded with weddings between two of the class and two of the graduates of the girls' school, amid great rejoicing. In the festivities we tried to adopt in large measure their old customs and ceremonials. The people, even when accepting evangelical truth, cling to their old customs. They would not consent to a double wedding, as they never saw such a thing, and the old women were afraid the bad luck of one would fall on the other. Both afternoons the men assembled as the groom's guests and the women as the bride's—the latter at the girls' school. Several hours passed in tea drinking and eating fruit. Among the latter cucumbers served whole are a favorite. To the assembled women guests each bride exhibited her outfit and they chatted and gossiped about her dresses and ribbons and kerchiefs and dolls, admiring this and envying that, and secretly discussing the prices. They knew just how much the bride paid for the groom's coat, and the groom for the bride's dress, and the number of articles she was provided with. When the garments were exchanged the boys serenaded the groom while he put on his new suit, and the women helped to decorate the bride. They took off the flat cap of girlhood and put on the embroidered crown, the symbol of the married state. The girls like to sing, "There's a crown for me, there's a crown for you."

THE MARRIAGE CEREMONY.

After dark the procession formed at the groom's home to conduct him to the bride. By a singular mishap the first night we started without him, and had to loiter on the street until he could be found. In front of the procession marched the schoolboys bearing candelabra and singing songs, while others went ahead announcing, "Behold, the bridegroom cometh." We entered the bride's house amid songs of rejoicing, continued even into the parlor. There a flaring artificial bouquet was pinned on to the groom's coat, the couple were brought face to face, and I put the bride's right hand in the groom's, saying: " As God placed the right hand of Eve in the right hand of Adam," and followed with a prayer. Then the procession marched to the church, the bride moving at a snail's pace as if utterly unwilling to go. The church was decorated with flowers, and the organ welcomed us with a wedding march. We had planned to make the ceremony long enough to please them. A Persian couple married in the American style would scarcely believe themselves well joined. We had three hymns, three prayers, several selections from both the Old Testament and the New Testament, a sermon and the ceremony proper. No one criticised us this time for brevity. Marching from the church, songs rent the air, rockets shot up in front of the column, sightseers looked on from the roofs along the narrow streets. Some of them threw bouquets and some dust. One man drew his horse across the way to extort *bakhshish*—a present from the bridegroom. Arrived at the latter's house, the bridal party pledged each other with sherbet, rose water was sprinkled about, the guests seated themselves on the carpets, and a bountiful supply of roast sheep, rice, and other dainty dishes, prolonged the festivities until midnight.

At one of the weddings the native dance found a place. It is in no sense a promiscuous dance, and is entirely too chaste and modest to please western civilization. The boys and girls in separate rooms, and with slow gliding motion, and each one independently, follow the native airs and add to the joyousness of the occasion. Our adoption of Armenian customs gave universal satisfaction, while all that seemed contrary to truth and sobriety was eliminated. May we follow many more such torch-light processions and see the setting up of many more evangelical homes in Persia. The happy couples spent a few days in Tabriz and then went to Khoi and Miandoab, where their work of Christian teaching has been blessed.

In the following year another class of seven was graduated. Of these two classes, some consecrated themselves to the ministry and a theological class was organized. They seemed earnest in spirit and well prepared intellectually.

We did not think it best to give Greek and Hebrew to them for the present, but gave them a theological course through the medium of the Armenian language, sometimes using text books in English. I gave instruction in Bible history, general and special instruction, interpretation of Romans, Hebrews and Revelation, theology, church history; also lectures on church government and pastoral theology, in connection with the pastoral epistles. Mr. Nicoghos Guleserian has instructed them in Armenian church history, homiletics, types and Messianic prophecies, with interpretation of Daniel, Ephesians and Corinthians. Mrs. Wilson taught them in John and Thessalonians, and in comparative religion.

It was a day of rejoicing for us who had watched over them from their childhood, to see them sent forth as well trained ambassadors for Christ.

In 1890 our quarters became very cramped. Thirty-five boarders and the teachers were living in rented houses. The proper superintendence of the boarding department was impossible. To supply the need, Mrs. Wm. Thaw, of Pittsburgh, Pennsylvania, most liberally donated funds, which enabled us to build and fully equip the Memorial Training and Theological School, as a memorial of the philanthropist, Mr. Wm. Thaw.

First a large property was secured, well situated between the Mussulman and Armenian quarters of the city. It has ample grounds for the present and future uses of the school, for a hospital and missionaries' residences. On one side was a distillery, built for the manufacture of whisky from raisins, but never used, owing to the government prohibition. This has been refitted and made into a dormitory suitable for forty boarders. The grove of large mulberry trees gives the boys a shady, delightful campus. On another side was the anderoon or zenana of a noble family, where the women led their secluded life and in one of whose rooms the guests of the khan feasted. It was in a dilapidated condition, but being repaired it will do for the teachers and their families. But the main interest centers in the new recitation hall, which stands in the orchard and is a fine-looking building for Persia. It is two stories high, of red brick, has six class rooms, a chapel and library. In the following year a residence for the missionary in charge of the school was built. This is a very complete equipment and will be a lasting memorial institution, giving the blessings of Christian education to many of Persia's young men and exerting through the teachers and preachers trained in it a continually increasing influence.

The boarding department is very simple. As most of the boys are poor, we aim to keep them on the same plane of life, that they may return with ease to their homes or go to villages as teachers. The rooms are nicely whitened and have the cement floors which are in universal use in Azerbaijan owing to the lack of wood. On this floor is woven a split-cane matting, which protects the carpets from the dirt. The carpets are the one essential article for rooms. No tables, chairs or bedsteads are necessary. A lamp is provided, and in winter a wood stove made of sheet-iron brought as barrels filled with petroleum from the Caspian coast. Each boy brings his bed, consisting of a narrow mattress, a cylindrical pillow, and some comfortables. These are generally stuffed with wool, which, at five cents a pound, is slightly cheaper than cotton. Pillow-cases and sheets are considered unnecessary luxuries. The bed is spread on the floor at night, rolled up into a bundle in the morning, and placed at one end of the room. A boy on entering his room leaves his shoes in the hall and sits down upon his heels, puts his lamp on the floor, his pencase by his side, his paper on the finger-tips of his left hand, and writes with a reed or with a steel pen his Armenian from left to right, his Persian from right to left. For his books, shelves in the takhtchas or niches of the walls are provided. Four or five boys occupy a room. In the summer they spread their beds on the flat roof, and the free play of the mountain breeze drives away the mosquitoes and sand-flies.

Formerly the boarding arrangements were in the hands of the pupils. They took turns week by week in preparing their food. Now we have a regular Persian kitchen, with an *ojak* or fire-place built in the wall, in which charcoal is used for cooking. The baking is done in a kind of underground oven, an earthen jar the size of a hogshead open at the top, and with a flue from the bottom to the floor at some distance away. The smoke goes out of a hole in the roof. This oven is heated with twigs, grapevines and dried manure-cakes called *yapma*. How much trouble bread-baking is in Persia! First, samples of wheat must be bought and dickering over the price completed. Two hundred or three hundred bushels at thirty or forty cents per bushel are brought on donkeys to the school-yard and weighed on a steelyard. The grain is poured on the pavement and men or women come with sieves and board platters, sift it and throw it with a circular motion, until gravel, dust and straw have been cleaned out. Then it must be lugged indoors to escape rain, while an opportunity is sought to mill it. After the miller has broken two or three appointments, his donkeys and bags finally appear and the wheat is weighed and loaded. A man is sent along to watch the miller lest he substitute a poorer quality or barley, lime and dirt for the wheat. Another man is sent along to watch the first one and to take turns in sleeping, for the mills of Persia grind slowly, even though not exceeding fine. On returning the flour must be weighed, put into a bin and stamped down by a man in his bare feet, though you may vary the custom by putting a sheet over it.

When a day has been set by the busy baking women, whose trade calls them everywhere, they come and mix and leaven two or three barrels of flour and knead it. The oven is heated. The women sit on the floor around the oven. One kneads the dough, another rolls it and slings it on her arms until it becomes as thin as pie crust and about two and one-half feet long. She puts it on a cushioned board. A third woman casts it against the side of the oven, where it adheres. By the time she has thrown a sheet on every side, the first is baked, and is taken out. The process is continued; the floor and walks are covered with the thin, crisp sheets of bread, laid out to cool. It is delicious, sweet and wholesome bread, though of unbolted flour. It is piled on a rack in the cellar, a stack of bread five or six feet in every dimension—a supply for the school for some weeks.

Laying in stores is no light matter. Look into the store cellar. From the ceiling is hung a ton of grapes, which will keep until March and cost less than a dollar a hundred weight. Around the walls of the store-room are large jars ranged on wooden frames. Some are filled with clarified butter. It was made in the villages or by the wandering tribes, from sheep's, goats' or cows' milk indiscriminately. It is brought to the city in sheep skins, weighed in basket balances, stones and pieces of brick being used to offset the inequalities. When clarified by boiling, it keeps fresh and palatable all winter. Three or four hundred weight of this is laid in during the cheap season at seven dollars a hundred weight. Cheese is another article that is much used. It is white and unpressed, and is preserved in brine and soaked in fresh water before using. Other jars are filled with dried peas, beans, rice, cracked wheat, pickles, salt, and a pile of onions occupies a corner. Other storerooms are filled with thorn bushes for kindling, *yapma*, charcoal, wood and petroleum. Buying wood is another great annoyance. Orchard wood, preferably almond and apricot, is brought on donkeys, weighed on the steelyards by a combination of rascals, who have innumerable tricks, and sold at four dollars a ton. The *baltachis* or woodcutters use an ax weighing fifteen pounds, in the shape of a wedge, the thick end being three or four inches square, and split the wood rapidly. They generally like to go off concealing a few sticks under their coats as *mudakhil*. In making these and other preparations for the year, the steward or cook lays by for himself against a rainy day. The all but universal dishonesty is one of the trials of life in Persia.

In the dining-room a width or two of calico or muslin is spread on the carpet, and the boys sit down on their heels. Sheets of bread are placed before each one, with a wooden spoon and here and there a salt-cellar. For breakfast, they have bread and cheese with tea in tiny glasses without cream, but sweetened and steaming hot from the Russian samovar. For the noonday meal, bread with cheese or *yogurt* (sour milk, Armenian *matsun*) or some herbs or fruit are eaten. Grapes and watermelons are especially common. For dinner at dark, a fragant meat stew (*shorba*) is the favorite dish. Each one breaks his bread in a plate of the stew, and takes it up with another fold of the bread or with his wooden spoon. *Dolma*, another palatable dish, is a dumpling in which meat and rice, highly seasoned, are enclosed in a cabbage or grape leaf or in a hollowed-out cucumber, egg plant, tomato or fruit. Another favorite is *pillau* (boiled rice and butter). Frequently in eating this both bread and spoons are dispensed with and the fingers do effective work. Once I was called upon to settle a dispute between some of the boys. The offense on the part of one, which became almost a cause of war, was thus stated: "He has no manners; he eats with five fingers." "And how should he eat?" "Why, with three, of course; only a boor eats with five." The offender was duly counseled to observe the rules of polite society.

On this fare the boys thrive, and have better health

than the average boys at home. This simple way of living may not seem very civilized to some, but it has several advantages. It keeps the pupils on a plane with their people. Should they acquire the habit of sitting on chairs, eating with knives and forks, and having other artificial wants, it would be difficult afterward for them to return to their villages. It is economical; for a boy who furnishes his bed, books and clothing can thus be supported for the school year for a small sum, for food and fuel. Some of the boys are able to pay part toward their own support.

Though the dormitories are furnished thus simply, the recitation hall is equipped with desks, globe and maps, physiological and astronomical charts, physical apparatus and kindergarten outfit. There is the beginning of a library in Armenian, Persian and English.

In the new buildings we have little so far to record. A few months after they were opened, the mustashar-i-donlah, Mirza Javat Khan, the foreign agent, visited and examined the school. With his gift a feast was made to all the scholars. In the autumn of 1892 the recitation hall was sealed by the government. In the following year, on the anniversary of the sealing, the nadmi bashi, principal of the government school, with several officials, made a friendly visit to the school. Bearing greetings from the crown prince, he requested that we furnish a teacher of English for their school, that one of our ladies teach music, embroidery and languages to the prince's children, that Dr. Vanneman give medical lessons in their school, and that I visit their school from time to time to give advice concerning it.

The Week of Prayer (1893) was full of encouragement and blessing. The Monday evening school meeting showed that the Spirit was with us in power. I requested the scholars to make the meeting one of confession and prayer. An Armenian Catholic arose and with trembling voice said: "I have been the Jonah in the ship. I have resisted the truth. During these years I have always prayed in the names of the Mother of God and Peter, of Gabriel and Raphael, but last night, when Rabi Benyamin talked to me, I was melted to tears on account of my sins. I cried until midnight, but at last my eyes were opened, and I looked to Jesus Christ as the only Mediator, and found peace. Pray for me." He sat down with tears in his eyes. Another who had been a probationer, but had backslidden, said: "I used to love my Bible and had several times tested God in prayer and found him ready to hear, but last year I fell into temptation; I associated with evil companions. I began to drink, though I had never done so before. I quit reading my Bible and determined to use all my power to destroy this work. But in the summer, when associating with evil companions, the thought came to me, "If I continue this course I shall be like these men." I abhorred their conduct and determined to repent. I now wish to serve God, and with the same energy with which I was determined to fight against his work, I desire to wage warfare against evil."

Another, only a boy, not finding words and composure to express himself, simply ejaculated, "I am a great sinner, pray for me," and sat down with tears. Others spoke in the same strain. An encouraging feature was that every one of the fifteen connected with the school, who professed conversion, desired to unite with the Evangelical Church. One boy is the son of a priest. Some Gregorians were heard talking in the street. One said, "What! a priest's son become a Protestant?" The other answered, "Well, they have true faith in Christ; but what do we believe?" Of those received into the church during the past ten years in Tabriz, four-fifths have been from the schools.

In Haftdewan, Salmas, is a prosperous school for Armenian girls. It was begun in 1886 by Miss C. O. Van Duzee. The last report gives the average attendance as forty-three, of whom twenty-three are boarders. "The chief difficulty encountered in the education of the Armenian girls in this field is the custom of early marriage, many becoming brides at the age of twelve or fourteen years. Effort is made to follow them up after they have gone to their new homes, where the most dense ignorance of religious truths and life prevails, to foster their habits of Bible reading and prayer. While in the school, every Sabbath afternoon the older ones have a prayer meeting among themselves. It was a joy to those in charge to

SALMAS SCHOOL-YARD

have four of them this year develop sufficient intelligence and spiritual character to warrant their being received into the church."

In the villages of Salmas and Urumia and in Khoi and several out-stations of Tabriz, there are a number of day schools for Armenians, and in the Eastern Persia mission, boarding and day schools among them are increasing in prosperity.

CHAPTER IX.

REFORM OF THE GREGORIAN CHURCH.

A PROMINENT Armenian in Tabriz is reported to have remarked, "We are aware of the need of reform in our Church, but we do not wish to have foreigners do it for us. After a while we will gradually reform our own Church." The first idea of missions among the Armenians was to assist toward and inspire reform from within. The aim now is not to make Presbyterians, Congregationalists, or Anglicans, or even a denomination of Evangelicals.

If real reform were accomplished in the Gregorian Church, the missionaries and boards would cease their operations and recommend their evangelical congregations already formed to reunite with the Reformed Gregorian Church. We are simply striving to lead the people back to the doctrines of the gospel and to a spiritual life. While the old Church remains as it is, not ministering to the growth of the Christian life or the edification of believers by the means of grace, it is necessary that believers should unite themselves in evangelical churches. Plants will not thrive in a cellar.

It is not uncommon to hear Gregorians admit the necessity of reform. In many cases, the light spread abroad by the missionaries has revealed to their eyes the errors of their Church. We watch with eagerness for such a spirit working among them. From time to time enlightened Armenian papers voice their expectations and desires for reform.

The *Mourj*, a monthly magazine of Tiflis, sets forth that the hour calls for the fulfillment of grave duties. It demands first *the reformation of the priesthood*. "The clerical order must be purified from its bad members, the congregations from their unworthy pastors. The moral and mental plane of the clergy must be raised. The declension of the clerical order is evident to all, and accusation on this point is not new. Who, except Kremian as catholicos is able to begin authoritatively the work of moral cleansing, to begin in such a firm manner that it will be impossible to return to the old, the rotten, the stinking? It is necessary to breathe new life into Holy Etchmiadzin, to prepare cultured, progressive, patriotic pilots for the offices of bishops and their inferiors. It is necessary to put away from the field the incapable and unworthy vartabeds and priests and replace them with those more suited to the demands of the times, that the congregations may be instructed by the mouths of incorruptible preachers." The *Shavig* of Teheran joins in the same cry, "To say that the Armenian clergy of Persia, with few exceptions, are unworthy to fulfill the spiritual offices rightly, would be to repeat a fact of which every single Armenian complains." The condition of the priests is truly deplorable. As a class they are men of good intentions, and are not so responsible for their condition as the higher authorities who ordain them. They do not comprehend their higher duties. The standard has been low and nothing has been expected of them. They are chosen from any occupation and very limited qualifications are demanded. A peasant, a blacksmith or any artisan is suddenly made a priest. The cook of our boys' school has been ordained a priest.

Without special training the village priests are but little above the ignorant people. They are merely able to read the forms of the Church in the ancient Armenian. They go through the forms of prayer with often not more than two or three worshipers. I have seen a village priest mumble through the service by the light of a single wax candle and without a hearer save our party. They at times practice divination. At one place a Mussulman woman with a sick child, for whose recovery she had tried the charms of her own religion, desired me to write a prayer or consult our books for a magic remedy. While I was telling her the true doctrine of prayer, she turned to the Armenian priest, who showed a readiness to consult the Book of Solomon on her behalf and to take her silver. One priest in Karadagh was asked, "Who was Jesus, and who was Christ?" He replied, "They say that Hesous was a brother of Christos." Another priest, taking hold of the Gospel which we had been reading, declared it to be falsified, and all the people believed him, though his proof was from the change of spelling of words in the modern Armenian. Even the superior priests are deficient in Bible knowledge. One taught religion in the schools of Erivan. The subject of Christ's life after the resurrection, came up. A Protestant pupil said that Christ ate after his resurrection. The priest denied it, saying, "It may be in your Bible; it is not in ours." Ancient and modern versions, Russian and French Bibles, were brought. The priest was convinced and said, "My child, I had no information of it."

They are lax, too, regarding the keeping of the commandments. It is sad to see them buying provisions and overseeing the building of their houses on Sunday. I have gone to a village and found the priest and his flock harvesting wheat on the Lord's day. Sadder still is it to hear of their excess at wine, and of a priest falling drunk in the street and being jeered at by Mohammedans. At weddings and funerals intoxicants are abundant, and excess is a temptation to which the priests, with a few notable exceptions, yield. The priests must drink the wine after mass. "Drink ye *all* of it." In one city a priest sold liquor to Mohammedans and his daughter was bartender. Once at a wedding, under the influence of liquor, the priest rose and danced a vulgar pantomime and passed around the hat for his own benefit. The priests are all married and are comparatively free from impurity, though if Armenian novelists are to be trusted, their monasteries are full of vice.

The result of the condition of the priests is that they are despised. Even though the people continue to kiss their hand, they do not honor them. A priest took a boy to apprentice him to a tailor. The tailor said, "Oh, this boy is no good; make a priest of him." It is hopeful that there is a call for a remedy. The *Shavig* advises that several boys be sent from every village and town to the seminary in Etchmiadzin to be educated as priests. Some have been sent, but they afterwards declined to be priests, seeking more lucrative and independent occupations. Educated men dislike to be bound down to the observances of these rites and to be dependent on them. One desired to be a priest if he could be excused from wearing the robes, another if he could be a preacher and not have the burden of ceremonies. The bishop answered him, "But then how would you earn your living?" for the fees from funerals, masses, baptisms, weddings, house blessings, saints' days and church collections make up the priest's income. Some therefore advocate a fixed salary for the priesthood. But the priests are quite comfortably supported. The real difficulty with the educated young men is that love for souls and the necessity of laboring for their salvation is not in their thoughts and has probably not been set before them as a constraining motive. Some educated men seem inclined to become priests to acquire political influence over the people.

Another demand is for *the revision and reform of the judicial procedure of the Church.* The *Mourj* says " The judiciary of the Church is in a very pitiable condition. It is not paternal, but corrupted and debased. Bribe 'eating' is spread abroad; judging according to law and good conscience, is despised; taking unlawful gain for decisions is the rule. Just judgment has become almost impossible." It must be remembered that the bishops in Turkey and Persia are judges of many cases. They receive fees for their decisions and advocacy, and this writer plainly accuses them of corruption. Dispensations from the marriage laws are also a fruitful source of revenue. The prohibition of marriage is to the seventh degree of consanguinity or affinity. In one instance, a paper of dispensation was given to a man to carry to a priest with instructions in a postscript to take a certain fee from him. The man outwitted his " holiness " by cutting off the postcript.

Lately a case created considerable excitement. The acting bishop, for forty dollars granted a dispensation for fornication, with the privilege of marrying another than the injured girl. The circumstances of the case aroused public indignation, and the elders went to the bishop and told him to leave the city inside of twenty-four hours. He had the dropsy and begged for mercy, saying, " I am sick ; give me fifteen days to leave; or if I die, bury me." He died on the morrow. Then to honor the office, though they despised the incumbent, they gave him a funeral, splendid beyond all precedent in Persia. For eight hours prayers and chants were continued in the church, on the streets, and at the grave, while a military band and representatives of the consulates, Persian government and mujtehids added to the pageant.

Some even deny justice to the poor unless paid for it. A bishop was appealed to by a poor woman against her brother, who was taking her property. He heard her case and wrote a decision in her favor, but refused to give it to her unless she would bring him five loaves of sugar, which she was unable to do. A Mussulman eloped with a Christian girl from Erivan. The latter became a Mussulman. Afterwards for legal purposes he needed a certificate that she had died a Christian. He applied to a priest for it. The priest said he would give it, but he would not sell the truth for less than five monats. Finally, for eleven krans, he gave a certificate that he had given the girl the last sacrament as a Christian, though he had never seen her.

This love of money manifested by the clergy gives them an undesirable reputation. The native opinion of their bishops may be seen in the following from a leading newspaper: "Oh, if I had two hundred thousand rubles," said a bishop in the circle of his acquaintances, "I know what I would do." "What would you do?" asked one of them. "What would I do? First of all I would hire a cook who would cook so that you would eat your fingers afterwards," (alluding to the habit of eating with the fingers). "Afterwards?" "Afterwards I would buy a good carriage with four horses; afterwards I would rent a fine house, and would have everything in order." "With these you would not have expended the interest of two hundred thousand rubles. What else would you do?" "Afterwards I would bring from Stamboul high-priced silk fabrics, fine ointments, costly soaps of the best quality." "Afterwards what? Your money is not yet finished." "I would buy bank bonds and have the interest on the money, and after some years the two hundred thousand would become two hundred and fifty thousand." "After this perhaps you would found a school or do a work of philanthropy or help the poor?" "What poor? What school?" said the bishop excitedly. "To whom am I indebted? I will keep it for myself."

Because of the venality of the clergy the *Meshag* reiterates, "We desire a reformation which will abolish the bribery of the clergy and their unworthy conduct, and take away those antiquated laws which prevent a prosperous condition."

Another demand is for *the religious instruction of the people, and that the priests should become preachers of the Word.* The *Artsagank*, of Tiflis, says: "Every Catholic and every Protestant before being deemed worthy of receiving the holy communion for the first time is instructed in the confession of the Church and is examined and after that is counted a member of the

Church. This rule is of great importance, because it is not possible to be a Christian without a knowledge of the faith. Only a small part of the Armenian people are instructed in the principles of the faith, the greater part are ignorant of them. It is a duty of the Armenian Church to correct this evil. Armenian ecclesiastics must conceive well their calling and not be *ritualists*, but preachers of the living divine word. They must continually teach their people the confession, traditions and ceremonies of the Armenian Church, in public and at home. That priest who only performs the rites and does not teach the ignorant people, has a great accountability to men and God.

"Certainly it would be a perfectly heathenish arrangement if our priests were only for the celebration of religious rites. All formalism is contrary to the spirit of the Christian Church. Christ claims that one must love and serve God with 'the intent of the heart,' not with 'lips only.' Such a Christianity is worse than heathenism, and that church is very far from the primitive Christian Church. It is the chief of all the important duties of our parish priests to care for the spiritual necessities of their parishioners, to instruct them in the truths of the faith, and afterwards to receive them to the communion.

"Our spiritual government must exercise much care concerning the religious instruction of our people. Until every priest turns into a teacher and every house and church turns into a school, it is impossible to scatter this darkness of ignorance."

Rev. J. L. Barton writes; "Perhaps it is not fully known that there is considerable movement toward a certain kind of reform in the old Armenian Church. Recently, men who were regarded as infidel, have furnished leading articles for the principal Armenian papers, calling for gospel preaching and an educated ministry in the Church. One in particular, who is a leading educator and an author of no small note among Armenians, recently discussed, at considerable length, the reasons of the great falling off in the attendance upon the services of the old Church. His conclusion was, 'That there was nothing edifying in the services of the Church; that the clergy remain where they were a generation ago, while the congregations have become much more enlightened; that the service is simply bare ritual and form, very little of which is understood by the masses and into which the clergy put no soul; that there is nothing in all the service to inspire to devotion or instruct the people, and very little in the clergy to command respect.' He calls for an educated and enlightened clergy which shall be able to preach the gospel of Christ, and explain the Bible, 'which,' he says, ' is the foundation of our faith.'

"Several others have written on this same line, and their articles have met with acceptance from many leading Armenians throughout Turkey. They voice the sentiment of the progressive party in the old Church, which appears in all parts of the country, in the form of a demand for better schools, the preaching of the gospel, and the gradual adoption of the methods of the 'evangelicals.'

"This movement does not meet with general favor among the clergy, for they well know that their day for education has passed, and that in a reformed Church there would be no place for them."

The Independent had the following condensation of a letter of Rev. H. O. Dwight:

"The death of the Rev. C. H. Spurgeon has been the occasion of a discussion in the Armenian papers of Constantinople as to the reason why there are not great preachers in the Armenian Church. One writer draws a painful picture, saying that the Church is regarded as a shop, its altars and ornaments as implements of trade, and that the clergy are too absorbed in money-getting to give time to feeding their flock. He instances one Christmas sermon of fifteen minutes in length, the same identical homily which the preacher had repeated from memory every year since his ordination, which was followed by an impassioned appeal of half an hour for generous contributions for the priests. After the collection by deacons of the contributions, the discussions over the amounts collected grew so eager that the congregation had to entreat that they remain quiet until after the communion service. The article closed with an earnest appeal to the patriarch to cause the people to be fed with gospel sermons which should foster a more spiritual religion. This letter was replied to by a letter in another paper, which claims that it is wrong to lay so much stress on preaching; that the real need of the Church is more attention to religious education of the children, fasting, confession and other rites and ceremonies of the Church. The rejoinder in the first paper was that the ecclesiastic who wrote the second letter knew only the outer shell of religion; that rites and fasting and ceremonies cannot make a man a Christian, nor develop children into good and pure men. What is needed, he claims, is less ceremony and more gospel; and what is looked for among the Armenian clergy is higher, more spiritual and more Christian views. The possibility of such a discussion in the orthodox Armenian papers is indicative of the change that is going on in the Armenian Church."

Another demand is for the *revision of the Prayer Book and a relief from ritualism*. The *Mourj* continues, " Who but Kremian as catholicos is able with full authority to take in hand the book of Church ceremonies, that is, to examine the Prayer Book and separate the necessary and obligatory parts and relieve the Church ritual of the additions and corruptions of the centuries."

The *Meshag* of Tiflis makes the following severe arraignment of the priesthood for ritualism: " If you do not know your duty, Holy Fathers, let us teach you. To be ministers of Christ does not mean merely to repeat memorized prayers, to fulfill outward ceremonies, to cause the people to burn candles before the pictures and kiss the covers of the Gospel, without having the gift of interpreting its solemn contents, and to exhort the people not to brotherly love, but only to more bountiful gifts for your personal living. No! Christianity is not this! Has there indeed remained in you the real Christian spirit, a feeling of mercy, love and self-sacrifice, or has that long since been exchanged for selfishness? Have we not a right to say that, leavened with the bureaucratic spirit, you have killed the evangelical spirit of the Church and of Christian teaching with dry and barren rites, written prayers and outward ceremonies? Yes! Instead of the great contents of the gospel, its mere externals rule; instead of the light of Christ, ruble-bought candles; instead of the spirit, form. It is dead; yes, the Christian spirit is dead, the meaning of the divine teaching is gone; and in their place, by the grace of Christ's ministers, there now rule two entirely different principles—dry, barren, empty, lifeless formalism, and money-worshiping, debasing covetousness."

Some Armenians would have the Church books translated into the modern tongue, and the Sunday-school introduced. Many would relegate pictures to the position of ornaments and abolish the adoration of them. Others would do away with the fasts, which occupy nearly half the year. Indeed most of the people now disregard them. Bishop Jermakian made a feast during Lent, and when some found fault with him said,

"We bishops established these fasts and we can abolish them." The sacrificing of sheep at the shrines is falling into desuetude. Bishop Andreas denounced the custom as contrary to the gospel. Such festivals as the purification of the Virgin are still kept up in villages, but are modified in cities. Superstitions are lessening their hold on the people.

Again there is a *doctrinal tendency toward evangelical truth.* There is not much discussion of doctrines. There is on the part of many an ignorance of the position of their own Church. Many reject transubstantiation, and denounce the celibacy of the higher clergy. There is one tendency to skepticism and another to approach near the gospel. The poet Aghayantz, in his "Story of My Life," says: "As a child I had all sorts of superstitions, believing all I heard. They presented the mother of God (Virgin Mary) as the intercessor before God. They said that she pleads and beseeches God and with tears moves his mercy, that he may take away the punishment from the world and forgive men's sins. From this I had come to imagine that the mother of God was full of mercy, but God was an unmerciful tyrant. Therefore I was afraid of God, and did not love him. My protector was the God-bearing mother. Now hating, I hate this belief of intercession. With the infinitely good Father and his Son, no intercession is necessary. We must love him with the whole heart and soul without dread. I would that all would so believe, and so teach their children and pupils, for so must be the faith of the true Christian."

The evangelical tone of the new catholicos, Mugerdich Kremian, has been marked. In addresses to the clergy and students of the seminary he has emphasized the spiritual duties, and the necessity of knowledge of and obedience to the gospel. There is a marked absence of formal and traditional teaching. I have examined his first encyclical and find in it sixteen mentions of the titles of Christ, and twelve of God and the Holy Spirit, and not one of the Virgin Mary, nor any intercession of the saints.

In another chapter I have referred to the demand there is for a version of the Bible in the modern tongue under the authorization of the catholicos and the favorable prospect of its being accomplished.

Altogether the demands made and the spirit manifested are hopeful indications for the reform of the Armenian Gregorian Church. The leaven of the gospel is working in the mass. Mr. Dwight says: "Thirty years ago the man who dared write such things about the Church would have been killed. Now they strike a cord which vibrates through the Armenian community. There could be no more telling proof of the leavening effect of the long preaching of the gospel than the change of view here revealed. The yearning of spiritual religion is under this cry for gospel preaching. God give us means to foster the yearning and supply it!"

CHAPTER X.

MISSION WORK AMONG THE JEWS.

MOST Jews in Persia are doubtless children of Judah, but some call themselves Beni Israel, and say that they are not of Judah. I know no reason why they may not be regarded as of the ten tribes. Israel was carried captive and placed in the "cities of the Medes," "by the river of Gozan." Some find Gozan in the Guzul-Uzum, the longest river of ancient Media. Besides the early transportations, Shaphur II. brought Jews from Armenia to Persia. They are widely scattered in Persia. Going southward along the western border they are found in Salmas, Urumia, Sulduz, Soujbulak, Mianduab and Sakkus, making one thousand two hundred and fifty houses in Azerbaijan. They are found also in Sennah, Kermanshah, Hamadan, Kashan, Khorasan, Ispahan, etc., making a population of forty-five thousand souls. These remnants have survived the persecutions of centuries. The Jews were driven from Tabriz by reason of an old slander, which is renewed in the present day, even in Europe. Some renegade reported that the Jews had killed a Mohammedan child and drank its blood. An infuriated mob followed into the courtyard of the former kalla-begi, a Jew accused of this crime. The police had snatched him from the mob, who were yelling for his blood. The kalla-begi applied the bastinado to appease the mob. The English consul remonstrated with him for beating an innocent man. He replied that it was the only way to save his life. At that time the Jews fled from Tabriz. In Urumia in the time of Dr. Perkins a Mohammedan infant was found in front of a Jew's door. He was accused of murder and arrested. The Mohammedans collected in an angry mob and for several days surrounded the governor's palace, demanding that the whole Jewish population should be put to death. To appease the mob, the Jew was delivered to them, beheaded and burned.

In Meshed, Jews had resided for centuries, though it is the sacred shrine of the Iman Reza. It was one of their rabbis there (Tus), who made the first version of any part of the Bible into Persian, in the eighth or tenth century. In 1840 it was reported that the Jews had killed a dog in ridicule of the ceremonies of the festivals of sacrifice. A mob rose, killed fifteen Jews in cold blood, tore down some of their dwellings, and finally gave the rest the alternative of Islam or the sword. In fear of death they accepted an outward profession of Islam.

At Balfurush, in Mazanderan, in 1866, a massacre of Jews occurred.* The cause may have been the lack of rain, for which the Mussulmans thought the scattering broadcast of the dust of a Jew would be an effica-

---

* Mounsey's *The Caucasus and Persia*, p. 274.

cious remedy. For this or for some unknown cause, they rose one night, set fire to the Jews' quarter, and killed eighteen men and six women. Two of the men were besmeared with petroleum and burnt alive. The rest, to the number of four hundred and fifty, escaped to the woods. The British minister made representations for redress. The shah gave orders for the punishment of the culprits, and the indemnifying of the Jews. But the mollahs rose in wrath that any one should be punished for injuring "a dog of a Jew." Popular fanaticism ran high in Teheran. An attack on the British legation and on foreigners in general was even contemplated. To appease the mollahs, the shah dismissed some foreign officers from his service. Finally the Jews were partially indemnified for their losses.

When I was in Hamadan in November, 1892, there was a reign of terror for the Jews. The Mussulmans turned their wrath upon them as the supposed cause of the cholera. A mollah, who desired by some means to gain a reputation, as some had done by opposing the tobacco monopoly, instigated the attack. Several Jews were seized and beaten. The mollah in order to disgrace them and restrict their liberty commanded that the Jew should wear a cloak of two colors; should have a badge of red on his coat to indicate his race; should not come out on a rainy day; if while riding he met a Mussulman, he should dismount until the latter passed; that the Jewish women should wear black veils; that the houses of the Jews should not be higher than those of their Mussulman neighbors; that Mussulmans should not barter with Jews nor call their doctors. Some of the Jews in fear took refuge with powerful Mohammedan friends, others fled to the telegraph office and appealed to the shah and the English legation. A crowd of Mussulmans collected and paraded the streets, shouting, "Ya Ali! Ya Ali!" They surrounded the refugees in the telegraph office and frightened them so that a dozen accepted Islam. The Jews in Bagdad, hearing of the disturbances, appealed to their friends in England. Lord Rosebery, secretary of foreign affairs, inquired of the shah concerning it. The governor had been out of town on account of the cholera and had done nothing. He returned, and was about to send the mollah to Teheran, when the mob interfered and prevented it, guarding his house day and night. The governor was not averse to settling the disturbance by persuading the frightened Jews to become Mussulmans. Among the Jews who were surrounded by the mob and pressed to become Mussulmans was a young convert who is a pupil in the mission school. He stood his ground as a Christian and afterwards gave before the governor the reasons for his faith. A month passed in this confusion, and the Jews continued in distress. The governor was removed and a stronger one arrived. After a few days he sent word to the mollah that the shah called him to Teheran. He said, "All right; I will go," and started, stopping at the nearest village. The next day some Sayids, or descendants of the prophet, went about, closed the bazaars, and called the people to go and bring him back. Soon the hill overlooking the city was black with people. In the rain and mud the crowd went out, and toward afternoon they returned, pouring through the streets with clubs and drawn swords in hand, carrying the black flag and crying out, "Ya Ali! Ya Ali! Shah Husain! Shah Husain!" so that they could be heard all over the city. Soon we saw the mollah, a weak old man, mounted on a horse led through the streets amid the hosannas of the multitude and taken to the mosque. Then some of the crowd went to the governor's and demanded pardon for the offenders. This was the priest's second triumph. A month passed, and one night mounted soldiers seized the mollah and started off with him, having a larger force waiting for them outside the city. Alarm was given and they were pursued. They threw the old man over a wall into a garden, where he was found and brought back. The crowd, now frenzied, attacked the governor. He fled from the city, but his house was looted, his cook killed, and several officers narrowly escaped. The mob also made for the Jewish quarter, crying "Kill the Jews!" But the door of their quarter was closed, and before they could get around to it they were dissuaded. There were rumors that an army would be sent to bring the mollah to the capital for punishment. Many of the soldiers cannot be relied on to fight against the mollahs. Finally it was arranged that the mujtehid of Teheran should invite the mollah to come to the capital as his guest. Thus he arrived at the foot of the throne and the affair was settled. Certainly in this case all friends of liberty must sympathize with his majesty in his effort to protect the oppressed Jews, and regret that after a reign of such honor and progress his old age should be troubled with such disturbances as have happened in the last two years. It is no wonder that a race that has undergone such oppression has a downcast mien and servile manner. Mr. Cohen, of Bagdad, wrote to the Anglo-Jewish Association concerning his own race in Persia: "Despised and persecuted, they are unable to command respect or to arouse feelings of humanity in the breasts of their oppressors. They passively submit to the vilest insults, while petty acts of persecution gradually become habitual. A Mussulman child may with impunity pull a Jew's beard and spit in his face. The word 'Jew' is considered a term of disgrace and is never used by the Persian without an apology for giving it utterance." On both visits of the shah to England addresses have been presented to him on behalf of the Jews. His first reply is given in Piggot's *Persia*. The shah has shown an earnest desire to protect all his subjects.

Even the native Christians, I am sorry to say, join the Mussulmans in abhorring the Jews. The Jews, in turn, hold themselves apart from all and probably in their hearts despise and hate all others. They largely maintain their dietary laws. I invited a Salmas Jew to send his boy to the Tabriz boarding-school. He replied that God had commanded the Jews not to eat the bread of other races.

I was invited with some Jewish physicians to a wedding at Zenjan. Separate dishes, as honey, fruit and bread, prepared by a Jew, were set before them. They sat apart and returned thanks for themselves both before and after meal. It is only with difficulty in Teheran and Hamadan that Jewish pupils have yielded their prejudice and begun to eat with their companions. Jews kill their own animals and extract all the sinews. If the liver is diseased, they sell the animal to the Armenians.

Jews are limited in their occupations. Very few are farmers. Many sell dry goods in the bazaar or by peddling in the villages. Some are goldsmiths and jewelers and dealers in antiques, both true and false. Some are physicians; the Mussulman, though refusing the Jew's food with abhorrence, takes his medicines. Many are liquor sellers, and are themselves much addicted to drink. On other points of morality they differ little from the rest of the population. They are polygamists as the Mohammedans and with the same results. Mrs. Wilson wrote: " Two Jewesses called, very richly dressed in purple and scarlet, with ornaments of silver and gold. The unmarried sister is betrothed, and later we had a call from a young woman who is the man's present wife. She is very angry because he is taking a new wife, has deserted him and her baby and gone back to her father's house." They regard Sabbath breaking as the sin for which they are suffering and will not light a fire on that day. They hire a Mussulman to come in and do it for them. They look for a national return to their own land when they shall rule over the nations. They have schools everywhere, taught by their rabbis. Most of the men can read Hebrew, though they do not understand it perfectly. Their spoken language is akin to the modern Syriac. They best understand the Persian Bible in Hebrew characters, part of which has been published.

The eccentric Wolff visited the Jewish communities in Persia in 1825 and again in 1828–33. The London Society for the Propagation of the Gospel among the Jews sent out in 1844 four missionaries to Bagdad as a center. Two years later Mr. Stern, of this company, took up residence in Ispahan. A state of anarchy compelled his withdrawal. In 1852 he again visited Persia and in 1853 again in company with Mr. Bruhl. In 1866 this mission was suspended.

Work for the Jews has been carried on in part by the American Mission in North Persia and by the Church Mission in Ispahan. In 1894 a German Mission arrived in Urumia to labor among the Jews.

Beginning at the north, our mission has an Eastern Syrian evangelist among the five hundred Jews at Kuhna Shahr, Salmas. In Urumia among the twenty-five hundred Jews there have been some interesting events. In 1875-78 there was a movement among the Jews. Twenty-five families rejected the Talmud and traditions, and stood up for the Old Testament alone. This made a great commotion and the new party was cast out of the synagogue. Persecution followed, some were fined. They finally came to the missionaries to put themselves under their instruction and protection. A school was opened among them. Various difficulties arose and the government strove to prevent our getting a foothold among them. In 1888 this work had a fresh impulse. A boy's school was opened. A sewing and Bible class was organized with thirty or forty Jewish women and a girls' school with thirty-two pupils, in charge of Miss M. K. Van Duzee. Again a storm was raised, the government closed the school for boys and only fifteen of the girls dared to continue in attendance. As a result of these labors, four young men openly professed Christ in 1892, and stood out in spite of beating and expulsion from the synagogue. An evangelist is working among them at present.

In Nakada, Sulduz, there are about one thousand Jews, and an evangelist preaches to them as well as to the Armenians. Once a story was circulated that they had celebrated the Passover by drawing a picture of Christ on the cross and insulting it. The Mussulmans collected and nearly tore down their synagogue.

I was invited to this synagogue one evening. It

is a plain, mud-plastered room, with a raised platform in the center, upon which I and the rabbis, with their open Hebrew Bibles, sat down, and about fifty Jews stood around. I attempted to set before them Jesus as the Christ, but one cried one thing and one another, as in the theater at Ephesus, and soon it became evident that they were nearly all tipsy, as the more sober ones said, "Come in the morning," which recalls Peter's proof of the sobriety of the apostles. In upper Kurdistan, including Soujbulak, Mianduab and Sakkus, there are about two thousand Jews. In Soujbulak we have a school among them and evangelists there and in Mianduab.

At Soujbulak I attended morning prayers at the synagogue. On the door post, inclosed in a glass tube, were the ten commandments. In the one corner were the benches for circumcision and the bier. Each worshiper had bound on his arms and forehead with long leather cords, portions of the law, and thrown over his turban a thick white veil which hung down over his shoulders. The service, led by three or four rabbis, consisted in prayers from the Psalms and Talmud and reading of the law. Each man held an Old Testament in his hands, and they read in concert or responsively with frequent hearty amens to the prayers. The attitude was varied, being sitting, standing or bowing prostrate. The climax of the service was reached in the procession of the law. The manuscript roll of the law was inclosed in a cylindrical case covered with scarlet broadcloth, topped off with two silver pomegranates, with pendant silver bells, such as hung from the high priest's robe. It was moved in procession through the synagogue, each one devotedly kissing it; and the women who had previously stood aloof, true to their nature, came forward to engage in this ceremony. Then they sang psalms and the people joined in petitions for the coming of the Messiah.

In Mianduab an interesting case occurred. Rabbi Benjamin had been an opponent. In discussions I had with him in his school, he stoutly maintained his position. At last he was led to accept Jesus as the Messiah, and preach him in the synagogue. His income from the people, fees as teacher and portions for slaughtering the animals, were cut off. His wife wished to drive him from the house. He appealed for support. Having been deceived by a number of "loaves-and-fishes" converts, we insisted on his finding some way of supporting himself, our idea being to employ him if, after a year or two, he continued faithful. He was not reduced to want for he had his household goods, etc. Meanwhile the Jews persecuted him. Among other things, they took him to the river and ducked him, to exorcise the "evil spirit" which the Christians had put into him. Finally he yielded and went back to Judaism. The Jews immediately presented him with a sum of money, a donkey and a cloak. He went into a vineyard, bought some grapes for winter use, loaded them on his donkey and covered them with his cloak.

Coming out of the garden he was detained a few minutes and when he bethought himself, donkey, grapes and cloak had been stolen. He said, "That is a punishment to me for denying Christ."

A Jew who has an interesting history was received into the church at Tabriz. I give its details because they show so many phases of Persian life. While a young man in Shiraz he discovered in a fallen wall a jar of old coins. Little by little he was trying to sell them, but the purchaser, a Jewish goldsmith, suspected that a treasure had been discovered, and cautioned X——'s brother about it, for a treasure-trove belongs to the king. X——, after many lies told in trying to conceal the fact, at last confessed. The older brother sold the coins for three or four hundred dollars. The goldsmith over his cups told the story and officers heard of it. The brother fled, but X—— was captured and tortured to reveal the treasure. Finally he confessed that he had found a treasure, but it was spent. He was beaten and tortured in various ways. Sticks were put between his fingers and the ends pressed together until the blood oozed out. Irons were heated and he was threatened with burning. Finally a mediator suggested that he become a Mussulman and escape these tortures. He refused. He was then taken before a mollah for examination and claimed the privilege of sanctuary. The mollah protected him, keeping him at the outer gate, because, as a Jew, he was unclean. After a few days he was persuaded at night to try to escape, but it was simply a trap. He was captured in the street and taken to prison again. To save himself he pretended to be a Mussulman. Afterwards he became an eye-doctor and was in the service of the zil-i-sultan, who daily provided for him from his table, but, instead of eating the food, he had Jewish food brought him secretly. Afterwards he went to Ispahan and back to the Jews, but when the zil-i-sultan became governor there, he was discovered and compelled to keep up the appearance of being a Mussulman. In order to bind him, they proposed to give him a Mussulman wife. He chose a blind one, thinking she could not discover his hypocrisy. Shortly after they were married, she questioned him about why he went up to the second story for so long a time each day, saying she had followed him to the room and found him praying in a strange tongue (Hebrew). "What religion are you of?" she asked. He was afraid to tell her lest she might report on him and he be killed, so he affirmed he was a Mussulman. Finally, after several days, when she said she would be of whatever religion he was, because he was good to her, he told her that he was still a Jew. He still feared for some time that she would betray him. It is no uncommon thing in Persia. One day he was called to Dr. Bruce the C. M. S. missionary at Ispahan, where some other Jews were writing a petition. He read from the Hebrew Old Testament and had it explained, and in course of time was convinced that Jesus is the Christ. After a time he came to Tabriz and was baptized and received into the Church.

Mr. Bassett in his *Eastern Mission*, pp. 167 and 233, mentions some interesting facts about work for Jews in Teheran. In 1886, after the date of his writing, a letter was written from the chief rabbi of Jerusalem to the shah, complaining against the Protestant school in Teheran for turning away Jews from their faith, and especially accusing Rabbi Baba the teacher. Baba was thrown into prison* by order of the minister of foreign affairs, was cuffed and beaten, his head shaven, a chain put on his neck and his feet made fast in the stocks. Direct appeal on his behalf being unavailing, the good offices of the English and American legations were besought for him and his release secured. Others of the Jewish Christians were persecuted at the same time. Baba's father, a physician of note, was imprisoned, but a high official whom he had cured procured his release. This persecution had been instigated by a hostile Jewish rabbi in consort with an oppressive chief of police. Retribution soon overtook them. Within less than a month, this officer was imprisoned, bound with the same chain and treated in the same manner, because he had accepted a bribe to release a prisoner. He was fined two thousand tomans and dismissed from office. The persecuting Jewish rabbi was turned out of the city by his own people.

* See letter of Dr. Torrence, *Foreign Missionary*, 1886.

Among the Jews of Hamadan the work of evangelists from Urumia began to bear fruit in 1875, especially under Pastor Shimun. A considerable number professed an interest in Christianity during 1877-80. Popular slander reported that the evangelist had mixed powder in their tea, which had such influence as to induce them to become Christians. They met with much persecution, were ostracized, excluded from the baths and schools; their business was interrupted and their shops threatened. Appeal was made to the authorities in Teheran to put a stop to these persecutions. Repeated orders were given. I insert the full text of one, translated by Mr. Potter. It is of permanent value as a declaration of religious liberty for non-Mussulmans.

"Oh thou near Royalty: The government of Hamadan has been frequently written to concerning certain Jews who have chosen the Christian faith — and the other Jews have quarreled with and persecuted them—that the oppression of certain Jews on the part of the Jewish congregation is by no means according to custom. That the other Jews should oppose and quarrel with those of themselves who choose another faith and not permit them to go to the bath, and in other ways afford them a ground of complaint and trouble, is very bad.

"*Let a Jew choose the Christian faith or a Christian accept the Jewish faith, they should not incur opposition or molestation from anybody.* With all these (previous) injunctions, what reason is there that some arrangement has not been effected for removing the oppression on the part of the Jews toward those certain persons?

"You yourselves know that *this conduct of the Jews is very much opposed to custom*. Assuredly this time you will give such exertion and attention to the matter that *hereafter eternally no hindrance shall be placed in the way of those* certain individuals and persons of the *Jews and Armenians who wish to enter another faith*. And in other respects, also, you will take care that the Jews and Armenians dwelling in Hamadan shall enjoy rest and quietness. What further writing is necessary?

"In the month of Safar the victorious, 1298."

Notwithstanding these orders, persecutions continued. Several of the prominent converts were arrested on a false charge, imprisoned and fined. The chief officer went repeatedly to them in prison, beat them and said, "You have become filth; turn now and be Mussulmans." They answered, "If you cut off our heads, we will not deny Jesus." Word of this was telegraphed to Teheran by Pastor Shimun, and the following day the imprisoned brethren were severely bastinadoed. Inquiry was made from the foreign office at Teheran, and the governor in a rage called the pastor, reprimanded him for sending word and having taken seventy tomans from the Jews, commanded the pastor to telegraph a message of satisfaction and that the governor had taken nothing. On his refusal he commanded him to be bastinadoed.

His feet were bound to the pole, but on the entreaty of Dr. Rahim, a Jewish brother, who was in favor, he was released. The congregation addressed a complaint to the minister of foreign affairs concerning the dishonor thus put upon their pastor, and he, fearing further violence, took refuge with the khan of Sheverine and afterwards fled to Teheran. He was able to go back with a proper order for his protection.

In the hope of securing better protection and schools than we were furnishing them, a petition was addressed by these Jewish Christians to the London Society for Jews. Dr. Bruce endorsed the appeal. In the autumn of 1881, Mr. Lotka, a converted Jew, arrived from London and took up his residence in Hamadan, about the same time that Mr. Hawkes went from Teheran to reside there permanently. Mr. Lotka was beset with difficulties, and was even arrested with a number of Jews He was withdrawn in 1884, having reported to his society that the American mission was quite sufficient to do the work.

In 1881 the congregation of Jewish Christians was reported as forty men, thirty women, and twenty children. Prominent among them was Rabbi Hyim, who, as a teacher and evangelist, has labored among them many years. Another was Dr. Aghajan. An account of his life by Pastor Shimun is translated by Rev. Dr. Labaree as follows:

"Dr. Aghajan was a Jew about fifty years of age. He was a native of Hamadan. He was a man of great zeal for the commandments of the fathers in Judaism, and quite familiar with the Old Testament.

"My first interview and conversation with the Jews of Hamadan, 1875, was with this man. Our first discourse together left a deep impression on him. He could not throw off his hand from the verses I had quoted to him.

"He came and went continually, and found for himself two companions, and gradually gathered a little company (of believers in Christianity), whose numbers have increased now to not less than two hundred.

"He was urgent to be baptized, but we kept him in probation two years.

"When Mr. Bassett came here, and baptized three of his companions, he was absent. On his return home in November, 1878, I baptized him. His joy was great; he made a feast which he closed with prayer.

"From that time on he has shown great energy among the Jews of Hamadan and has written to those at a distance. With boldness he has confessed Christ before mollahs and Mohammedan rulers. He was a doctor and had access to every class, and was highly respected. He ceased not his discussions with the Jews, until he finally opened his own house for open discussions and prayer.

"The chief men of the Jews became his enemies and

traduced him to the principal persons in the town, hoping to make him ashamed or afraid.

"He, however, counted all these as trials to purify him. The company of believers suffered much persecution, but he ever gave them heart, 'Be not shaken; Christ is with us as he promised.'

"Now he has departed from death unto life—in the year of Christ 1880, December 5 (O. S.). He has left a widow, two daughters, and a son. These also are believers in Christ.

"His sickness lasted four months. His bed was made rough by the Jews who came to urge him to return to Judaism. His word to them was: 'Christ, whom our fathers have looked for these three thousand years, I have found. I cannot throw my hand from him. If you wish to find him, he will not come except you search the law and the prophets—in whose writings you will discover him.'

"During his last illness we observed the Lord's Supper. I told him, 'This is our week of prayer before the Lord's Supper.' He replied with sighings, 'I cannot come to the meetings. If possible on Sabbath I will come.' I replied, 'Perhaps you can come on an animal. I will send the brethren to bring you.' He answered, 'I will see by that time.' He came afoot. I asked him why he had done so, and he replied, 'I did not wish to come to the memorial of my Saviour's death riding, for he suffered greatly for me.'

"After this he grew much worse. I often visited

him with the brethren, inquiring carefully as to his hope. He declared himself happy in the confidence that at his departure he should be received into the bosom of Christ.

"He was often saying to the brethren, Armenians and Jews—'Work—be not grieved—I am sorry I did not do more for my Saviour. I commend to your care this blessed work of Christ.'

"Two days before his death he sent for me and gave his family into my charge. 'Do not,' he said, 'neglect my children.' He asked for my hand, which he wished to kiss, saying, 'I shall not forget your kindness.' We kissed one another on the mouth and I came away.

"The Jewish rabbis went to him and asked him 'Who shall bury you, and where will you be laid?' He replied, 'Pastor Shimun will bury me. He will know where—if possible, by my mother.'

"At his death I was not, as I desired, with him. They sent for me to come and conduct his funeral. I went with a company of the Armenian brethren. We found it impossible to hold any services at the house. More than four hundred souls, men and women, were present. The graveyard was about half an hour distant from the house. We carried the remains with singing all the way, through the market and the streets of the city. When we arrived at the burying-ground, about three hundred persons were present, Jews, Armenians and Mussulmans. There was preaching and prayer. The silence was amazing. For an hour and a half, all, the Jews as well, listened most attentively to me to the last singing and benediction.

"The governor of the city, of his own accord, showed the favor of sending two officers to be near lest the Jews should make some trouble, and ordered, 'If any man speaks a single word of disrespect to the priest (pastor), bring him to me for punishment.'"

Some of these baptized Jews proved to be timeservers. Some became Babis, accepting Baha-ullah the captive at Accho, as their divine guide. One of these had been a student in the school. The truth seemed to have borne no fruit. His younger brother, who was a Christian, continued to pray for him. Finally a sermon by Mr. Hawkes stirred his conscience to a sense of his sin, and rejecting Baha, he found a refuge in Jesus as the Messiah.

Converts who have been trained in the schools are usually more stable. They are led in childhood to cleanly and correct habits. These influences reach to their homes and affect their parents. The Jewish converts have a congregation separate from the Armenian Evangelicals.

The Jews by becoming Christians subject themselves to double persecution, from their own people and from the Mussulmans. The latter wish to hinder them, that they may become Mussulmans. If they do so, to escape oppression, they frequently by a change of residence resume their former faith. Persian governors are now very liberal in allowing them to return to their own religion.

CHAPTER XI.

MEDICAL MISSIONS.

CHRIST sent forth his disciples directing them "to preach the kingdom of God, and to heal the sick." Luke 9: 2. Modern missions in Persia were established by the preacher and physician in association. Rev. Justin Perkins and Dr. Asahel Grant opened up the work in Urumia. Dr. Grant was a remarkable man, and his influence and power for good in Persia and the mountains of Kurdistan were far-reaching. Dr. Wright, his successor in Urumia, and Dr. Lobdell, among the mountain Nestorians, were strong men. Dr. Lobdell in three years made a deep impression on the people, and his scientific researches and published articles gained him wide distinction. Dr. Van Orden, after some years of able service, resigned, and has since been itinerating in the heart of Central Asia, enduring hardship, earning his living in Tartary and Mongolia, both preaching and healing.

Let me briefly indicate the present force of missionary physicians, the places and equipments, that the account of their work may not be interrupted by such details. Dr. Joseph P. Cochran took up the work in Urumia in 1878, and has prosecuted it with remarkable success. The utility of the work was greatly increased by the building of the Westminster Hospital in 1883. It stands in the same inclosure as the college. Its main building is 75 feet by 30, two stories high, and will accommodate thirty patients. On one side is the public dispensary, with rooms for medical students and assistants; at the other, the Howard Annex for women, built in 1890, by Mrs. George Howard, of Buffalo. Connected with it is the residence of Dr. Emma Miller, who arrived in 1892, and beyond, the residence of the physician in charge. The whole constitutes the first and for many years the only well-equipped and regular hospital in Persia.

Medical mission work was opened in Tabriz in 1881 by Dr. G. W. Holmes, who had been in Urumia from 1874 to 1877. Dr. Mary Bradford, arrived in 1888. Dr. Holmes having accepted an appointment as physician to the crown prince, Dr. Wm. S. Vanneman succeeded him in 1891. In Tabriz there are two dispensaries, one for men and one for women, and each physician has set aside a room in which hospital patients are received.

Dr. W. W. Torrence was the pioneer in Teheran (1881), was reinforced by Dr. Mary Smith, in 1890, and succeeded by Dr. J. G. Wishard in 1893. Under Dr. Torrence's supervision the Ferry Hospital was erected, named in honor of Mrs. Ferry, of Lake Forest, who gave liberally toward it. One of the shah's viziers first made a donation of ground for it, but as the gift implied partial control, the ground was purchased. The corner-stone was laid in June, 1889, amid a concourse of Persian officials and European diplomatists and friends. The corner stone was inscribed in Arabic and English characters, and was the gift of U. S. Minister E. Spencer Pratt, who, having been a physician, took great interest in the hospital and made an address on the occasion. Patients were first received during the cholera epidemic and regularly since 1893.

Previous to this Dr. Wishard, with several assistants, had labored among the mountain Nestorians, supported for three years by Mr. Morton, a philanthropic gentleman of London. The medical department at Hamadan was begun by Dr. E. W. Alexander in 1882. For a time he conducted a small hospital in addition to his dispensary. Dr. Holmes succeeded him in 1893. Dr. Jessie C. Wilson entered the field in 1890. Dr. Yohannan Sayad, a graduate of the Urumia Medical College, and also at New York, conducts the medical work in Salmas.

Dr. Hoernle established a medical mission at Ispahan under the Church Missionary Society in 1879.

Special emphasis has been put on the work of women physicians. The necessity for them is obvious in a society constituted as Persian society is. Women, as a rule, have neither desire nor permission to state their complaints to men. Proper diagnosis is impossible when the pulse must be felt or the tongue looked at, while the person remains behind a curtain. They may learn to consult male physicians for some cases, but for many complaints they must remain unministered to. The midwives do fairly well in ordinary obstetrical cases, but critical cases can have none of the alleviations of true medical science, unless physicians of their own sex are at hand. Some Persians do scornfully say, "What! can a girl be a doctor?" But women doctors are almost universally welcomed, and have not to encounter as much prejudice as in more civilized lands. Under ordinary circumstances they treat only women and children. One man seven times requested in vain to have his eyes examined. Another offered to come blindfolded if the lady would feel his pulse and prescribe for him.

The work of missionary physicians is varied, and valuable in several ways. One form of work, though aside from their great object, is very important. *They render efficient service in caring for the health of the other workers.* This is specially so in fields like Urumia, Salmas and Hamadan, where there are no European physicians. Embassies, telegraph and other companies have physicians in many places to care for their force. It is wise for a missionary society to exercise similar care. The record in Persia is remarkable. Through medical skill, favorable climate, and God's providence, but two missionaries in our Persian missions have died within the last fifteen years, and one of those, Mrs. D. P. Cochran, after forty-six years of service. There have been many long terms. Rev. Dr. Perkins spent thirty-three years in the field, Dr. Wright twenty-five, Mr. Breath twenty-one, Mr. Coan thirty, Mr. Cochran twenty-four, Dr. Labaree thirty-three, Dr. Shedd thirty-eight,* and the wives have in most cases survived their husbands by many years. Mrs. Perkins, the first American woman to enter Persia, 1835, is still living.

It is a remarkable fact that among the fifty or sixty boarders in our Tabriz school during past years, there has not been a single death, though epidemics of scarlet fever, diphtheria, smallpox, cholera and other diseases have carried off hundreds in the city. The prompt attention of our physicians has much to do with this.

In the general *work of relieving sickness and suffering* the medical mission is a grand agency. At least twenty thousand patients are treated each year. Their treatment is beset with special difficulties. Patients are ignorant, careless and superstitious. They wish to know if they should apply the pill externally, or swallow the paper in which the powder is wrapped, or, if the paper should be dissolved in water along with the powders. Several doses of medicine will be bolted at a swallow, to hasten the cure, or all the eye-wash poured in at once, and complaint made that the eyes were burnt out. After several days' prescribing, inquiry brings out the fact that the medicine has

* News of Dr. Shedd's death is lately received.

not been taken, because, as the patient was preparing to take it, he sneezed once—a bad omen. Sneezing twice would have made the time favorable. Others "eat" medicine from two or more physicians at the same time. Conditions of life are unfavorable to treatment. The patient is found lying on the floor, in a room occupied by the whole family, the air stifling, a crowd of children and visitors about, even when the disease is contagious. Care, quiet and cleanliness are not present to aid the physician. Much of his time, too, goes in mixing his own medicines, as there are no proper drug stores. In spite of these difficulties much is done to relieve suffering and restore health. Dr. Alexander narrates a case of a young sayid, upon whom native doctors had exhausted their skill without success. He was weak, half paralyzed and in a delirious state. His reason seemed hopelessly gone. Medicines and care were wonderfully blessed and he was soon in fair health, and his reason quite normal. The result was that all his friends and relatives came pouring in with their diseases. Dr. Bradford had a case of a boy, born a cripple, and who had reached the age of sixteen, only able to move about on his hands and feet. By a continued course of local electrical treatment, he was, after some time, enabled to walk upright, though still hunch-backed; he learned to read and became a book-binder. Dr. Alexander wrote: "Fully one half of our patients come from villages around us from two hours to three or four days' distant. It is pitiful to see them bringing their sick on donkeys when they are burning up with fever, or so weak that they can scarcely sit on their animals. A man came twenty eight miles suffering from an ugly wound. I wondered how he ever reached the city. It came near killing him, but he is now quite well and strong."

Dr. Wilson tells of a woman whose husband had struck her on the head, and who was confined to bed. Afterwards she was paralyzed and unable to walk for eight months. She was brought to the dispensary on a man's back. The woman pleaded for her cure, saying that her husband threatened "to take another wife if she did not soon get well." The doctor treated the case with electricity, massage and medicines, and the woman recovered. Afterwards when she could walk, she entreated for medicine to make her beautiful, for her husband now threatened to take another wife if she did not have a pretty face.

To reach cases distant from the dispensary, tours are undertaken by the physicians. When people see any foreigner traveling, they are likely to call out, "A doctor has come." Mrs. Bishop took her medicine-chest with her and ministered to the sick. I have made it a rule not to attempt it, except to recommend pure water for foul sore eyes, and occasionally give a dose of quinine. Even that is not always a success. After taking quinine, a boy with fever ate unripe grapes and grew worse, and of course attributed it to the quinine. The physician's opportunity is great. Dr. Cochran has, on a tour, found the sick gathered at the road-side and blocking the bridge where he was to pass. Of a tour by Dr. Cochran and Mr. St. Pierre in the Kurdish mountains in 1894, the latter writes: "The state of the mountains was very mixed, and bloodshed, robberies and oppression were of daily occurrence, and yet we passed through it all safely. The most rival factions showed us a very friendly spirit and gave us abundant opportunity to preach and counsel and administer to their present needs in the way of medicines. Hundreds flocked to our tent for treatment and sat attentively before the exposition of the word." When Dr. Bradford was traveling in Kurdistan, in passing a village, a man came out and ran along shouting, "Who is there? Is there a hakim (doctor)?" Finding she was a doctor, the man followed on foot four or five miles. While waiting for a boat on the Jagatai, she got out her medicines and gave him some for his eyes. He returned home and that night used some of it. It smarted and he began to beat his breast and tear his hair, saying: "Alas! alas! Vy! Vy! I could see only a little before, and now I shall be blind." In the morning he exclaimed, "My eyes are cured, I can see everything. That is a good medicine. Oh, my daughter, your eyes are also sore. Arise and go after that hakim, if need be many days, and she will cure you." His daughter followed crossing one river in a boat and wading three others waist deep. Others followed the doctor from the villages where she had been, often coming twenty miles. She writes: "In the first village during the whole afternoon, one room was filled with women. We prescribed for about thirty of them. The next morning a Kurdish sheikh sent an escort of fourteen horsemen to take us to his home. Such a crowd I never saw, and what fun it was to watch them! They all wore big, baggy trousers, some white, some sky blue, others dark, that filled out like balloons as they rode. One had a lemon-colored coat, with wide, white girdle and long, flowing shirt-sleeves. White drawers and blue and white turban completed his costume. How they did ride, capering everywhere, wheeling about, or flying ahead at full speed and throwing their heavy lances! Our party numbered twenty before we reached the village and there every one turned out to see us. The men drew up in line on each side of the street; the women and children crowded the roofs. The sheikh met us at the door, and the lady at the women's apartment. She had been a patient of mine in Tabriz and she gave us a cordial welcome." From village to village Dr. Bradford was constantly surprised to see how the Kurdish women followed her and begged for healing.

The form of work which missionary physicians prefer and which is most effective for healing as well as for evangelization is the hospital. In it care and medical and antiseptic appliances do much to insure the success of the treatment. Experience proves that surgical cases attempted in the houses of the people are rarely successful. Unsuccessful operations may result in a demand for blood-money. For this reason, some physicians take a quitclaim before the operation. The history of the Westminster Hospital has been one of remarkable success. Of the yearly average of three hundred in-door patients, nearly all have recovered. The greater part are Nestorians, but many are Persians, Turks, Kurds, and a few Armenians and Jews. Many come for wounds received in affrays. Operations on the eye are frequently necessary. Dr. Cochran writes: "One day there came a company of men, Turks, Armenians and Nestorians from Van, in Turkey, nine in all, five of them with sore eyes— ten of the worst eyes I ever saw together. They had experienced all sorts of difficulties by the way, from cold at night, and heat by day, from robbers and passport and customs officers on the frontier, and had at last reached us after ten days' journey. For two of these we could do nothing; the rest were helped more or less. One, who was wholly blind, went home seeing enough to get about, by the help of an artificial pupil, as happy a man as one could wish to see."

Dr. Cochran gives another instance. "We have had several interesting cases of cataract, interesting because the patients, being blind, were so rejoiced to see. One, a little girl, perhaps fourteen years old, a Moslem, had been blind for a year. I removed the cataract from one eye and by the time she had the bandages taken off and saw well it was the date of their great feast, their New Year, or the Ides of March. Her father, who often visited her and reported her progress at home, asked leave to take her there, so that her mother and friends, who did not believe that her sight was restored, could have a 'great feast of thanksgiving together.' Nergis left the hospital on a donkey which her father drove. As they approached their village, parties on the lookout ran ahead calling: 'Nergis has come and she can really see!' This was the signal for men, women and children to come out to meet her with fife and drum. Dancing, singing and waving their silk handkerchiefs, they escorted her to her home. New Year's day all who came to call on her brought little gifts, but before presenting them they would require her to tell the colors of different objects about her, count their fingers, etc. When Nergis came back to have her other eye cured, she told me her father cried from joy all the time that her friends were making such an ado over her."

The missionary physician has a great work *in promoting true medical science*. At the present time native medical practice exists side by side with the science of Europe and America. Native practitioners are of various grades. There are the regulars, if I may so speak, men who have learned from their fathers in the practice of the dispensary whatever knowledge of disease and drugs has been handed down from past ages. Their books are mostly old, and the older the better, according to the idea of some. The works of Avicenna (ob. 1037), are in high repute. The use of skeletons and dissection is not thought necessary. The bearing of physicians is dignified, their robe long and wide-sleeved, peculiar to the office. Fees are not usually charged for visits but for the medicine given. Some family physicians look to the New Year's present for their fee, the amount being left to the liberality of the patient. Sometimes bargains are made for certain cases, so much as a retainer, and so much when the cure is effected and nothing in case of failure.

Surgeons or *jarrahs* are distinct from physicians or *hakims*, and are held in less esteem. Their knowledge lacks scientific basis. Jewish and Armenian surgeons are much sought after. Their establishments are very simple. I visited a treatment-room of one of them. The doctor was seated on a cushion on the carpet, with two boxes near by containing salves and powders. A few bottles on the niches constituted his additional stock. His clinics were very simple. A man came in to have his eyes treated. He stretched himself on the floor, with his head near the doctor. Quickly a little powder was sprinkled in the eyes and he sat up. A boy with a crushed arm arrived. His arm had been treated previously and bandaged with calico. The boy squatted on the floor and unwrapped the bandages. Some salve was taken up with a case-knife, put on a piece of rag and placed on the wound, the lint was renewed, and the elbow exercised a few times while the boy screamed. It was then rebandaged and put in a sling. Some more ointment was put on a piece of cloth and given to the boy. A mother brought her child with sore eyes. She placed the child's head on the doctor's knees and held its hands. The treatment was speedily finished. Then the doctor reached under the edge of the rug, drew out a rumpled sheet of paper, and wrapped some powder in it. One wishing a liquid medicine brought a tea-glass for it. There seems to be no call for bottles, pill-boxes and fancy wrappings. The doctor had everything within reach, and sat on his heels and treated a number of cases with great expedition. His fee in each case was probably a few coppers, possibly a dime.

Another class of doctors are old women, who have belonged probably to a doctor's family and are left without support. They seem to have a lively practice, especially in treating eyes. Worse even than they, are the itinerant quacks who peddle brick dust through the villages and probe cataracts. One of them wished to buy the zinc lining of a box out of which to make eye lotions. The barber, too, tries his hand at surgery. He circumcises the children, pulls teeth and lets blood for the whole community. Not least in importance are the *mammas* or midwives, from whose province the doctors are excluded by rigorous custom.

I have never fathomed the theory of medicine among the regulars in Persia. Diseases, medicines and foods are all classed as hot or cold, according to their essence, not as a matter of temperature. Medicine and food of a quality dissimilar to the disease must be given. Diagnosis is made by feeling the pulse and observing the tongue. Large doses are used. Castor oil is administered by the tea-glassful. Many European drugs are used. Quinine, called "qina-qina," is now widely known. Bleeding by cup and leeches is very frequent. Massage and even trampling on the body are practiced to relieve pain. Blistering and canterizing are extensively in vogue. For croup and diphtheria the throat is gouged with an inserted finger. For dysentery exhalations of lime water are breathed. Virtue is attributed to snake flesh. An official out hunting killed a large snake, and sent it to Dr. Vanneman to examine. A Mussulman procured it and ate it. Afterwards the official remarked that a snake, to be good for the health, should be killed without being enraged.

Among diseases, smallpox is one of the most common. Every child is supposed to have it as a matter of course. It is not considered dangerous, but people disfigured and blind from this cause are not few. Vaccination is being gradually introduced. Venereal diseases are frightfully common. Leprosy is not uncommon. In Azerbaijan lepers are segregated in a village. One day a woman was brought to a physician for treatment. She was a leper. Her neighbors said she must go to the leper village. Her family said they would go with her. The owner of the village did not wish to lose such an industrious family. Being a doctor he offered to give her a medicine that would kill or cure her in eight days. His intention was to poison her. Fright is a frequent cause of sickness and death. A man who had accidentally wounded a prince was so frightened that he died in a few days. An Armenian in Suhrul had gone to a blacksmith to have his horse shod. A Mussulman came and took his turn. The Armenian threatened him, that he would die before a certain day. The superstitious man became frightened and died at the set time.

Some special causes are conducive to disease. Impure water is largely drunk. Running open through the streets, it is polluted, clothes are washed in it, it stands in the *ambars* or cisterns and is drunk even after its smell is very bad. The public baths are a cause of disease. The central plunge-tank is used by hundreds indiscriminately, and the water in it changed at long intervals. It is a source of contagion. Another cause is the disbelief in contagion. Mothers will take their children to see those sick of the scarlet fever or diphtheria, and laugh at the idea of disease being communicated. Coupled with this is the belief in the doctrine of kismet, or fate. "If it is his lot to be sick or die, he will; you cannot prevent it," they will say. They ridicule the idea of microbes and even think precautions are irreligious, a sort of defiance of God. Ideas are changing gradually. An incident will show the old and the new ideas in conflict. A child died of diphtheria. The church authorities refused to have the funeral from the church on account of the danger of contagion. The mother became angry and appealed to the Chaldean Catholic priest, who allowed the child to be buried from his church.

There is a great deal of superstition in the treatment of disease. The conjurer and astrologer are still the companions of the physician. The Vendidad of ancient Persia says: "If several healers present themselves, namely, one who heals with a knife, one who heals with herbs and one who heals with the holy word, it is this one who will best drive away sickness from the body of the faithful. The surgeon must practice on the infidels and prove success before he can treat the faithful." Frequently now as in those times the astrologer and doctor are called for the same patient. The former consults the stars as to the favorable opportunity for calling the latter, and which one of several shall be called, and whether the medicine shall be given and when. If the die is not favorable the medicine will be untouched. A nobleman living at Urumia consulted the astrologers as to what physician he should consult. The lot indicated Dr. Holmes, so leaving the help at hand, he took a five days' journey on horseback to Tabriz, and by being cured was confirmed in his faith in the omens.

A Persian doctor was called to a case of difficult child-birth. He could only stay in the next room and send in directions through the midwife. He asked them to call the woman physician. There were half a dozen women about when she arrived. They were so fanatical that she could hardly get her hands washed, lest she defile the bowl. The diagnosis being made, it was decided to give chloroform. The father was willing but the mother opposed. Meanwhile a mollah led a sheep into the room and around the couch of the woman. It was then sacrificed for her life. The doctors left without doing anything. Sometimes the priest will write a prayer and the patient will swallow the paper or dissolve the writing in water and drink the solution. For cases of melancholy or insanity the priests are called, as the devils are supposed to fear the mollahs or sayids, who wear clothes of the holy blue or green color. They sometimes exorcise by beating in a barbarous manner. Others are taken to the shrines and shut in a dark pit for some days to cure lunacy. Others make the long pilgrimage to Kerbela, hoping to be healed by being tied to the portico of the shrine.

The deficiency of the old medical practice is recognized by enlightened Persians and foreign science is cordially received. From the time of Abbas Mirza, European physicians have been in attendance on the royal family. Dr. Tholozan, a Frenchman, has for forty years been physician-in-chief to the shah. Others have been professors in the Royal College at Teheran. The physicians to the legations and telegraph companies have helped to spread the knowledge of medicine. A few Persians, Armenians and Eastern Syrians have been graduated in the universities of Europe and America, and are in the service of the crown prince, the zili-sultan and other princes, or are engaged in general practice. Twelve graduates of the Urumia college and hospital have had their diplomas sealed by the government and are in successful practice. But what are these few score among so many? Our missionaries not only try to promote a knowledge of hygiene and sanitation among the people, but to assist the native physicians to arrive at a higher standard. Recognizing their capability and holding toward them an attitude not of rivalry but of helpfulness, they are frequently consulted by them and are able to promote their usefulness.

Again medical missions *directly promote the kingdom of Christ*. Medical missions are not merely nor essentially a charitable work. They are indeed benevolent and beneficent but they are more. They are essentially *evangelistic*. Their final aim is to reach the soul. A system of charity would be restricted to the poor, or to those who could not be reached by any other physician; a missionary work aims to reach all. Our missions reach the learned and the great to influence them to a better life, and to gain their influence and friendship for Christ's kingdom. One incidental benefit of this is that the fees from the well-to-do enable the missionary to do more work for the poor.

Medical missions promote Christ's cause *by removing prejudice*. Kindly ministry in times of weakness wins hearts from their old hatreds and fills them with love. Dr. Grant referred to his work as follows: "As I have witnessed the relief of hitherto hopeless suffering and seen men's grateful attempts to kiss my feet and my very shoes at the door, both of which they would literally bathe with tears; as I have seen the haughty mollah thanking God that I would not refuse medicine to a Moslem, and others saying that in every prayer they thanked God for my coming, I have felt that even before I could teach our religion, I was doing something to recommend it and to break down prejudices." Experience through many years confirms this. Dr. Cochran writes: "A Jew, an old man from Kurdistan, who was led to the hospital totally blind, could not express his joy and gratitude on being able to go home without a companion. His strongest expression was, 'May Jesus in whom you believe, bless you and give you long life.'" Mrs. D. P. Cochran, for many years the loved and honored matron of the hospital reports:

"One day an old man, a Mohammedan, having his arm badly gangrened, came and lay down at the gate of the hospital, and asked for the physician. Dr. Cochran sent for him to come into the dispensary where he could be examined. 'No, no,' replied the man. 'I have been a faithful Mohammedan. I have fasted, and prayed, and taken pilgrimages, and now near the end of my life I am not going to forfeit my right to enter paradise by contamination with Christians.' The doctor protested against his remaining outside, insisting that he must at least come into an outer room where he could be treated. The man said he must not defile himself by touching Christian food or eating off Christians' dishes. So, at first, he was treated at the gate, but later was gotten into the hospital and placed on a bed in the ward, where he could receive full attention from nurse and physician. One night the man was much worse. The nurse called the doctor, who worked over him a long time. When somewhat relieved the man burst into tears and said, 'How could I think what you should do for me would keep me from paradise? Here you have cared for my sores with *your own* hands, forgetting your comfort in easing my pain. How kind you are! How good you are!' Over and over he expressed his confidence in the doctor, and humbly implored forgiveness for having thought that contact with so good and wise a man could injure his prospect of paradise. Afterwards, alluding to his former fear of contamination, he said, 'I will eat your food off your dishes.' Thus the old man's prejudices were removed, and when he left, it was to tell others of the good he had received at the hands of the Christian missionaries."

Medical missions help to *maintain and strengthen cordial relations with the government and its officials.* They win and keep the friendship of the khans and owners of villages, thus opening new doors for gospel work, and relieving the work and converts in times of difficulties and persecutions. An indication of the shah's appreciation of the work of the physicians may be seen in his conferring the decoration of the Lion and the Sun on Drs. Cochran, Holmes and Torrence. Dr. Cochran by his influence with Sheikh Obeidullah at the time of the Kurdish raid was the means of preserving the lives of many Christians. By his intercession he obtained a delay in the attack of the sheikh, and saved the city of Urumia from pillage and massacre. Again after the war a prince, a son of the shah, conveyed to Dr. Cochran a formal expression of thanks for his kindness to the army while stationed at Urumia. The sequel to the story of the Kurdish raid is remarkable. At that time two sons of Sheikh Obeidullah, Sheikh Abdul Kadir and Sheikh Saduk, followed their father's standard. The latter vowed vengeance upon Dr. Cochran as the instrument of defeating their purpose. Of this Mrs. D. P. Cochran reports:

"Later Sheikh Saduk wrote a letter to Dr. Cochran, asking that his wife and daughter be received into the hospital. They soon arrived, attended by men and women servants. The presence of a Mohammedan mollah, whose watchful eye guarded the entrance to the lady's chamber, showed her lord's care for his cherished wife, as well as the sacredness of the retreat to which he had consigned her. We made her stay with us as pleasant as possible, seeing that nothing was wanting for her comfort. After a stay of some two weeks, she left in health and with the profuse thanks of her husband to the doctor. Soon after, desiring to send a teacher to the Christians in this Kurdish chief's district, a letter from the physician, we felt sure, would secure his protection. The roads, too, through his villages will be safe for us and for our people. Such passports through these wild regions are of no little account, though the pecuniary profit of such patients to the hospital is very small. Sheikh Saduk sent a mule laden with honey and tobacco."

Other incidents illustrating the same point and showing the influence of the hospital are given below:

"A Persian general was for some time under the doctor's care. Hearing that he was soon to leave for America, the general sent to his door three camels laden with rice, flour, bread, cheese, potted quails, butter and lambs. The season before he had sent two mules laden with fruit, vegetables and fowls. Presents thus brought to the medical missionary are turned over to the hospital for its use, or an equivalent credited to that institution.

" Another officer in the Persian army, a fine specimen of a military gentleman, was sent to the hospital by the prince governor. He had been wounded some weeks before, and now his arm was swollen and the bones broken and diseased ; his blood was poisoned ; he had no appetite and no strength. The doctor was hourly expecting a telegram to call him to a critical case some distance away, and replied that the officer could not be received. But he plead as a man for his life—'If you stay here but one day or one hour, let me remain till you go.' To this, consent was given, and he was installed in the best quarters we had for air and attention. One personal servant together with his young wife was suffered to come with him. Providentially for him no telegram came for the doctor. It was a long and hard fight against fearful odds. I would go in to find him seated in an easy-chair, with his wife fanning him, when with mingled praise to God and his physician he would talk till he would sink back exhausted. As he grew stronger, he would have his wife go with him into the yard, where he would sit on cushions under a tree. He liked best to sit where he could hear the singing in the college chapel. One Sabbath, as I returned from service there, he told me how much he had enjoyed the music, and added, 'I wish they would pray for me. Please tell them to.' One of the medical students went to the evening meeting and made known his request, when his case was most earnestly remembered. The medical students took turns daily in reading the Scriptures in Persian to him. When he left, no one was more earnest in expressing gratitude for healing mercies than was this man, and we can depend on him to aid the work of our preachers wherever he has any influence.

"The Mohammedan ruler of a farming village had been bitterly opposed to having any Christian work done among his tenants, even among his nominally Christian subjects. The missionaries sent a preacher to his village. The ruler ordered him away; that not availing, he ordered the preacher's goods and furniture to be put out of the house into the street. Later the ruler's son was sick. He needed to have an operation performed, for which he must be taken to the hospital. The father accompanied him and afterwards kept visiting the hospital, occasionally spending a night, thus keeping well acquainted with all that was done for his son. He watched the workings of the establishment. When well enough the son was sent home, and later the father called for a Christian preacher in his village, and attended service himself, carrying his own Persian Bible, a translation made by Henry Martyn, often comparing passages and asking questions, and discussing the Christian faith. This course excited comment. Mohammedans asked, 'What does this mean? Recently you drove the preacher from your village, and now you are attending services and reading the Bible.' 'Well,' replied the ruler, 'I will tell you. I did not know these people. My son was sick, and I sent him to their hospital, and I got acquainted with the missionaries, and I know they are good people, and I wish their teachers, and I am going to have them.' That man will never again oppose the missionary work.

"There was an old Kurdish chief and robber, who, with others, had repeatedly perpetrated outrages on Christians. Redress was sought by the missionaries, and some of the robbers, among them this old chief, received punishment. Dr. Cochran had been instrumental in obtaining this justice, and the chief vowed vengeance upon him, even threatening the life of the 'Christian dog.' While breathing out his hatred a cataract blinded his eyes and he felt compelled to seek the hospital for help. He was kindly welcomed. 'The Christian dog' removed the cataract; the chief recovered his sight. Later the doctor visited the village where the chief lived, and as he sat in one of the houses reading the Bible aloud, there was a sudden stir among the people. A passage was quickly made and this chief passed up between the rows of people to the doctor, who stopped reading, but the chief bade him resume, adding he was glad to have him preach to his subjects, and he himself wished to learn more of Christ. Thus the once proud, cruel man sat down a humble listener at the feet of the Christian whose life he had threatened. He could well have said, 'One thing I know, that whereas I was blind now I see.'"

When Dr. Wishard reached Mosul, he was immediately called to treat many patients, winning the favor of the officials and of men of influence. Pressing invitations came from all quarters. Among those who invited him were the powerful sheikhs of Berwer, either of whom had it in his power to prevent mission work for the Nestorians of Berwer and Supna. Of the visit made to them Mr. McDowell writes: "We first went to Telee Beg, who did us the honor to meet us outside, and who during our stay of three days did all in his power to show his friendship. He paid Dr. Wishard honors which are reserved for the very highest. Many sick were treated and an operation on an old and very influential Kurd created a favorable impression. Dr. Yohannan Sayad had done much to secure us such a favorable reception. He had visited and treated this man. . . . We spent two days with the other great chief, Mira Mohammed. He expressed himself as pleased with the idea of Dr. Wishard's giving to his people the benefit of his medical skill, and invited us to make his village our headquarters in passing. Our reception by these two men will have a great moral influence upon all classes. . . . Dr. Wishard's work is making itself felt in places hitherto inaccessible to us. From Ashitha, Dr. Grant's village, which has so long been closed to us, comes an earnest invitation for Dr. Wishard to visit the place on behalf of the sick. A similar invitation comes from Malek Ismiel, the most powerful man in Upper Tiary."

In Hamadan an incident occurred which shows how doors of opportunity may be opened up. Dr. Alexander wrote in 1888: "The Armenian Gregorians of Sheverine, who are completely under the influence of their priests, and have always stoutly opposed our work in their midst, succeeded in enlisting the lord of the village in their cause. For a time their triumph was complete. Our school was closed and we appealed to the khan in vain. Soon, however, one of his children was taken sick. Native hakims were called, but failed to restore the little patient. The child's mother knew that I had saved her little sister's life some time before, and so at the eleventh hour sent for me. The efforts to save the child were blessed and she made a rapid recovery. In return the khan sent a nice present to the dispensary and gave us a permit in writing to go on with our work in the village. He had received orders from Teheran to the same effect, but without his personal permission we could do nothing."

The history of Dr. Holmes' work in Tabriz further illustrates the influence of the missionary physician. As soon as his arrival became known, many of the chief men of the city called to give him their salaams. The native medical fraternity, too, received him with the utmost cordiality, welcomed him to frequent consultations, and seemed glad of his instruction in their cases. He found among the Persian hakims some with a much more full and accurate knowledge of medicine than we had supposed them to possess. Those acquainted with some European language had become familiar in a measure with the science as we possess it, and abandoned many of their crude theories. They seemed unusually free from Mohammedan prejudice, and fully appreciated the superiority of Christian learning. An acquaintance with them led us to number increased knowledge of medical science among the advances which Persia is making. Appreciation of Dr. Holmes' coming was shown by rich and poor alike. The dispensary was crowded from morning till sundown. Among the persons treated was a young prince who was afflicted with frequent epileptic fits. It was a case of long standing and great severity. Through God's blessing the disease was arrested in a marvelously short time; and in their gratitude they hesitated not to exclaim, in the language of Oriental hyperbole, that "the hakim sahib had raised their son from the dead."

During the following years Dr. Holmes so commended the religion of Jesus that even an infidel was heard to remark, " If there is a heaven, Dr. Holmes will go to it." In the palaces of princes, the houses of the mollahs and mujtehids, in the homes of the people of all classes, rich and poor, learned and unlearned, he was invited constantly to explain the principles of our faith and listened to with respectful attention. In 1887-8 several cases of severe illness occurred in official circles. The governor-general was so seriously ill that in view of his advanced age, it was the settled conviction that he would die. It was even said that his successor was designated. Through God's blessing, medical skill accomplished his recovery, to the surprise of all. Shortly afterwards a child of the crown prince was attacked with meningitis. Her life was despaired of. A month of special care and watching saw the patient convalescent. Dr. Holmes received the public thanks of the crown prince, and for a second time a *khalat* or robe of honor. After this he was requested to accept the position of physician in chief to his highness the vali Ahd, and the governor-general, the amir-i-Nizam. It was deemed wise that he should accept this position. Dr. Holmes was moved by no selfish ambition. His life was consecrated to the service of Christ, and a position in the palace seemed a fitting sphere for the exercise of this service. After spending a day in fasting and prayer for divine guidance, Dr. Holmes accepted the position, it being expressly stipulated that no restriction should be placed on his engaging in Christian work as heretofore. At the end of the first year, 1888-9, the hope of prolonging Mrs. Holmes' life necessitated her being taken to Europe. After the time of the furlough had expired the vali Ahd telegraphed several times, urgently requesting Dr. Holmes to return. But Dr. H. Adcock, a well-qualified and experienced English physician, who was in the employ of the telegraph company, Imperial Bank, etc., having agreed to perform the duties for half the sum which had been paid to Dr. Holmes, the half was offered to Dr. Holmes and refused. Dr. Holmes was then invited to return as a missionary physician either at Teheran, Salmas or Hamadan. He chose the latter for personal reasons. Soon after his arrival he was called to go to Sennah to see the amir-i-Nizam, then governor-general of Kurdistan. He was right royally entertained by the amir, who urged him to take up his residence in Sennah, and gave authority to open a school there, as the Jews had for some time been requesting. In parting he embraced the doctor in the presence of a large concourse, sent a handsome rug and a hundred tomans in cash, and gave him an escort of horsemen to accompany him home.*

Finally, medical missions are *a direct means of evangelization and of the conversion of souls*, by conversations in visits and by the sick-bed, by public exercises in the dispensaries and in hospitals. The direct sequence of a period of treatment in the Urumia hospital has not seldom been the true repentance of the patient. I have observed striking instances. Reports contain such items as the following. "The other Armenian, the son of an old church-priest, received no help for his heart disease, but he expressed himself as far better satisfied with what he had found than he would be with physical health alone. One was a Nestorian from the independent mountain tribes, a man who was warlike and has the reputation of constantly stirring up quarrels in his village. He was with us several months; he was never happier toward the last than when the Scriptures were read and explained to him. He went home cured of a distressing skin-disease and professing Christ. Recently one of our church members

---

*Dr. Holmes' successor in Tabriz, Dr. Vanneman, notwithstanding special difficulties, has won the favor of all classes and laid the foundation for a great work.

from his district was down here and remarked: 'Really, Aaron is not the same man we used to know last fall.'" "A young shepherd was deeply interested in the truth, but was not inclined to believe anything without the strongest evidence. One of the hardest things for him to accept was Christ's free forgiveness of sin. With his hot blood he could not see how God could forgive until he had first taken revenge. He one day heard the passage read where Christ likens himself to the good shepherd. The young man eagerly asked, 'Does Jesus truly love me as I love my sheep?' and then added, 'now I can understand how he can forgive my sins.' Toward spring he returned to his dark mountain home, where pillage and bloodshed were scenes of almost daily occurrence. Good report came constantly of his Christian-like deportment, although exposed to great peril from his friends for his confession. He has lately returned to the hospital, and desires to profess his faith. In other parts of the mountains of Kurdistan, difficult of access, missionaries and native helpers on recent tours have found old hospital patients giving them a hearty welcome, and ready to promote their mission of gospel light."

Again, "Among the women who have come to the hospital have been those whose lives were full of suffering and sorrow, and the Christian atmosphere and kind care received, have made the place seem to them like the very 'gates of paradise,' as one and another have testified. One woman came with a fatal disease, and while here her faith was quickened by what she heard and saw. Later, when back in her humble home,—a poor, mud hovel, she patiently bore her sufferings and met the approach of death with triumph and joy." God be blessed for the results of medical missions!

The question has been raised: How does medical mission work compare in its results with other kinds of work? J. D. Rees, in the *Nineteenth Century*, 1889, speaking of Persia, says, "The American medical missionaries are most useful, and deal very successfully with ophthalmia, conjunctivitis and other diseases of the eye. It would be well if all classes of missionaries were like the American doctors, and combined like their great Exemplar Jesus Christ, the healing of the sick with the saving of the soul." In the London *Christian* the remark was made, "In some countries the medical missions are the *sole* means of overcoming the local prejudice against Europeans, *particularly in* Persia." Doctor Robert Bruce commenting on this statement wrote, "They are very far from being the only means, indeed I doubt very much whether they are the most valuable and effective means for that purpose. Invaluable work has been done by medical missionaries in Bagdad and Ispahan, and in large cities like these, the work of medical missionaries is of unspeakable value, not as a sole means of evangelization, but as a most useful auxiliary to the other branches of the work." I need not enter into a detailed discussion on this point. The end and aim of all is evangelization. I believe that pulpit, Bible, press, school, and dispensary are all efficient means and are owned and blessed of God.

CHAPTER XII.

DROUGHT AND FAMINE.

IN 1879-1880 there was a failure of the crops for two successive years in Northwest Persia, due to lack of rain. This resulted in scarcity and in great distress, which was aggravated by much grain being sold for army supplies during the Russo-Turkish war. Then another drought brought on a veritable famine throughout Azerbijan. In Tabriz some Persian merchants supplied the bakers for some months and enabled them to sell at not more than double the ordinary price. But the bakers were dishonest. The merchants quarreled, a murder resulted and they were called by the shah to Teheran. After this bread in Tabriz rose to nine times its usual price. Much of it, mixed with bran, almond husks and clay, was unfit to eat. Meat was beyond the means of the poor. Women and children went to the fields to gather clover and grass to satisfy the cravings of nature and some died from dysentery as the result. Men fell in the street in a famished state. Horses and other animals became lean and bony as in Pharaoh's vision, and travel by caravan and the transport of grain was costly. Distress was aggravated by the rich keeping the grain for a further rise.

In Urumia the condition was extremely deplorable. Grain was unobtainable; the price of bread was high beyond precedent. The majority of the population were without food, without work, and without anything to sell. They lived on from week to week on a mere handful of grain, with a little meat, herbs, milk, blood, entrails of animals, anything they could obtain by selling their very houses, or household furniture and clothes, or by begging and stealing. The digging of roots and herbs in the field was the occupation of thousands of women. One thousand people died in a day within sight of the mission station. To an appeal of a band of women, begging at his door, a nobleman was reported to have said, "You have not yet eaten your own children."

The condition was evidently one to move the sympathies of the Christian world. Appeals for aid were liberally responded to from England and America. The shah sent five hundred tomans through the British consul to the missionaries in Urumia for distribution. In Tabriz, Mr. Wright of the mission and Messrs. Ziegler & Co. distributed flour, bread and money, and employed poor workmen to pave the streets and build the wall of the Protestant cemetery. Deceptions were guarded against. One woman was discovered coming the same day in three different costumes. Several came asking for money to bury their dead. No dead were found at their houses. When distribution ceased there was danger of the crowd breaking into and plundering Mr.

Wright's house. A display, amounting almost to violence, was necessary to induce them to depart.

In Urumia forty thousand dollars were systematically distributed in relieving the famished, besides four thousand dollars distributed in Tabriz, Khoi and Maragha. Inquiry and calculation by Mr. Oldfather, led to the opinion that every four dollars saved a life. Notwithstanding this, it was said "that twenty per cent. of the population of Urumia died of famine and its consequent sickness." Two or three thousand Christian families received relief for the three months preceding harvest, yet in spite of all efforts more than five hundred Nestorians and Armenians died. In the mountain district of Mergawar one-fifth of the Nestorians died. Without the assistance of their fellow-Christians of other lands, the death rate would have been more appalling. Some of the Evangelical churches made commendable efforts to care for their own poor. In Geogtapa fast days were observed in which the provisions they would have consumed at home were brought to the church and distributed to the poor. Offerings were collected, cotton was bought by their committee and given out that, by weaving and knitting, some might earn their bread.

Relief was distributed to thousands of Mohammedans. The soup-house in the city was thronged. Mohammedans forgot that Christian food would defile them and gladly ate of it. But religious prejudice is very strong. One poor woman dying in great pain said: "Alas! I have eaten bread made unclean by the hands of the infidels and therefore I cannot die easily." This exhibition of Christian philanthropy impressed many Mohammedans with the spirit of our religion and is gratefully remembered. Some contrasted it with the conduct of their own priests. A Persian writer says: "One of the clergy, in Teheran, living in an odor of sanctity and enjoying universal respect, had in store enough corn to satisfy all the people of the city. The shah wished to buy his wheat at forty tomans a *kharvar*, and sell it at cheap rates to the people. But this reverend exponent of the law withheld the people's food in the hope that its value might rise about forty tomans."—(New History, Browne, p. 189.)

CHAPTER XIII.

THE CHOLERA EPIDEMIC OF 1892.

CHOLERA used to be epidemic in Persia with considerable frequency. It seemed to come in periods of six or seven years. In 1835, it raged in Tabriz, when the active services of Rev. Mr. Haas, the German missionary, among the sick and dying were greatly appreciated. In 1847, from four thousand to seven thousand died of cholera in Urumia. It prevailed in 1871. Since that time it did not appear until 1889, when it came from Bagdad into the regions of Kermanshah and Hamadan. In the latter city, three hundred died. The usual theory is that cholera starts from India, but Dr. Holozan, the shah's physician for thirty years, is reported to have concluded, "that the real center or focus of cholera is not India, but Central Asia, *i. e.*, Samarcand and Bokhara."

In 1892, it reached Persia through Afghanistan, being first virulent in Meshed, where seven thousand died. Thence it came by the new pilgrim route, that is, by the wagon road from Meshed, the Trans-Caspian Railroad and Caspian steamers, to Baku. It traveled by steam, not by slow caravan as previously. I had occasion to go to Batum early in July. It had just broken out in Baku and the railroad was overcrowded with fugitives, scattering through Trans-Caucasia. The trains were delayed for medical inspection. As a sanitary measure the Russian government sent home several thousand Persian laborers, and this was one means of scattering the disease quickly in Persia. It soon appeared in Ardebil and Resht. Sanitary measures are impossible in Persia. Some feeble attempts were made. Orders were issued to clean the streets. Quarantine was established on the road between Ardebil and Tabriz. It was simply a laughing stock. Minor officials made it an excuse for levying on travelers for permission to pass the cordon. Some men are said to have paid the government from two hundred to five hundred tomans for the privilege of being quarantine agents. One party, threatened with detention, were passed when two *krans* a person were paid. This caused it to be called *krantine*.

The reliance of the Mohammedans was on religion, not on sanitation. It was about the time of the Muharam celebration of the Martyrdom of Husain when rumors of the approach of cholera became universal. Then religious frenzy reached a higher pitch than usual, in efforts to appease God and especially to obtain the intercession of the Imams. The mosques were crowded, the chain-bands and sword-bands were more earnest in self-tortures, even the women marching through the streets with loud cryings and supplications. The multitude assembled at night in the open plain for religious ceremonies. As cholera had already begun in the city, these efforts only increased the danger of contagion. It was telegraphed everywhere that a revelation had been made at the tomb of Abbas at Kerbela, that at 4 o'clock on the Ashura, *i. e.*, the 10th of Muharam, cholera would cease. The people were greatly encouraged in the assurance of safety by a telegram from Khorasan. A mujtehid had seen a vision. The Imam Reza had appeared to him in traveling clothes. He asked, "Where do you come from?" He replied, that he had gone to protect Tabriz from the cholera, because they stood so firmly for the faith in the matter of the tobacco monopoly. But how vain these efforts and promises! The cholera had come and by direct course and quicker than usual, from the shrine of this very Imam.

But religion had not yet exhausted its means of protection. Korans were hung over the streets that by passing under them safety might be assured. At one place forty-one Korans were placed in a sheet and suspended from a pole stretching from roof to roof. To the astonishment of the faithful some one dared to steal the sheet at night. At Zenjanab a dream revealed to an old woman, by the mouth of Ali, it was said, that whoever would drink of a certain new spring indicated would escape the cholera. People went sixteen miles to obtain the water; even high officials were said to have sent for it.

Prayers were printed (lithographed) and thousands

of them posted on the streets above the doors of the
houses. I obtained copies of two kinds. They were
in Arabic. The larger one, after mention of the names
of God, Mohammed, Fatima and the twelve Imams,
narrates that Abdullah, son of Abbas, had a tradition
concerning Mohammed as follows : He said, "I heard
from Gabriel the faithful, that in the time of Jesus a
severe epidemic of cholera occurred in which eleven-
twelfths of the people of the world died. Gabriel said,
'In the last times your people will be subject to this
plague.' The prophet put his head upon his knees in
perplexity and prayed to God and said, 'Keep my
people from this cholera.' Gabriel answered from God
and brought this prayer and said : 'Whoever wishes
to be free from liability to the cholera, let him buy a
sheep with lawfully gained money and read this
prayer seven times upon it, and kill the sheep and dis-
tribute it to the people. God will keep from the
cholera the owner of the sheep and whoever shall eat
of the meat. And again, whoever shall paste this
prayer upon his door, the cholera will not come to
that house. Whoever shall write it and keep it about
his person shall be safe, and whoever reads it once a
day for seven days shall be exempt. And whoever
shall write it and put it in a cup of water and shall
drink of that water, the disease of cholera will not
reach him.'"

Then follows a long prayer. It is in many respects
admirable, pleading with God by his many titles and

attributes in detail and in beautiful language. Toward the end it says: "We ask this for the sake of these" (naming the fourteen holy ones of the Shiahs); "may this cholera turn from us for the honor of these names, and we send greetings to Mohammed and his sons. Oh! Thou who deliveredst Abraham from the fire. Oh! Thou who didst enlighten the eyes of Jacob when they were blinded. Oh! Thou who didst take Joseph out of the pit and the prison, etc., etc., save us from the cholera and the pangs of death. Forgive us, forgive."

The second prayer was very similar. Its introduction stated that in one year in Bagdad the cholera came twice severely. Twelve thousand young men of the faithful died, besides women and old men. A merchant and his family remained in safety. They inquired of him the reason, and he said, "There is with me a prayer spoken by Imam Jaffar Saduk for preservation from cholera." The Khalifs procured it and sent it everywhere. We are told that whosoever shall repeat a certain surah three times, say the creed, write certain Arabic words and swallow the paper shall be preserved. These words are a mystery. There are other cabalistic or talismanic signs in the prayer. Many Mohammedans were quite confident of their safety and said, "We by our prayers and by the intercession of Husain will be the means of preserving you, Armenians or Christians." A Sayid stonecutter told me that as long as he was working for me, no evil would befall me.

But neither faith, superstition nor fatalism could save them. Cholera began in Tabriz before July 29th. The first known cases were among the Mohammedans. Its presence and power were emphasized by the sudden death of a servant, a tutor, a sister and a daughter of Mr. Bernay, the French consul. Mrs. Hogberg, a Swedish missionary, her infant and nurse were taken down. The former died inside of twenty-four hours. Mr. Hogberg, returning from a tour, was met by words of condolence in the street, but no one would tell him the evil tidings. Crossing the threshold, he saw which one was missing and the truth was known to him. The infant died also. When this household was sick and a nurse was needed, Mrs. Yeghisabet, the wife of Rev. Gregor Guergian, came to Dr. Bradford and said, "I want to go and take care of Mrs. Hogberg." The doctor said to her, "You know the danger." She answered, "Yes, but I cannot leave them alone." She assisted also in the last offices for the dead and the same day was taken sick, coming very near death's door, but was happily spared.

Meanwhile the disease was spreading rapidly. The polluted water supply, public baths, ceremonial ablutions and other causes promoted the disease.* Ignorance of sanitary laws, and disbelief in infection or the

---

* The sanitary condition may be inferred from some rules framed by physicians in 1889 to prevent the spread of cholera.

1. Baths must be cleaned and the water in them changed every three or four months. Waste from the baths must not run into the drinking water.

much spoken of microbes, assisted its spread. It was not many days until people were dying by hundreds in every quarter.

At the first alarm, multitudes escaped the infected city. The crown prince, with the officials and their retinues, consuls, Europeans and many others camped on the Sahend mountains. The Armenians fled to Muzhumbar and Karadagh. Mussulmans scattered themselves everywhere, many returning to their native villages. Thousands abandoned business and daily bread, even leaving their property unprotected, showing that "all that a man hath will he give for his life." Mussulman belief in fatalism seemed much weakened. They would frequently ask: "Is it right to flee?" They seemed glad to be assured that it was. I think they will never question hereafter the wisdom of leaving the city; for those who left had comparative exemption. Many of the poor said, "We cannot flee, therefore we must trust God!" Trusting God and keeping your powder dry seemed to them somehow inconsistent.

Our mission tents were pitched on the side of Sahend, near Zanjanab. Dr. Vanneman took charge of

2. Tanneries must be outside of the town and hides must not be washed in the drinking water.

3. The waterways must be covered and clothes must not be washed in the drinking water. Waste from coffee-houses, etc., must not run into the drinking water.

4. In the baths, the fuel must not contain bones and other things (as carcases) which give a disagreeable odor.

those precious lives, while Dr. Bradford, Miss Holliday and I remained in the city. The Memorial School for Boys was quarantined in a general way, and the school-girls, with Miss Holliday, occupied the recitation hall, and the boys and teacher the dormitory. A month's supply of groceries, flour, etc., was laid in; a cow, some sheep, and a flock of hens were bought with provisions for them, and we ceased to buy food from the market. Even fruit from the trees in the yard was interdicted. All drinking water was boiled and a few drops of acid put in each glass. Whenever I went out to visit the sick or to attend a funeral, I took a carbolic acid bath and changed my clothes before returning. These precautions secured our yards from the infection.

Dr. Bradford lived at the dispensary ready to minister to the sick night and day. For a few days, Dr. Casparian attended patients, but was attacked himself. After convalescence, he was removed to Muzhumbar. Dr. Bradford then remained the only physician of foreign training in the city. Her hands were full, her heart brave, her faith in God sustaining, and many were benefited by her treatment. The exigencies of the time necessitated her breaking her rule of attending only the women. Among her patients was a Greek gentleman who happily recovered, and through his grateful mention of her work in writing to his brother in London, her devotion to the stricken city was mentioned in the press of Europe and America with highest appreciation and unstinted praise. Of

LADIES STARTING FROM TABRIZ ON TOUR

Miss Holliday mounted, face invisible under white veiling. Dr. Bradford, ridingwhip in hand, about to mount.

this she modestly wrote, "You give me more credit than I deserve, for I did only my duty and what came to my hand, and as I look back, it seems to me we might have made it (the cholera relief), broader and more useful."

One day word reached us that some Americans had arrived in the city, sick of the cholera. I immediately went to see them and found Mr. Theodore Child, author, and Mr. Edwin Lord Weeks, artist, on a tour of Persia and India in the interests of *Harper's Magazine*. They were in miserable lodgings, and they and their dragoman were all suffering from the cholera. We invited them to occupy the large, airy rooms of the girls' school, which were turned into a temporary hospital. Mr. Weeks wrote in *Harper's Magazine*: "It was to Dr. Bradford's constant care and untiring energy as well as to the devotion of our Armenian friend (the nurse Yagut) that our party owed their recovery." Afterwards they proceeded on their journey, but Mr. Child, whose attack had been very severe, had a relapse with typhoid symptoms and died near Ispahan. Of this Mr. Weeks wrote: "The kindly and sympathetic welcome which I found at the mission did much to render more endurable the painful circumstances attending my return to Julfa (Ispahan). Had I brought the cholera with me it would have made no shade of difference in the warmth of my reception either by Dr. Bruce or by the ladies of his household." Mr. Child was much admired as a writer of fine ability, especially in descriptive travels, and greatly beloved by a select coterie of literary friends in New York, Paris, and London. These raised a sum of more than eight hundred dollars to be used by Dr. Bradford as a memorial of him. The intention is to endow a hospital room for sick foreigners when a hospital is built in Tabriz.

Another traveler, Mr. Van Ketel, a Hollander, arrived sick of the cholera and died inside of ten hours. His passport, which showed that he was of the Reformed faith, was brought to me. With no one but Hosef, an Armenian Protestant, who acted as undertaker, the Turkish *hamals* bore his body to the grave. That they might understand, I held the service in Turkish. A couple of days afterwards, word was brought that Hosef was attacked, and in the morning he was dead. A few days before, when I had called on him, as I did on each church member once a week to pray with them and strengthen their hearts in those trying times, I had found Hosef reading and meditating on the Psalms. He was the only one of our little flock that died. We went to conduct the funeral services, invited by the daughter and granddaughter, who were Protestants. The Gregorian priest also came, called by the wife, who was a Gregorian. An altercation arose, led by a relative, an old vixen, who used to come to her gate and curse when she saw a man passing to church carrying Bible and hymn-book. She would revile him for carrying the " Devil's books." She led the war of words, backed by a dozen wine-excited Armenians. The granddaughter answered with strong words, affirming that Hosef had chosen the spot in the Protestant cemetery where he wished to be buried. The priest, too, joined in, reviling the girl with words which need not disgrace this page. Finally we told them that we desired no fight about it, that if they would not do what was right they might do as they pleased, and we stood by while the priest waved his censer and read the unintelligible prayers.

Of the Armenians who remained in the city, mostly the poorer class, one in eight died. They had the idea that alcohol would prevent the cholera and many were under its influence. Some resorted to religious ceremonies. Many sacrifices of sheep were made and distributed. In a village thirty sheep were sacrificed at the festival of Mary "the Mother of God." On the same day many women visited the cemetery of Nana Mariam (Mother Mary) in Tabriz. They lamented their sin in not having kept strictly the fast of Mary, and kissed the stones of the shrine with such fervor and at such length, that the priest enjoined them to cease. Processions with certain rituals and prayers were made around the churches. The tradition was brought to mind that if the supposed hand of Thaddeus were brought from the monastery beyond Khoi, the plague would be stayed. But it would be on this condition, that a priest should go and bring it, and that priest would certainty fall a victim after his return. Though no priest went for the hand, yet it is due to the priests to say that they unflinchingly did their duty in this time of danger. On some days so many persons died that one priest remained at the cemetery and another in the city to officiate. The innovation was adopted of sending the bodies on horseback. It was in superintending the loading of a body that Bishop Stephanos was attacked with the cholera. He had made his loads up in order to leave the city, when he was reproached by a poor man of his flock for abandoning them. The word struck his heart. He remained and did much to encourage his people. When he became sick, Dr. Bradford was called to treat him. We were all glad she could have the opportunity of kindly ministering to one who had so bitterly opposed our work. Dr. L. Castaldi, an Italian physician, most generously took the trouble to come down from Naamatabad. But their efforts to save the bishop's life were unavailing. He was greatly mourned by his people. They held his funeral from the church and showed their affection by kissing his hand, forgetting prudence. Some of them said, "It is expedient that one man should die for the people," and expected the cholera to cease.

The Protestant Armenian preacher, Mr. N. Guleserian was, during these trying times, exhorting many and ministering to the sick and bereaved.

The epidemic raged about a month. We could not tell the exact number of deaths. On the worst day possibly one thousand died in the city, and in all ten thousand to twelve thousand. In one family eleven died. In one house the father had died, and one night the neighbors heard the children crying, and entered to find the mother dead also. They were silent days. Business and pleasure were alike suspended. Official and private life were at a standstill. Fear and death reigned. Funerals were passing day and night. Before many doors carpets were spread and the mourners sat in the street for prayer and lamentation. At night the reading of the mollahs and the wail of the mourners could be heard on every side. Though officials and their servants who act as police were largely absent, and possibly by reason of this, there was little crime. One case was reported where a party was seen carrying a bier at night. Noticing that the corpse seemed large and heavy, a guard approached the funeral procession. The bearers dropped the bier and ran. It was full of household goods which they had stolen.

As time passed, the sanitary condition of the city became worse. Ten thousand bodies buried within the city in shallow graves would have polluted the atmosphere, but even worse than this was the custom of putting corpses on the ground, and building a casement of brick and plaster over them with the idea of transferring them to Kerbela or Meshed to rest in sacred soil.* The stench from the cemeteries polluted

---

* The following year some grave-diggers in Teheran disinterred such a corpse, and were fatally attacked with cholera.

the air. Men passed them holding camphor or garlic in their hands to make the stench less perceptible. One day early in September a wind and dust storm filled the city with a horrid odor like the quintessence of putrefaction. It seemed as if the smells from the city had been collected, concentrated and blown down upon it. It was due to the bad condition of the city that Mrs. Wilson and I had slight attacks of cholera after I brought her down from Zenjanab.

Cholera invaded the mountain retreats, though partial quarantine was kept up with sulphur fumes and carbolic acid. Efforts were made to smuggle watermelons into the Vali Ahd's camp, concealed in straw. At one place envelopes were wiped with a cloth soaked in carbolic acid. Afterwards the water tasted of carbolic acid and it was found that the cook had used the cloth as a stop for the water jar. A score died at Muzhumbar and at Zanjanab. At the latter place a European lady was at the point of death, but recovered under Dr. Vanneman's care. Medicines were sent by Dr. Bradford to Maragha, Mianduab and Soujbulak, and some lives were saved by the teachers and preachers distributing them. At one place the postmaster appropriated a duplicate lot of medicine and then cast lots as to whether he should use it. The lot fell that he should use the pills but not the powders. At Soujbulak two dervishes seated themselves in the public square and declared that they had brought the cholera and their departure would take it away.

They were given a present and told to go away. In Salmas the cholera was light. Dr. Yohanan Sayad and Mr. Mechlin did good by distributing medicines. In Urumia, Dr. Cochran, in anticipation of its coming, had prepared a pamphlet, setting forth the nature and causes of cholera and giving advice as to its prevention and treatment. It was of great value and its suggestions were acted on by the nobles and people. The cholera came in its lightest form. By that time stories of the cholera riots in Astrakhan, and other places in Russia, were in circulation, where physicians were killed and hospitals burned. They said that the physicians were poisoning men at the first symptoms of sickness and burning their bodies in chemicals almost before they were dead, that the disease might not spread. These horrible and incredible tales were rehearsed with vividness and detail and the people believed them. The result was that though Dr. Miller and an Eastern Syrian physician went from house to house in the city of Urumia, offering medicines, the people refused to take them and many closed their doors against the doctors. In a village which they visited, all refused the medicines except the Protestants. Of more than five thousand Protestants but one died. In Mosul people gladly received the medicines from Dr. Wishard.

The cholera reached Teheran, by way of Khorasan, a few days after it appeared at Tabriz. It was even more violent at Teheran. The missionaries in Teheran organized efficient aid. At the suggestion of the American *chargé d'affaires*, the Ferry Hospital, lately completed, was opened for the sick. Dr. Torrence, who but a short time before had resigned his connection with the mission, took charge of it. Mr. Ward and Mr. Esselstyn acted as head nurses. A corps of boys from the school from fourteen to twenty years of age volunteered to assist, and with faith and heroism as true Christian Endeavorers did every duty. Messrs. Taylor and Janson, English traders, did efficient work in the dispensary. Ninety patients were taken in, some of them from the streets in a dying condition. Mr. Potter acted as city visitor, going to the poorer quarters of the city, distributing medicines and in certain cases bringing word to the busy doctor and taking back directions. In one short alley he found thirteen houses with cholera. Five hundred homes were visited. They also distributed medicines in the public squares, with written and oral directions, to two thousand five hundred. The expenses of the hospital and dispensary work were met by the European colony to the extent of one thousand tomans. Mr. Watson R. Sperry, under appointment as U.S. minister to Teheran, raised in America a fund for hospital relief which was distributed to various points for medicines and other expenses.

Several European physicians were at work in the city. Dr. Smith attended the sick in the mountain villages and came into the city two or three times a week to see the Christian women. Of those engaged in ministering to the sick none died. The greatest number of deaths in one day was a thousand. The total deaths were from thirteen to twenty thousand, of them two hundred and fifty were Jews, one hundred Armenians, and twenty or more Europeans. The Imperial Bank kept its doors open and suffered greatly. Of a force of one hundred, ten died.

The cholera extended its course toward the center of Persia, reaching Hamadan and Ispahan late in the season. Dr. Wilson ministered to the sick in Hamadan. The total deaths in Persia were well up toward one hundred thousand.

The efforts of the missionaries and others to minister to the stricken ones, were not done to secure the praises of men. The shah, however, made grateful mention to the U. S. minister of the hospital and dispensary work. Mr. Rabino, manager of the Imperial Bank, wrote to Mr. Weeks: " I inclose various reports from the American Presbyterian Mission, for whose courageous and devoted labors, I, an Englishman and a Catholic, can find no words to express my admiration. The hospital was positively the only organization for the help of this terribly visited city."

Mr. Weeks wrote in *Harper's Magazine*, January, 1894: " Whatever arguments may be brought forward, justly or unjustly, against the utility of foreign missions in general, there can be no shadow of doubt as to the beneficent results of their work in Persia. During the epidemic at Tabriz, the medical department of the American Mission, then under the direction of Miss Bradford, did noble work. After hearing so many sensational histories of Kurdish atrocities from Europeans along our route, a new light was thrown on that subject when we met at least two American ladies connected with the mission, who had traveled about among Kurdish villages, regardless of exposure, healing their sick and striving to better the condition of their women. Whatever sect they may belong to, the men and women who have devoted their lives to this cause have shown themselves to be absolutely fearless in the discharge of duty; their record is one of self-sacrifice and pluck, and they represent most worthily the Church militant."

On the other hand, a strange bitterness developed, especially in Teheran. Mr. Ward wrote: "Now, people say that the medicine we gave was intended to kill our enemies. The mollahs and rabbis are doing what they can to detract from the example of Christians, so opposed to their own lack of mercy. Instead of confessing their sins, they say the scourge was sent by God because of adopting European clothes and habits (others said the tobacco monopoly was the cause of the cholera). We thank the Lord for giving us this opportunity of service, though men may not be grateful; and we bless him for his guardian care." There was not a single case of cholera in the village where the missionary ladies of Teheran were in retreat, but there were many in the surrounding villages. The people explained this fact by saying, "In answer to their prayers, God is visiting his wrath upon us." They became enraged and fanatical over the thought. They spat at the ladies, called them "Christian dogs," and even once collected in a crowd and threw stones at them.

It is worthy of note that none of the American missionaries and not one per cent. of the converts in Persia died of the cholera. Trust in God, giving a peaceful mind, lessens the danger of attack and is a real assistance to wise sanitary precautions.

CHAPTER XIV.

BIBLE TRANSLATION AND DISTRIBUTION.

THE history of versions of the Scriptures in the Persian language up to the year 1882 is fully presented in "Persia: Eastern Mission." Up to that time there had been made in Persian, "one version of the Pentateuch, two versions of the entire Old Testament, five versions of the four Gospels and three versions of the whole New Testament." The most memorable of these versions was that of the New Testament by Henry Martyn. It was presented to Fath Ali Shah, in 1831, at Tabriz by the British envoy. In acknowledging it, the shah wrote as follows:

"In the name of God, the all-glorious! It is our exalted will that our dear friend, the Right Honorable Sir Gore Ouseley, etc., should be apprised that we have duly received the book of the gospel, rendered into the Persian tongue by Henry Martyn of blessed memory. We hold worthy of our high appreciation this work, presented to us in the name of the learned, worthy and enlightened society of the Christians, united for the purpose of diffusing the divine books of the teacher Jesus, to whose name as to that of all the prophets, be ascribed honor and blessing! For many years indeed the four Gospels of Matthew, Mark, Luke and John have been known in Persia, but now the whole New Testament is translated, an event which must be of great satisfaction to our exalted soul. By the grace of God, the all merciful, we will commit to those of our servants to whom access is granted near our person, the function of reading the aforesaid writings before us from beginning to end, that we may hear their observation thereupon. Express to the members of the above mentioned enlightened society our deserved thanks.

" Given in Rabi-il-aval in the year of the Hegira, 1229 (A. D. 1831). Fath Ali Shah Kajar."

Henry Martyn's version with Dr. Glenis of the Old Testament have been most largely used. Dr. Robert Bruce, of the Church mission at Ispahan, has given much labor to their revision. The New Testament on which Prof. Palmer was associated with him before his murder in Egypt, was published in 1882, and the whole Bible in 1894, by the British and Foreign Bible Society.

Secondly. *The Turki versions.* After Persian, the language most extensively used in Persia is the Turki, or Tartar, called also the Azerbijan or Transcaucasian Turkish. It is the vernacular of Northwest Persia and is well understood as far as Teheran and Hamadan. The Persian as in the other parts of Persia is the language of literature and government, the Turki is the vernacular. Turkish tribes occupy several provinces of Persia. In the eighth century the Khazars made a permanent settlement. The dynasties of Saman and Ghazni, and the Seljuks were Turks. After the Mongols of Ghengis Khan, the Tartars of Tamurlane, the Uzbeks and other hordes had overrun Northern Persia, few Persians remained in that region. Many of the Turks or Tartars, who settled in Azerbijan, were called *Guzul Bashi*, golden or red-headed from the color of their head-dress. There were seven of these tribes, the Ustajali, Shamli, Nakali, Baharli, Zulkudar, Kajar, and Afshar. The Shamli inhabit the region of Maku and the banks of the Arras; the Afshars, the regions of Takhti-Suleiman and Urumia; the Kajars, the tribe of the royal dynasty, live in Mezanderan. Another tribe lives around Ardebil, and Khalkal. It was organized *de novo* by Shah Abbas of volunteers from various tribes for his own protection, and called Shahsevans or king-lovers.

The Turki is spoken with remarkable uniformity in three or four provinces of Persia and in the Caucasus, by three and a half millions. It is a dialect of that great branch of the Turanian or Scythian family which reaches from the Danube and the Adriatic to the Lena and the Polar seas, a distance of ninety degrees in the parallel, and which besides is found scattered in China, Thibet and India, in Syria, Egypt and Barbary. The Turkish family, occupying so large a space in the vast continent of Asia, and holding an important position in Europe, is very diversified in religious belief.

In Siberia some are orthodox Christians. The Yakuts are Shemanists. In the Chinese Empire some are Buddhists, while from Chinese Turkestan westward they are Mohammedans. The various Turkish dialects are said to be so nearly akin that the Yakut of the icy sea can make himself intelligible to the Turk of this region or to the dweller on the Bosphorus.

The ancient literature of the language is meager. It was cultivated to some extent on the table-lands of Central Asia. Its alphabet was akin to the Syriac, being derived from the Nestorian missionaries, who, centuries ago, penetrated the far East, but it was abandoned for the Arabic character on their conversion to Islam. The Jagatai Turkish has some valuable literature, especially an autobiography of Baber, the conqueror of India, and a fine poem, called Najâyi. The Tekke-Turki is used by the Turkomans of Trans-Caspia. The Osmanli is rich in literature and is a cultivated and copious language. The Azerbaijan Turki is rude and uncultivated and without much literature. A newspaper, called *Kashkol*, was published in it in Tiflis. In it have been written some books of the Ali Allahis, tales of dervishes, poems, and *marseyas* or lamentations. Some religious books, also have been published in this dialect.

The construction of the Turki is easy. The verb is remarkably regular, with only euphonic variations and one conjugation. The participial construction is preferred to the relative clause. The inflections are made by prefixes and suffixes. Nouns, pronouns and verbs are alike treated in this way. For this reason it is called an agglutinated language. The vocabulary is meager and many words are drawn from the Arabic and Persian.

The Turki is the mother tongue to one million five hundred thousand in Persia, and to a large number in Trans-Caucasia. In 1883 Mr. M. A. Morrison, A. M., agent of the British and Foreign Bible Society for Southern Russia, wrote: "Of people called by the government Azerbaijan Tartars there are nine hundred and eighty thousand. These are all south of the Caucasus range and north of the Arras. To the north of these mountains there are one hundred and forty-two thousand Turkish-speaking Tartars. The Tchetchenes speak a dialect of the Turkish; they number one hundred and sixty-four thousand. Almost all the Lesgian races understand and quite one-half speak Turkish or Tartar dialects. They number half a million. We have thus fully a million and a half on this side of the Arras for whom a version is needed." It is the aim to give every people the Bible in the perfectly understood vernacular. In the Osmanli Turkish the entire Bible in Ali Beg's version, and in Dr. Schauffler's, and afterwards the revision of it, has been for many years in the hands of the Mohammedans of Turkey. Besides these are the versions prepared with the Greek and Armenian character for Christians of these races who speak the Turkish language. In Russia the New Testament, and in some dialects portions of the Old Testament are prepared in the Kazan, the Kirghese, the Orenburg, the Karas or Astrakhan. The Gospel of Matthew in the Jagatai or Tekke-Turkoman was prepared by Mr. Bassett in conjunction with a Jew of Meshed. Mr. Hohannes Avedaranian is taking preliminary steps to a translation into the Tartar of Kashgar.

The first attempt made to translate the Scriptures into Trans-Caucasian Turkish was under the superintendence of the Basel missionaries at Shusha. The translator was Mizra Ferukh Amirkhaniantz. He had a remarkable history. Born of Armenian parents in a village on the Arras and named Haritun, he was led captive as a boy in 1810 by a Mohammedan khan of Karadagh, who crossed the Arras and plundered the village. He was made a Mohammedan, named Ferukh, and sent as a present to one of his captor's wives. She having lost a son, adopted Ferukh, and educated him in Persian literature. After eight years he was taken by his master to travel through the kingdom. Still mindful of his race and parentage, when the Russian war of 1828 broke out, he escaped. Afterwards he returned to the religion of his fathers. Coming to the German missionaries to learn Russian, he became evangelical. As their translator he worked in the preparation of tracts and books, assisting Dr. Pfander in the preparation of the Mezan-al-Hak. He translated the New Testament into the Trans-Caucasian * Turkish. In 1836 the Gospel of Matthew was published. The German missionaries having been expelled by Czar Nicholas, the rest of the manuscript seems to have been lost sight of for more than thirty years.

The son of this translator is Rev. Abraham Amirkhaniantz. As a youth he was sent by the missionaries to Basel and educated, and returned as an ordained minister of the Lutheran Church. For a short time he was a missionary in Tabriz and afterwards became translator for the Bible Society at Tiflis, for which work he is admirably qualified. During his travels in the Caucasus, he accidentally came across a manuscript portion of the New Testament in Turkish. He recognized it as the work of his father. This discovery led to an inquiry and search, and the remaining books, except Romans, were found stowed away in the archives of the Bible Society at London. He translated Romans and revised the whole, which was published in 1878. This version has been used in Persia, but differences of idiom rendered it somewhat unsatisfactory to Azerbijan Tartars.

In the meantime the Gospel of Matthew (1872), of John (1876), and of Luke (1884), were translated by Rev. Dr. Labaree and others, and in 1885 the four Gospels were published by the American Bible Society. Dr. Labaree undertook their publication in Constantinople,

* Smith and Dwight's Researches, vol. 1., p. 306.

but met with unexpected difficulty in obtaining permission to print. At every point of the negotiations he met with delays and vexations. Willing to submit to anything rather than be refused, all the minutiæ and troublesome regulations were fulfilled, and even a promise was given that none of the books should be sold in the Turkish empire. But it was all in vain, for after many of the steps were successfully passed, the absolute refusal of one of the officials to affix his seal abruptly ended the negotiations. Finally arrangements were made to have an edition of five thousand printed at Leipsic. The Psalms had also been translated. At this point a conference was held in Tiflis, and grammatical and orthographical differences were compromised and a standard adopted. It was decided that Rev. A. Amirkhaniantz's manuscript should be revised by Rev. Mr. Wright and several Turki scholars of Azerbaijan, and by Dr. Sauerwein, of Germany, and published by the British and Foreign Bible Society. This was done, and, in 1892, the Old Testament and, in 1893, the New Testament were printed in Leipsic.

Thirdly. *Armenian versions.* When modern life began to move the Armenians, the spoken language had many dialectic variations. These have finally been reduced to two, one called the Constantinople, the other the Ararat dialect. Three millions in the Turkish empire use the former, and one million in Russia and Persia the latter. It is not more than thirty years since the Ararat gained acceptance as a literary language. Now it has a rapidly increasing literature, original and translated, issuing from the press in Tiflis, Moscow, Etchmiadzin and other places, and a number of newspapers are printed in this tongue. The written language has almost acquired definite form, but every valley has some peculiarities of dialect. This is increased by the habit of the people using the vocabulary of the dominant race, Persian, Turki, Russian, or Georgian. The differences in the two Armenian dialects consist of different meanings attached to the same word, variety of terminations for declensions and conjugations, and different sounds given to letters of the alphabet, especially to mutes. There are thirty-eight letters, three each for the sounds expressed in English by *b* and *p*, *d* and *t*, *g* and *k*, *ds* and *ts*, and two out of each group of three are pronounced differently in the two dialects. But the resemblances are manifold. Educated men can easily understand each other's speech and literature. Efforts which are being made to agree on one standard have so far been futile.

The first translation of the Scriptures into the Ararat Armenian was made by Mr. Dittrich of the German Mission at Shusha. The Russian censor refused his permission to print unless the synod of Etchmiadzin approved. After much trouble and a visit of Mr. Zaremba to Etchmiadzin (1833) the Gospel of Matthew received the imprimatur of the synod, but for the other Gospels it was refused. This translation was printed in parallel columns with the ancient version of Mesrob in Constantinople (1855). A revision (1879) of this by Rev. A. Amirkhaniantz has passed through several editions. The entire Bible, completed by him, was published in 1883 by the British and Foreign Bible Society.

This able leader of the evangelical Armenians of the Caucasus fell under the condemnation of the government. He had been offered a professorship at Etchmiadzin Seminary, but refused unless he could be permitted to teach evangelical doctrines. But the cause of his trouble was from the Russian Church. An orthodox priest in Tiflis challenged the adherents of other churches to a public religious discussion. One of the implied privileges was freedom of speech. Mr. Amirkhaniantz took part and stated plainly the objections of Protestants to images and saint-worship and other errors. At this the authorities took umbrage. Later he was accused of converting some of the orthodox fold.

One morning he was awakened by a violent knock at the door. The police summoned him before the prefect. He was informed that orders had come from St. Petersburg for his arrest and imprisonment. After about ten days an order came from headquarters that he with two other evangelical preachers should leave in three days for Orenburg, to remain in exile four years. The morning of his departure the street of the German colony in which he lived, was filled with a crowd of spectators, saying farewell and expressing their regret and sympathy. His wife and seven children went forth across the snowy Caucasus toward Ekaterineburg on the Siberian frontier. Since his exile expired he has been elected professor of Oriental languages in the University of Helsingford.

It is very desirable that the Armenian Gregorian Church should itself sanction a modern version of the Scriptures. Constant objections are made to the versions printed by Protestants as partial, inaccurate, and changed. While devoid of fact, these objections have great influence with the people, and many from sheer prejudice refuse the blessing because of the hand that brings it. Efforts have been made to procure the sanction of the Catholics and Armenian synod to a modern version. Mr. Morrison has several times visited Etchmiadzin for this purpose. He is understood to have proposed that the synod should prepare the version and the Bible Society would bear the expense of publication and aid in its distribution. The prospect of success in this effort is favorable.

In the *Meshag*, a secular Armenian newspaper of Tiflis, January 13, 1894, reference is made to this subject. It says: "The importance of such a translation is evident, and the *Meshag* has often spoken concerning it. The Protestants say that the ecclesiastics of the Armenian Gregorian Church purposely prevent a version in the modern tongue because it will open the eyes of the people. It is true individual clergy have done so, but not all. Bishop Sallantian sanctioned the editions of 1833 and 1856. But it has not had the highest sanction. The deceased catholicos George IV. committed to a celebrated author to translate the Gospels. In the *Monthly Ararat*,* No. 3, 1879, it is said: 'Two years ago the eminent catholicos, wishing the holy gospels to become known to the entire people by translation into the modern tongue, committed to an exegete to translate them into true and easily understood language. It is now finished, and he himself, notwithstanding his care and business, will pass every line under his own eye with every attention. Making known with joy the good provision of the *Holy Father* we also make known that it will be printed after a little while, and the Armenian people will receive the gospel of Jesus from the press of the Throne of Mother Ararat, at simple cost, an authentic translation into the vulgar tongue, which will be a glorious monument of the zeal for national enlightenment of our magnificent catholicos.' As this design was not fulfilled, we have no doubt the present catholicos is determined to accomplish it. Let it be done quickly."

Fourthly. *The Syriac Versions.* As early as 1829 the four Gospels in ancient Syriac were printed by the British and Foreign Society. But the first version of the New Testament in modern Syriac was translated from the Peshito by Dr. Perkins and published at Urumia in 1846. It was in parallel columns with the Peshito. The Old Testament from the Hebrew was published

---

* Organ of the holy synod and catholicos.

in 1852 and a second edition in 1858. It was the size of a large pulpit Bible, weighing six pounds. A pocket edition of the New Testament and Psalms was printed in New York in 1863. This translation was in the language of Urumia. In 1886 Dr. Benjamin Labaree, in company with Profs. Yoshana and Baba, able Syriac scholars, began a revision, having in view the needs of the mountain and Mosul Nestorians, using a universal and purer diction. This version of the whole Bible was published in New York in 1893, the type-setters having come from Persia to do the work. It is a beautiful edition in small compass, with maps and references, and a noble monument of the efforts of those engaged upon it. The joy of the people on receiving it beamed upon their countenances, as in finding a treasure of great price.

An edition of the four Gospels in the Elkosh dialect of the Syriac has also been published.

Fifthly. *Kurdish versions.* The only population of any extent which has not yet received the Scriptures in their tongue is the Kurdish race. Some attempts have been made at making a translation for the Armenians in Turkey who speak Kurdish, and a portion has been published in the Armenian character. Steps are being taken toward a translation but a great difficulty arises in the different dialects of the tribes.

Sixthly. The Scriptures in *Hebrew* are sold in considerable numbers, during some years even more than those in Persian. Altogether the Bible in ten languages is in demand in Persia

In the distribution of the Bible the American and the British and Foreign Bible societies are both at work. The former has an agent, Rev. W. L. Whipple, residing at Tabriz, the latter was represented by Rev. Robert Bruce D. D., and now has its work in charge of the Church Mission at Ispahan.

After visits by the Rev. E. M. Bliss, assistant agent at Constantinople, to Persia in 1878-79 the American Bible Society decided to establish an agency. Mr. Whipple was given as an object the putting " of a Bible in every town and village and establishing of depots at central points." The latter object has been fulfilled, first by locating central depots at Tabriz, Urumia, Teheran and Hamadan, with booksellers in the bazaar and subsidiary depots at Resht, Meshed, Kum, Yezd, Kasan, Zenjan, Maragha, Soujbulak, Dilman and Khoi. In the superintendence of these depots the agent has made many long and difficult journeys.

General distribution is accomplished by colporteurs itinerating either on foot or more generally on horseback. It is safe to say that there are few regions in the northern provinces of Persia which have not been visited by them. The same is true of the southern provinces on behalf of the British Society.

The work is one of special difficulty in Persia. One cause is the ignorance of the people. In many villages of Azerbijan only two or three men can read. Another reason is their poverty, which makes them hesitate about buying, even much below cost. A New Testament which printed in a foreign language costs a dollar, is sold for ten cents, but this latter sum is a day's wages for a laborer. They at times offer to exchange hay or chickens for it.

Another difficulty has been to get trusty colporteurs. Some have been faithful, others have belied their profession. Some have inflated their accounts, or remained at ease, and reported difficult and dangerous journeys, or acted as quacks and peddlers instead of attending to their business. One at least cast the Bibles into wells and sold them to be ground into pulp for the manufacture of *papier maché*, and covers to bookbinders. Purchasers have destroyed other volumes or used the paper to cover windows. The agent estimates that perhaps five thousand copies have been destroyed.

But even stray leaves sometimes do good. A man became so interested by reading a portion on his window, which constantly fell under his eyes, that he purchased a Bible at the next opportunity. A lady presented the shah's retinue in England with elegantly bound Persian Bibles. Many were destroyed, the covers being used for albums. Others were sold to an Armenian for a nominal sum. Once a colporteur to the dishonor of his book but true to his Persian surroundings, gave a mollah in a village a Bible and some money for his recommendation. With the latter he sold many books and immediately left the place before they could be returned to him. But not all are false to their profession. Some are true and endure hardness, as good soldiers of Jesus Christ.

Of some of these Mr. Labaree writes as follows: "Some years ago, in my circuit among the villages of Urumiah, I became deeply interested in a class of young men uniting with the church in Ada about the same time. Out of this class there have gone forth three colporteurs, who have made an interesting record for themselves and greatly advanced the cause of Christ in Persia.

THE YOUNG HERDSMAN.

"One of these was a very poor boy, who gained his livelihood by tending the village herd. The missionary riding over the grazing lands of that village was pretty sure to have a visit with Shimun. He had learned to read in the mission village-school, and his New Testament was his constant companion as he tended his cattle. He usually had a question to ask upon some verse or passage. His memory was a remarkable one. It was almost impossible to mention a verse or sentence of which he could not tell the chapter and verse. *He was a living concordance.* He ultimately was graduated from herding cattle, took a short course of study, and entered the colporteur service. I believe he is in it still. In this capacity he has traveled much, and has been the agent of circulating very many copies of God's word among all classes.

His wonderful knowledge of the Scriptures has been a recommendation for him among aliens and enemies, greatly increasing his opportunities for good.

"Of the second man, Deacon Tomma, I will only say that he remains a tried and successful agent of the American Bible Society, by whom he has been employed now for several years.

THE APOSTOLIC COLPORTEUR.

"The third man has been for a long time in the service of Dr. Bruce, of Ispahan, as one of the British and Foreign Bible Society's colporteurs. He has probably sold in Persia more copies of the Christian Scriptures, in whole or in part, than any man living. Rather short in stature, thick set and well built, his head large and firmly placed upon his shoulders, his face full of resolution and his eye twinkling with good nature, you read at once the lion-hearted, enterprising, genial colporteur which his remarkable record proves him to be. Dr. Bruce seldom omits to express his profound obligation to the American missionaries for this noble Christian colleague. The annual reports of the British Bible Society contain large extracts from his most interesting journals. His travels take him long distances into the interior, away from all ordinary protection; now a month to the east and now a month to the west; to Bagdad, to Bushire on the Persian Gulf, and even into the kingdom of Muscat, among wild and fanatical populations. But he knows no fear. He has suffered great indignities at the hands of mollahs and fanatics; has been bastinadoed; his life has been in danger; but he finds his way back to these places of greatest peril another time.

"The report of the British and Foreign Bible Society for 1885, after narrating how, in a certain town, for the crime of selling the Scriptures, he was seized, and bastinadoed till his feet bled, goes on to say: 'It is not possible, without a sympathetic glow of feeling, to read Benjamin's entry in his diary: "When I think of those who will come after me, and be able to sell the holy word freely (for I hope there will soon be religious liberty in this country), I feel very glad and comfortable in thus suffering for Christ's sake. The same day," the courageous fellow adds, "I was able to sell eight copies in that bigoted town."'

"Another extract from his diary is as follows: 'October 8th. In —— the Mohammedans were very glad to see the Bible in their own tongue, for this was the first time they had seen it. . . . Our work being new in this place, the people were afraid to buy books openly; however, we sold twenty-eight copies that day. Thanks be unto God for his help and grace. We have made twenty-two marches from Ispahan to this place, and have had only six working days. In them we sold one hundred and eighty copies. Let us lift up our hearts to our heavenly Father and pray him to bless his word, which is being disseminated in this land, and make it bear fruit to the honor and glory of our Saviour.'

"Again he writes: 'November 27th. On our journey to this place we visited Neyriz. The people are more enlightened than in the purely Mohammedan towns through which we passed on the road, as many of them are babis. And many of them disputed with us about the sale of New Testaments. Perhaps you will be surprised at my saying they are enlightened, and then saying they disputed with us; but they did not dispute like the people in other places, but only for not selling more Testaments to them. Having sold twenty-five copies, we told them we must keep some for other towns. They said, "Do you think other people will have more desire to buy these books than we have?"'"

Another obstacle is the opposition of the mollahs. Sometimes they will say "The book is good," and commend it to the people. Often they condemn it, and even command the people to return the books already purchased. They say, "The gospel was brought down from heaven by Christ, and was taken up to heaven again. There is now no gospel on the earth." or "This book is not introduced by a 'Thus saith the Lord.' It is a mere bundle of traditions written down by the disciples." Others say, "It is not a genuine gospel. The Christians have changed it. The true gospel testified of the coming of Mohammed. He was the Paraclete." Others say, "The gospel has been abrogated, it is no longer of any use to you." Others object to its influence, "You would better not buy it;

your children will read it and turn from the faith."
A colporteur says, "We came one evening to a sheikh's
village in Kurdistan, and were received as his guests.
He was very much interested in our books and said,
'Yes, I must have a Bible in my house, I want my
children to read it.' As we were talking, a mollah
came in, and finding out what the book was, said, 'A
person who will receive that book deserves to have his
house burned.' The sheikh said, 'But this is the
word of God, the books of Moses and Jesus, whom we
acknowledge to be prophets.' The mollah would not
consent to the sheikh's buying one. Afterwards he
did, however." *

Mussulmans sometimes buy Scriptures to search for
prophecies about Mohammed. One of these, Jews are
said to point out to them in the verse, " I will multiply
thee exceedingly," the latter word standing for " Mohammed" because the letters of the word *exceedingly*,
they assert, count in Hebrew the same as the name
Mohammed. Not long ago a Mussulman got hold of a
Gospel of John, and read the words, " The prince of
this world cometh," and began to show it as a prophecy
of Mohammed. The preacher soon made him anxious
to deny the truth of his own interpretation.

At times they will wish to put the faith to a test.
Even the trial by fire has been proposed. One said,
" Let us pass through the fire ; whoever is unharmed,
his faith is true." The colporteur said, " All right,

* Dr. Bradford in *The Interior*.

come on." They went to the blacksmith's shop. "Now," said the colporteur, "you make the first test." At the last moment the Persian backed out. At another time the deacon was challenged by a dervish to the same test. He agreed and they built up a fire. Then the deacon walked around the fire repeating three times the Lord's Prayer in Syriac. Then the dervish, frightened by the unknown tongue, declined, saying that the deacon was using magic.

The opposition to colporteurs does not always confine itself to words. One entered the bazaar at Zenjan, carrying Bibles on his arm. A Persian merchant addressed him, "What have you there?" He said, "The word of God, the Toret and Injil." The man exclaimed in rage, "The mollah told us that whoever sold these books to subvert our faith should be killed. Beat him! beat him!" The crowd fell upon him, and beat him till the blood poured from his nose. Then the Persian said, "I will pour oil over you and burn you. Your book says, God has a Son; you are blasphemers." The colporteur answered, "When we say it, it is blasphemy. What is it, when you say it? Do you not say of Husain, 'By the blood of God and the blood of the Son of God?' What do you mean?" The man was perplexed and took him before a mollah, requesting an explanation of the phrase. The mollah to avoid entangling himself said, "It is written not to abuse the followers of the Book," meaning Jews and Christians. Finally the merchant repented of his conduct, bought the Bibles, paying for them in *henna* (red dye). The colporteur sold the henna and departed.

The following conversation was reported between a colporteur and a mujtehid before whom he was taken. The latter inquired, " What are you doing with these books ? " He answered, " They are the word of God; I am selling them." " Yes, but they are Christian books; why do you have Christian books ? " The colporteur asked, " Do we to-day obey Fath Ali Shah or Nasr-i-Din Shah ? " He answered, " Nasr-i-Din of course. He is the living king ; Fath Ali is dead." " Very well; is Jesus living or dead ? " " Living, certainly." " Is Mohammed living or dead ? " " Dead." " Then why should we not listen to the words of Jesus ? "

Persian officials, as a rule, befriend and protect the colporteurs. In Hashtarud a colporteur had sold many Bibles, when four or five men, instigated by a mollah, fell upon him as he was leaving the village and robbed him. He complained to the governor. His property was restored to him and the mollah fined five tomans. A colporteur at Khoi was attacked by a sayid and beaten and his books taken from him. He appealed to the governor, who had the books returned and told those present that in the king's bazaars anything might be sold. One governor kept the Bible beside him and decided cases between Christians by its teachings. A prominent governor bought the Persian and Arabic Scriptures in his judgment hall, and said to those around him, " Buy these books; by reading them you will find out their value." In another city a prince had been reading the Bible and called the preacher to his house to explain the long list of verses he had marked. On one occasion he said he dreamed that he, his friends and the preacher were seated on blocks of ice in the sea. To the preacher's block were attached great pearls, and in his efforts to reach them he awoke. The preacher explained that the truths of the kingdom were the goodly pearls. The prince told him to pursue his work, and that he would stand by him.

Mr. Whipple reports that: "Two of our colporteurs had started out for a three months' tour. The morning after they left, very early, before daybreak, they were attacked by five or six robbers and led off to the mountains, not far distant. The robbers held a council of war, to decide what they should do with them. Part were in favor of shooting them, but the others said no, that would not do; for the gun had a voice that would betray them. They said it were better to cut their throats. They, however, finally listened to the men's earnest pleadings to spare their lives: they would give all they had, and why should their blood be upon their necks? After beating them severely, and taking all their money and some of their books, the robbers left them blindfolded and bound. The poor men made their way back to the city and related to us their sad experience, thankful enough to escape with their lives. They were sick for two weeks, on account of the cruel beating and excessive fright.

"The case was reported to the amir-i-Nizam, the governor-general of Azerbaijan. Dr. Holmes was at the time treating him. We think on account of his friendship to the missionaries, and gratitude to Dr. Holmes in particular, he took up the case *con amore*. He called our men and questioned them particularly, and, obtaining all the information he wished, he sent his *ferashes* (constables) in search of the robbers. It was not long before they were apprehended and punished, and the loss sustained by the colporteurs was paid back. The robbers also had to pay for the Scriptures which they stole."

Among the few instances of official opposition was one under a former amir-i-Nizam (1882). A Persian colporteur was brought before him. He ordered him to be beaten. By paying a fine he escaped. The amir told him that he was doing the devil's work by selling the Gospels, as they would turn the people away from Islam. He threatened him with punishment if he continued. When colporteurs many years ago went to the city of Maragha and began to exhibit so many books, people were astonished. Where could they have got so many Bibles? Finally the suspicion arose that they must be robbers of churches, and they were arrested on this charge. At first no customs duty was charged; afterwards five per cent. was taken in kind. In 1886 the chief of customs at Tabriz laid down a rule that Scriptures in the languages used by Mussulmans would be detained; those in other languages would receive the seal of authorization from the censor on the payment of a shahi each. He gave as his reason, that the Scriptures were doing damage to Islam, and therefore their circulation would not be allowed. The affair was placed in the hands of the British consul, Mr. Abbott, who was the more willing to act as the editions in question were those of the British and Foreign Bible Society. After several months' delay, through the kind offices of Mr. Nicolson, of the British legation, the order was annulled and the chief of customs ordered to seal and deliver the Bibles free of charge.

In the spring of 1887 a Bible shop was opened in the bazaar in charge of a Mussulman. This was in addition to the Bible depot in the amir caravanserai. It caused much talk among the people. The Armenian bishop, too, procured a copy of the Mezan-al-Hak and sent it to the mujtehid, saying that we were distributing it. The mollahs began to say, "These men are filling the bazaars with the Injil, and wherever we go we find one." The mujtehid gave a *fatra* or decree prohibiting the sale. Itinerating colporteurs were arrested. The governor prohibited not only the shop in the bazaar, but the traveling of colporteurs in Azerbaijan. The order remained in force for a year. These events were exceptional. On the whole we have reason to be thankful to the Persian government, our experiences with the Turkish government having been more trying. In 1883, the colporteur at Khoi was invited by an Armenian priest near Bayazid to come to his village, as his people were in need of Armenian Scriptures. Without consultation, he accepted the invitation. When he arrived on Turkish soil, he was arrested and thrown into prison, where he suffered from hunger. Through the kindness of the Turkish consul in Tabriz, giving a letter to the governor of Bayazid, he was released, but his two hundred and thirty-six volumes of the Scriptures were detained. A colporteur in the Kurdish mountains was thrown into a filthy prison and almost starved and frozen before he was released. Even the agent himself, *en route* for Mosul was detained on the frontier and his Bagster's Bible and sermons retained as dangerous documents.

There have been but few controversial works written in Persia against the Bible. I know of but two in West Persia. One was prepared by an official and never published. The character of it may be inferred from an objection made in it to the Gospels that they narrate the death of King Herod and afterwards speak of him as alive. The author did not know that there was a family of Herods. Another book was written by a Mirza Husain, who taught Persian in our school for a while and in pique on account of his dismissal wrote a book attempting to show contradictions and discrepancies in the Gospels. Several officials acted as his patrons, enabling him to publish his book. But it had no sale, and the author came to want and died in a condition of extreme destitution. His wife afterwards came and wished me to buy up the edition.

The Nestorians and Armenians have retained through all the past ages a superstitious reverence for the Bible, with an almost total neglect of it. They are submissive to it as authoritative, and while sometimes objecting to our translations, they rarely actively oppose their distribution. Their reverence manifests itself in superstition. In Maragha there is an Armenian New Testament a few centuries old. It is carefully kept wrapped up in forty napkins. Every Saturday evening it is placed on a stand and a candle is burned before it as an honor. An ancient Gospel in Urumia was carried off by the Kurds. It was believed by some that it came back of itself through the air. It stopped at night in a village, directed a man to take care of it and dismiss it on its way in the morning. Kissing the covers of the Bible and pressing it to the forehead are considered pious marks of respect. This is often done at church. A Nestorian mukadasi, in the olden time, came to Dr. Perkins' room. Seeing a row of large books, he devoutly bent and kissed them, little supposing that his reverence was directed toward the Edinburgh Encyclopedia.

The people are inclined to take the Scriptures literally. Mr. Hogberg, Swedish missionary, read to a Jew the passage, "Give to him that asketh of thee."

The Jew, said, "Well, if that is true, give me your watch." Mr. Hogberg handed the watch to him. After a while he said to the Jew, "Give me that ring on your finger." The Jew gave it. Several days passed. The watch was worth much more than the ring, but the Jew, thinking he must have the worst of the bargain, because Mr. Hogberg said nothing, came and desired to exchange back. A Gregorian came up to an Evangelical who was reading the Scriptures and pointing to the words, "Whosoever shall smite thee on thy right cheek, turn to him the other also," smote him on one cheek. The brother immediately turned the other and was smitten the second time. He then said to the Gregorian, "You must read further." He read, "With what measure ye mete, it shall be measured to you again." He then returned the blows full measure.

The results of Bible distribution are already apparent. Correct views of Christianity are being received, and prejudices removed. Mohammedans are obtaining new views of the origin of the Koran. Some of the sects, as the Sheikhis, seem to have had their doctrines partially molded by the Bible. The Babis read it much, primarily to find prophecies and correspondences with their own dispensation, but attaining a familiarity with its contents which is hopeful. It spreads the light and truth. Nearly every case of genuine conversion has been in part due to the reading of the Bible.

CHAPTER XV.

THE MISSIONS OF OTHER CHURCHES.

THE first Protestant missionaries to Persia were the Moravians, Dr. Hokker, a physician, and Dr. Rueffer, a surgeon, who attempted to reach the Guebres in Kerman (1747) in the reign of Nadir Shah. They endured great hardship, were robbed, and found it impossible to go beyond Ispahan. Henry Martyn in 1810–1812 had his famous discussions with the mollahs of Shiraz and Ispahan, and came to Tabriz to present the Persian translation of the New Testament to the shah. The eccentric Wolff in his journeys to the Jews of the East passed several times through Persia, in 1823–1833. In Tabriz he wished to establish a school. Abbas Mirza approved of it and gave him a house. It was under the patronage of Henry Drummond. Nothing definite was accomplished. Mr. Groves and companion, of Bagdad, made tours into Persia in 1829. Dr. Pfander, of the Basel Mission Society, the translator of the Mezan-al-Hak, who was then residing at Shusha, journeyed through Persia in 1829 and 1833, and in the latter year Messrs. Haas and Hoernle, of the same mission, settled in Tabriz. Afterwards Mr. Schneider joined them. They planned a school which Abbas Mirza patronized and of which **Mohammed Shah** declared his warmest approbation. One of their pupils was afterwards governor of Tabriz. They intended to give higher education to the Persians, trusting to its influence to enlighten. Martyn's Persian New Testament was used as a text-book. They translated some works on science. A geography was prepared and presented to the king. French and English were taught. The Basel Society withdrew its missionaries, 1837, on the ground that the field was not sufficiently open for evangelistic work. Rev. H. Southgate * was besought by the young men to come and take up the work abandoned.

The Rev. Wm. Glenn, of the United Associate Synod of Scotland, who had spent seventeen years as a missionary at Astrakhan, came to Tabriz in 1838. He was engaged in the translation of the Old Testament into Persian, and in teaching a small school of Moslem young men. Afterwards he engaged in Bible distribution at Teheran. For many years the Americans were the only Protestant missionaries in Persia. In 1874 Rev. Messrs. Malcom and Amirkhaniantz, Armenians educated at Basel, were sent to Tabriz, but because the field was already occupied by our Board the Basel society withdrew them. A Nestorian convert, educated at Hermannsburg, established a Lutheran mission in a village of Urumia where his uncle, an evangelical and godly pastor of our mission, was laboring. He has gathered a considerable congregation, in

* Vol. II., pp. 8–9.

part composed of his uncle's flock. From 1889 to 1894 the Swedish Missionary Association had Mr. Hogberg and Mr. Larsen located at Tabriz. Finally on the ground of missionary comity they withdrew, and their mission was transferred to Kashgar. In 1894 German missionaries settled in Urumia to evangelize the Jews.

The Church of England has two missions in Persia. One represents the Church Missionary Society. It was established at Ispahan in 1869. Rev. Dr. Bruce, previously a missionary in India, first came to revise Martyn's version of the New Testament. The famine of 1870–71 engaged him in relief work. He distributed sixteen thousand pounds sterling. During this delay, his school and mission took root. In Ispahan there is a well organized and successful work, with schools, orphanage, dispensary, weaving establishment, etc. In 1893 the boys' school, had two hundred and fifty and the girls' school two hundred and ninety pupils, and the congregation numbered three hundred, of whom one-third were communicants. Much emphasis is put upon the distribution of the Scriptures. A station has also been opened at Bagdad. On Dr. Bruce's retirement, Rev. Mr. Tinsdale was transferred from India, and later Bishop Stewart has been sent to take charge of the work. The mission is evangelical and aggressive, and works in a spirit of love and comity with other Protestant missions.

The other English mission is the "Archbishop of Canterbury's Personal Mission to the Eastern Syrian Christians," "for the purpose of protecting the Old Nestorian Church from the Roman Catholics on the one side, and the American Presbyterians on the other." It is ritualistic of the extreme type. The missionaries, finely educated, are sent out for five years under vows of celibacy. They dress like monks. The "sisters" belong to an order, wear its garb, and submit to its discipline. These missionaries are not ascetic, with the possible exception of Mr. Browne, who resides at Kochanes. They have a large force of missionaries in Urumia, and have established many schools. Their attitude toward Catholic missions and our own is one of strong hostility. They look upon our work as destructive and perilous to souls. Their attitude at first can be seen in a remark of Mr. Riley, "We do not believe you are Christians, but we believe you will not lie." Mr. Wahl remarked somewhat similarly, "My wife was a Canadian Presbyterian, but after I married her she became a Christian," that is, an Episcopalian.

I need not enter into the details of their work nor tell of their contests with Catholics and Protestants: the latter name they reject. Their coming, while making our work more difficult and retarding self-support in the schools, seems to have had a good effect in toning up the Evangelical Church to stand more firmly on gospel principles and protest with more intelligence against rites and doctrines received as traditions of men. Of the Anglican mission, Mrs. Bishop, who is "devotedly attached to the Church of England," writes, "I have been reading Dr. Perkins' book with absorbing interest and understand better than before how your (American) mission long and earnestly labored to reform the old Church within itself and failed." She finds the Anglican mission "is on more ritualistic lines" than she knew, and says, "I have had many conversations with the Archbishop of Canterbury on this subject. My view is that his mission must utterly fail, because it condones superstition, exalts ceremonial, and having deserted the simplicity that is in Christ, cannot lead the people back to it."

The missions of the Roman Catholics in these lands date from the middle ages. Dominicans visited the commander of the Mongols in Persia in 1245. At their head was a monk, Ascelin. They bore a letter from the pope which was translated into Persian, and then into Turki, and presented to the commander. They gave offense by refusing to bow thrice before the commander, according to court etiquette, and by their assertion of the superiority of the pope to the great khan. The monks were detained several months, and then dismissed with a haughty letter to the pope, in which he was warned to take care if he wished to retain his own country.*

* See Neander's Church History.

About the same time, some Franciscans visited the great khan, and in 1253, Louis IX. sent William de Rubruquis on a mission. He passed through Persia, visiting the Mongol general, and had many religious discussions in the court of Mangu Khan. Again in 1291, the Franciscan, John de Monte Corvino, first appeared in Tabriz and then passed through to India and China. In the massacres of Tamurlane nearly one hundred Catholic monks were slain.

Intercourse of the Armenians with the Church of Rome was introduced by a personal visit of the first catholicos of Cilicia to Rome, in 1075. A formal union was declared between the two churches in 1197. Leo, who promoted this union in order to be crowned, afterwards expelled all the Catholics and their clergy from his dominions. In 1320, an extensive mission of the Dominicans was established among the Armenians with its seat at Nakhejevan, then a part of Persia. It met with success. Thirty Armenian villages embraced Catholicism, and an archbishop of Nakhejevan was consecrated. In the days of Chardin, 1673, the work was falling away. Twenty villages had returned to the Gregorian Church or emigrated, owing to the oppression of the Persian governors, due to the fact that a special embassy from the pope to the shah tried to withdraw the converts from Persian jurisdiction. In 1830, Dr. Eli Smith, who records these facts, found only empty churches.

In the sixteenth and seventeenth centuries Catholic

missions were established in many parts of these lands. The Capuchins occupied Kutais, Tiflis and Tabriz (1672) the Jesuits, Erivan, Shamokhi, Tiflis and Gori. To the two latter they came as physicians and the governor gave them a house. In 1830 they had a parish of six hundred at Tiflis, two hundred at Gori and a considerable number at Kutais. The last Russian census reports twenty-one thousand Armenian Catholics in Trans-Caucasia. The Latin priests have held possession of the convents at Tiflis, and the Armenian Catholics have lately made successful suit to obtain possession of them. In Ispahan (1598–1645) missions were established by Augustinians as representatives of Spain and Portugal, by Carmelites from the pope, by Capuchins from Louis XIV., by Jesuits, with letters from the king of France and the pope. An Armenian bishop and many of his flock were converted in 1688. They had three churches, the ruins of which are yet to be seen. In Tavernier's time there were six hundred Catholics in Julfa (Ispahan). The work was abandoned, and fifty-five years ago was again revived. Dr. Wills reports at present one Lazarist father poorly supported with a flock of two hundred staunch adherents. Now, besides this there are Catholic missions among the Armenians in Teheran, Tabriz, Salmas and Urumia.

The relations of the Church of Rome to the Nestorian Church became intimate in the sixteenth century. The Patriarchate of Seleucia, which had been moved to

Bagdad under the Arabs, finally was settled at Mosul or Elkosh. Several patriarchs of that century, whose title was Mar Elias, received consecration from the pope. In 1575, Shimun, bishop of the Nestorians of Jelu, Sart, and Salmas withdrew from the jurisdiction of Mar Elias and was elected patriarch of Kurdistan. After 1616, Urumia was added to his diocese. He resided sometimes at Diz, but the episcopal residence now is at Kochanes. In 1616, Mar Elias assembled a synod where he and five archbishops and one bishop endorsed the Catholic confession and declared in favor of union with Rome. His successors seem to have escaped from papal dependence, but in 1681 the metropolitan of Diarbekr quarreled with his patriarch, and was consecrated patriarch of the Chaldeans under the name of Mar Yosef. In 1775, Mar Yohanna, the successor of Mar Elias, was persuaded to submit to Rome, under threats of the Catholics who had seized his firman of succession. After a series of quarrels between these two Catholic patriarchs, Mar Yohanna was confirmed by the pope as sole patriarch of the Chaldeans. His successor in 1830 attempted to break the yoke of Rome, but was unsuccessful, and after suffering imprisonment, he recanted the Nestorian faith and renounced the patriarchate. During these years there were Dominican and Jesuit missionaries at Mosul.

These successive splits carried a number of the Nestorians of Persia into the Catholic fold. When our mission was established the village of Khosrova, and seventy-four families in other villages of Salmas and about two hundred families in Urumia were Catholics. This early start of the latter should be considered in making comparisons. Our mission has made much more rapid progress since its start in 1835. At that time there were Chaldean (Catholic) bishops at Salmas and at Urumia. The latter was making efforts to convert Mar Shimun. He was said to have offered him two thousand pounds sterling if he would turn Catholic. In 1833 Mr. Haas in Tabriz heard that he was about to accept the overtures and wrote him a letter of expostulation. Subsequently, Mar Shimun was promised the supremacy of all the Christians in the East if he would submit to the pope. At another time a Jesuit missionary laid claim to certain churches in Urumia and placed pictures and images in them. In the disputes that arose, the Nestorian bishops resorted to blows, and ejected the Jesuit and his pictures by physical force. Dr. Perkins (pp. 301-2) tells of an amusing discussion between the Chaldean and Nestorian bishops which they agreed to refer to a mollah for decision. Both argued their case before the representative of Islam. In 1841 the French Lazarist mission was regularly established by M. Theophane. Shortly before this, under an order from Prince Gahraman Mirza, M. Ozhene, a Lazarist, opened a school for Mohammedans in Tabriz. The Armenian catholicos at Etchmiadzin made an unsuccessful effort through the Russian government to have all the Catholic missionaries expelled by the shah. For many years it has been the custom to consecrate one of the French missionaries as bishop of Persia, with his cathedral at Urumia, and with the title of ambassador from the pope to the shah.

CHAPTER XVI.

INTEMPERANCE IN PERSIA.

PERSIAN history relates that wine was discovered in the reign of Jamshid. He attempted to preserve grapes in a large vessel. Fermentation ensued. The king believed that the juice was poisonous, and bottled it and labeled it as such. A lady of the palace, wishing to commit suicide, drank from it. She was pleased with the stupor that followed and repeated the experiment until the supply was exhausted. She imparted the secret to the king, and a quantity was again made that sufficed for all. Hence wine is called in Persia the *zahr-i-khosh* or "delightful poison".—(Malcom, Vol. I., p. 10.)

A story goes that Cyrus was on a visit to Astyages. Cyrus playing cupbearer, wished to give out the wine.

He filled the cup and gave it to the king. "Why do you not first taste it?" said Astyages. "Is not that the duty of a cupbearer?

"God forbid," said Cyrus. "It seems to me there is poison in it. Was it not when you had drunk yesterday that you did not know what you were doing? You had forgotten that you were king; the others had forgotten that they were inferiors."

"Does your father not get drunk?" asked Astyages.

"Never."

"Well, what does he do?"

"He satisfies his thirst with water only."

Wine was a common beverage of the Medes and Persians. Cyrus set a trap for the Massægetæ by deserting his camp and retiring into ambush, taking care to leave a plentiful supply of wine. The intoxicated enemies were easily vanquished. The cup was freely used in the palace of Xerxes. Esther 1 : 4–10; 7 : 2–7. The vineyards of Lebanon and distant provinces were laid under contribution by the Persian monarchs.

Drunkenness was checked by the Mohammedan conquest. The Koran declared that in wine " is great sin" and that it is an "abomination of Satan's work."

Southgate cites several stories of the origin of Mohammed's prohibition of wine

One is that the prophet's life was endangered at a feast given him by the Jews, where the company became intoxicated. Another account is, that at a nuptial feast, the guests were in a merry mood because of the wine. Mohammed saw them, inquired the cause, and blessed the cause of such cheerfulness, but returning later, he found fightings and confusion. Therefore he changed his blessing into a curse and made wine *haram* or forbidden. Others say the prohibition was given because Mohammed once saw a disciple unable to say his prayers because of liquor. He promised the faithful the reward of an abundance of unintoxicating wine in paradise.

According to tradition, one of the precepts of Mohammed was, "Whosoever drinks wine, let him suffer correction by scourging." For one thousand two hundred years the law of Persia has prescribed penalties for drunkenness of eighty lashes for a free man and forty for a slave. The stripes are to be administered if the offender is seized while intoxicated or while his breath smells of wine, and two witnesses testify that he has drunk wine.

This penalty of the bastinado is still sometimes enforced. Ayn-id-Doulah, mayor of Tabriz in 1893, had a man brought before him for drunkenness. He pleaded that he had been ordered by his physician to use wine. The mayor ordered him five hundred lashes and warned him never to be guilty again. In Khoi, not many years ago, some Mohammedans were whipped for drunkenness and two Armenians who sold the liquor were imprisoned and fined thirty tomans.

Not only is wine forbidden, but it is regarded as ceremonially unclean. Its touch renders impure. Strict shiahs will not use alcohol as a medicine or in the arts. I have been told that the Vali Ahd will not allow it to be used in painting or polishing his doors and furniture. A woman refusing medicine dissolved in alcohol, said, "What if I should die! I would go unclean into the presence of God!" The room in which wine is stored is defiled. Nay, more, an interpreter of the law has said, "If a drop of wine should fall into a lake, and its water should be used to irrigate a field of grass on which a flock of ten thousand sheep were grazing, it would not be lawful to eat the flesh of one of these sheep!"

But neither the sensible prohibitions, the punishments, nor the irrational traditions have been sufficient to prevent the use of intoxicants. Even some of the khaliphs of Damascus and Bagdad scandalized the faithful by their intemperate habits. A writer in the time of Harun-il-Rashid says, "Throughout the day our hands shed the blood of the wine cup, but the wine revenged itself upon our legs—a rosy liquor received from the hands of a gazelle-like nymph who seemed to have extracted it from her cheeks and then passed it around."

The poets of Persia, Hafiz, Saadi, and others, praise the wine cup and sing of its delights. Though Mohammedans, they invoke the muse of intoxication.*

> "Oh, that in some oasis green
> A fount of red wine gushed,
> While round the paradisal scene
> A boundless desert rushed.
>
> For to that fountain I must go,
> And pitch my life-tent there;
> That in its quiet I might know
> A bliss beyond compare."

* From Alger's "Poetry of the Orient."

"Fill up the goblet, and reach to me some;
 Drinking makes wise, but dry fasting makes glum."

"The sun of wine sank in thy mouth, where still its glory reeks,
 And left the flushes of its evening red upon thy cheeks."

"This lute to many a feast has added zest,
 This goblet waited on full many a guest.
 Believer, come! the wine house lures: come, hark,
 And drink; with cup and lute be wholly blest."

"The best ground is the ground of wet gold
  In the depth of a beaker;
 The best mouth is the mouth, from of old,
  Of the wine-praising speaker."

What the poets praised, the kings, their patrons, did not disdain. Hafiz says:

"Unnumbered kings have smiled to quaff this cup
 When anxious thought and woe their souls oppressed."

Take the Safavean dynasty, a line of sayids descended from Mohammed and defenders of the Shiah faith. Shah Abbas the Great is represented in his pictures as drinking. His wine magazine was one of the most costly edifices of Persia. Southgate says, "It consisted of a spacious hall, of which the entire roof was one magnificent dome. From the floor to the height of eight feet from the ground, the walls were of jasper. Above this on every side and over the whole interior of the dome, were niches of a thousand shapes, filled with vases of every imaginable form and material, appearing to the eye like incrustations on the walls. They were of crystal, cornelian, agate, onyx, jasper, amber, coral, porcelain, gold, silver and enamel, and were filled with the choicest wines."

Ismael Shah was a debauchee, and met his death through his indulgence in wine and opium, when rambling in disguise through his capital. He was found dead in a room over a candy shop, and the confectioner drunk at his side. Sufi Shah and several of his nobles got into a quarrel when drunk and he had them put to death. His successor, Abbas II. prohibited wine. "Drunkards were removed from office and strict sobriety and religion were the only recommendations to high station. The inhabitants of Erivan, alarmed at the abstemious and pious character of a governor appointed to rule them, petitioned the king not to send him. Their frailty, they said, led them to dread a water drinker. The fact was, the Christians of that city were remarkable for their drinking and were alarmed lest even a moderate use of wine should be considered a just ground for plundering them of their property or depriving them of life. The king was advised to attend to their petition. His reply stated that the drunkards of Erivan were quite unworthy of the holy man whom he had appointed to rule them, and he therefore had nominated one whose character was more suited to such sinners."(—Malcolm. Vol. I., 387.) Abbas II. himself, afterwards learned to indulge to excess, and many were the disgraceful and cruel scenes enacted in these drunken orgies. Shah Suleiman, his son, was even more of a drunkard. He compelled his prime minister to take opium to excess, that the latter's good example might not contrast with his own. In one of his sprees he ordered one of his favorites to be killed. The East India Company's agents presented this shah with some cases of European wines. Under his son, Sultan Husain, all the wine was cast out and the vessels which had been polluted by it were broken.

From what is recorded of the kings, we need not suppose the people were total abstainers. I conclude that there has been considerable intoxication in past centuries. When Drs. Perkins and Grant came to Persia, they saw evidence of its evil effects. One week previous to Dr. Grant's arrival, a caravan of liquors reached Tabriz, among which were eighteen barrels of New England rum. Dr. Perkins saw no other article of American manufacture in Tabriz, than rum. He says, "I sometimes see respectable Mussulman merchants falling down in the street or reeling in the rooms of their companions." Dr. Grant visited the governor of Tabriz. He found his excellency, though a young man, broken down with hard drinking. He requested Dr. Grant to prescribe for him. He was given medicine and told that he should drink no wine. The governor replied, "I can't go a day without my wine." Yet a change for the worse seems to have come in the past fifty years. Statistics of the number of drinkers and the consumption of liquors are unobtainable, but it is evident that the evil has increased. The wealthy, official and military classes are becoming more and more inclined to disregard restraints. I have seen Persians drinking in the house of an Armenian at the latter's festival until Persian and Armenian men began indiscriminately to embrace and kiss each other, and a chance sober guest would beat a hasty retreat. I attended a Persian wedding feast, and when the time came for the host to preside, he and a principal guest were excused from attendance because they were dead drunk in a side room. Drunken Mussulmans may sometimes be seen reeling through the streets. Once a drunken fellow attacked a foreigner, with a drawn sword, in the Armenian quarter of Tabriz. When the foreigner attempted to go away, the fellow drew a revolver and called a halt. He came up and threateningly demanded money. Just then his eyes fell on a bright object in the gentleman's hand. He seized it and walked away. His comrades returned it. Word was sent to the kalli begi, and he was arrested after making desperate resistance, and shooting the policeman through his coat. He was placed in a dungeon. In the morning it was discovered that he was a captain and son of a wealthy man. So they inflicted the bastinado and a heavy fine, and required a paper from him that he would forfeit his right hand if found drunk again.

While drunkenness is sadly on the increase, especially in cities and towns, on the other hand, there are tens of thousands of villagers and inhabitants of cities, who have never tasted liquor in any form, and who have an intense religious repugnance to it. They believe that alcoholic drink renders one unclean in the sight of God, and unfit for paradise. Besides hundreds of towns where no liquor can be procured, there are the sacred cities of Meshed and Kum, where its use is probably quite limited. Arthur Arnold says: "In Kum we found it impossible to refill our empty wine bottles. Intoxicating liquors appear to be absolutely unobtainable."

In general it may be said that the Persian who drinks goes to excess. His idea is that the pleasure is not in a gratification of the appetite or exhilaration of spirit, but in full intoxication, and that "there is as much sin in a glass, as in a flagon." He sees no stopping place between total abstinence and intemperance. A Moslem prince said to Arthur Arnold: "Why do you drink wine? I drink *arak*, it easily makes me drunk." This *arak* is a crude spirit, almost colorless, with a very large per cent. of alcohol. It is distilled from raisins, and is a veritable fire-water. Yet a traveler in Turkey was so much imposed upon as to write in a newspaper in praise "of the harmless and unintoxicating drink called *raki* or *arak*." Large quantities of this *arak* are distilled. It is the common drink of the Mohammedan topers.

The Armenian, Nestorian and Jewish inhabitants of Persia, with few exceptions, are drinkers, many indulging in "moderation," but great numbers excessively. Drinking is a matter of course, and almost a part of their religion. A Moslem defined a Christian as "one who drinks *arak*, and calls Jesus the Son of God."

Malcom says:* "The Persians often remark, 'It is the privilege of your religion to be drunkards and therefore attended neither by shame nor disgrace.' An English naval officer had come on shore at Bushire, and mounted a spirited horse to take a ride. The awkwardness of the rider, who was nearly falling at every bound the animal took, amused a great number of spectators. Next day a Persian, who supplied the vessel with fruit and vegetables, came on, and seeing the officer, said to him, 'I have saved your reputation; not a man who laughed at you yesterday has the least suspicion that you are a bad horseman.' 'How have you managed that?' said the gentleman. 'I told them that you were very drunk, otherwise you, like every Englishman, would ride admirably, as becomes a nation of soldiers.'"

No fast of the Oriental churches interferes with the free flow of liquor. Some missionaries were visiting a Nestorian bishop in time of Lent. He scrupulously abstained from the wine at dinner, *because the vessel that contained it* had been oiled, but urged them to join him in a glass of *arak*, as innocent, because it had not been contaminated by contact with animal oil. In the villages where the Nestorians and Arme-

* Vol. II., p. 423.

nians own vineyards, seven or eight barrels of wine are often set aside as the winter supply of a family. There are frequent carousals in the long winter months. One season, on account of excessive rains and the scarcity of fuel, the villagers made the grape crop into wine instead of raisins and molasses. During the winter high carnival reigned, even the women becoming intoxicated. Even when they had not bread to eat they had wine to drink. In one village Dr. Shedd found every man drunk and every woman bare-footed. Of one town on the Urumia plain it is said, that the walls get drunk and reel. This rural debauchery is caused by wine, not distilled liquors. At the New Year, Easter and other festivals, at weddings and sometimes funerals, intoxicants flow freely. One Armenian ordered wine to be furnished without measure at his funeral. His wine cellars were opened, all comers freely treated and many became intoxicated. A man in Sulduz, dying, told them to bury some bottles of *arak* in his grave with him. Accordingly his friends put in two bottles at the head of the coffin and two at the foot. Another man had one bottle of wine poured into his grave, and another bottle drunk at his grave. These three incidents are of course exceptional, but the drink habit among nominal Christians is almost universal. Coming from a county of Pennsylvania, where local option or wise judges have enforced prohibition of the liquor traffic during the most of the last quarter century, and where total abstainers are in large majority, it seemed strange to live among Christians where no feast, wedding, baptism, Easter or Christmas could be celebrated without almost universal drinking, and where a Christian who does not drink is an oddity to be remarked upon. It was said twenty years ago that there was not an Armenian house in Teheran or Hamadan in which wine or *arak* was not manufactured.

Nominal Christians are thus responsible for much of the corrupting influence that is being exerted among the Mohammedans. These scattered Armenian and Nestorian communities, which should be centers of gospel effort and virtues, are with the Jews at the front in the drink propaganda. In many a city the Christian quarter is the drunkard-making quarter. Tradition says that the mollah-bashi of Shah Abbas II., having turned all the races of the kingdom to Shiahs, thought to turn his attention to the Armenians. The king's council consulted, and were perplexed as to how the nobles could get their wine should this move be successful. They told the king that it was necessary to have some Armenians to act as salt in every city, and the king thus gave answer to the mollahs, and spared the wine sellers. Until recently it would have been impossible to find a Mussulman wine seller, and to-day none can engage in the business without contempt and disgrace. But love of money tempts Mohammedans to carry on the traffic where no Jews or Armenians live.

Open saloons are rare. In most instances liquor

is sold in private houses, out of the public view. Some shops in the bazaar are stocked with a quantity and variety of European liquors, and have back rooms in which dram drinking is permitted and where even Mussulmans enter and drink. Most of the latter carry the liquor home with them and consume it there. Curious stories are told of how mollahs at times resort to deception to obtain their liquor. A mollah called an Armenian wine seller before him and accused him of stealing his boxes of goods. The Armenian denied it. They told him they had seen the boxes taken to his house. Servants were sent with him. He was instructed to fill the boxes with bottles of wine. They were carried to the mollah as returned stolen goods.

The liquor traffic is not regularly licensed. When the Armenians returned to Tabriz after the treaty of Turcomanchai, 1828, an agreement was made with them that they should pay no taxes except five hundred tomans for the privilege of selling liquors. Afterwards, at the mujtehid's request, the shah annulled this regulation, and government sanction was withdrawn. But the Armenians continued to sell liquors, the aldermen collecting their perquisities through the police and overlooking irregularities. The tax is, I understand, two shahis per bottle of *arak*, which sells for twelve or fifteen shahis. Thirty-five years ago, when drunken rowdyism in the streets excited public attention, an attack was made by the Mussulmans in Tabriz against the liquor shops, the bottles and jars were broken and the drink was spilled. With this pretext the houses of many Armenians were looted. The enemies of the traffic continued their opposition for four or five years. In October, 1892, the Mussulmans made a raid on a wine shop in Teheran and poured its liquor into the street. The owner was a Greek under Russian protection, and the shah promptly footed the bill. A few years ago some prominent men in Tabriz imported machinery and built a distillery, intending to manufacture on a large scale, but the government refused its sanction. Each seller of spirits, as a rule, prepares his own supply. Fridays and Sundays, the two holy days, are the days on which the largest profits are made.

Nearly all the vast vintage of Persia is turned into raisins and molasses, a small part into wines. The native wines, with few exceptions, are inferior in quality. They are manufactured by the primitive process, the grapes being crushed by the feet, and the juice put into large earthen jars to ferment. The amount of wine consumed is small compared with the amount of *arak*. The possibility of having abundance of wine does not prevent the development of an appetite for stronger intoxicants.

The effects of drinking intoxicants are the same as in all the rest of the world. On account of their cheapness and the lack of amusements, a greater proportion of foreigners suffer from excess than in Christian countries. Its effect on natives may be illustrated by two **anecdotes**. One day the naib-i-sultaneh was going through the streets of the capital, when an Armenian reviled his princess, the queen and the royal harem in general. The prince restrained his wrath and reported to the shah, saying, "To what height of insolence will these Armenians go whom your majesty always praises as good subjects?" The shah ordered the Armenian arrested. He confessed his misdemeanor. The shah ordered him to be beheaded. The Armenian begged for delay, that he might bring his majesty the instigators of the insult. It was granted. He went home, put a bottle of *arak* in one pocket and a bottle of wine in the other and came before the shah. Presenting the bottles he said, "These are my instigators." His wit saved his head.

A story about the murder of Ali is curious. In Ramazan, Ibn Malzam came to Kufa to pay his respects to Ali. Ali said to him, "You are going to murder me." The man denied it, thinking, "Is thy servant a dog that he should do this thing?" Ibn Malzam loved a woman named Goudama, already married and an unbeliever. She was an enemy of Ali. She told Ibn Malzam that she would abandon her husband and come to him if he would do one of three things—first, kill Ali; second, burn a Koran; third, get drunk with wine. He thought to himself, "God forbid that I should kill the holy khaliph or destroy the sacred book, but to drink wine will not be so bad." He drank, and when intoxicated, burned the Koran and killed Ali on the same day.

Our mission takes a decided stand for total abstinence. Besides all reasons which enforce its necessity in other lands, in Persia it is necessary to commend Christianity and take away its reproach among Mohammedans. Our mission physicians rarely prescribe intoxicants as medicine; on the other hand they inculcate its injurious physiological effects. Dr. Hoernle, of the C. M. S. at Ispahan, takes a safe position when he writes: "Persian doctors often recommend wine and brandy. I, except when absolutely necessary, as resolutely prohibit them."

The question of sacramental wines has not been extensively agitated. The church at Hamadan uses the unfermented wine. Efforts are made to pledge all converts to total abstinence, for drinking is one of their besetting sins. Habitual drinking is a ground of discipline; drunkenness, of excommunication. Three-fourths of the evangelical churches enforce this discipline. Converts are hard to lead to this standard. The fact that Catholic and Anglican missionaries of Urumia and their priests and teachers almost all habitually use wine adds to the difficulty. Progress has been made, sentiment and conviction created, and many earnest advocates of temperance have risen among the evangelical Christians. The quickening of conscience by the Holy Spirit is a most hopeful sign. A late instance of this is most remarkable.

The grape harvest of 1892, in Urumia, was an abundant one. Early rains prevented its being made into raisins. Great quantities of wine were made. This was a subject of much solicitude, and the synod decided to persuade the people to pour out their wine. At the week of prayer, January, 1893, the hearts of church members were revived and many wicked men were brought to repentance. The religious interest took the form of a temperance revival. Of this Dr. J. H. Shedd wrote (in *The Independent*, May 18, 1893): "Drunkards gave up their drink, and every one who resolved to begin a new life gave evidence, if he had wine, by pouring it into the streets. Several hundred jars of wine, amounting, perhaps, to forty or fifty barrels, were thus disposed of, under no other pressure than deep conviction and earnest prayer. An old man arose and confessed: 'My one enemy is the wine. Come with me and we will turn out this enemy.' A crowd gathered on the flat roofs, and in the narrow streets to see the wine brought out. One of the brethren said: 'What a good opportunity for a meeting.' All were silent, and hymn, and prayer, and exhortation followed, and then another old man spoke in deep emotion: 'I have long been an opposer, but now my heart is broken, and I yield. Come on to my house and bring out my jugs of wine. I give that up, for it has long held me back from doing my duty.'"

Of the same occurrences Mr. Coan writes (*Women's Work for Women*, October, 1893,): "'Come on, boys,' shouted one, and with the command, boys and men rolled up their sleeves and soon emerged from the houses with vessels of every kind filled with the red and white wine, which began to flow in streams down the street. Soon every house but one had destroyed the poison, and the occupant of that, an old man of over eighty, who was keeping it for his stomach's sake, felt it so lonesome at the thought of drinking all alone, that he, too, gave the order and his wine helped to swell the stream. Many present from neighboring villages were impressed. One of these was a Mohammedan, who said, 'Please tell me what this means;' and again after he had heard the story, 'Blessed be God! would that I were a sacrifice to the religion that teaches such virtue.' As he went away he kept saying, 'That is the true religion.' The cheerful willingness of the people, who are very poor, to destroy their wine, from a conviction that it was wrong to use or sell it, preached a more eloquent sermon to that man than could be delivered from any pulpit.

"We found in other villages the same desire to throw away that which the people had been tempted to make to their harm. Entering one village I noticed a strong odor of wine. Wondering what it was, I saw Absalom, one of our indefatigable workers, appear with a pleased smile. 'Sahib, do you hear the waterspouts working?' Sure enough, there they were, put to a use they had never seen before, flowing with wine. In one village, so much wine ran down the streets, that some cattle, which were loose, took too much for their own good, and, unable to find their way home, got into the wrong stables."

With such religious convictions being formed, developing into such wise action, we can rest assured that Protestant Christianity will render a strong testimony for sobriety in Persia. It will be its mission, with God's blessing, to remove the reproach that has rested on Christianity before the Moslem world, as addicted to drunkenness and as purveyor to the appetite of debased Moslems. It is time that the malediction, " Woe to him that putteth the bottle to his neighbor's lips," should cease to rest on the Christians of the Orient.

THE END.

APPENDIX.

STATISTICS OF THE PERSIAN MISSIONS.

	1870	1890	1894
Stations.	1	5	6
Missionaries.	11	46	59
Outstations.	53	63	96
Native Preachers.	53	89	121
Organized Churches.	3	27	38
Communicants.	746	2269	2823
Boarding Schools.	2	8	10
Pupils in Boarding Schools.	60	403	450
Day-Schools.	54	139	109
Total Pupils.	865	2666	3502
Dispensaries.	1	6	9

MISSIONARIES IN URUMIA, 1870-1895.

* Died.   † Transferred from the American Board.   †† Transferred to another Station.

	Term of Service in the Field.
* Rev. J. G. Cochran †	1847–1871
* Mrs. Cochran †	1847–1893
* Rev. G. W. Coan †	1849–1879
* Mrs. Coan †	1849–1879
* Rev. J. H. Shedd †	1859–1895
Mrs. Shedd †	1859–
Rev. Benjamin Labaree †	1860–1890
Mrs. Labaree †	1860–1890
Miss N. J. Dean †	1860–1892
Rev. T. L. Van Orden, M.D. †	1866–1873
Mrs. Van Orden †	1866–1873
Rev. W. R. Stocking	1871–1879
* Mrs. Stocking	1871–1872
Mrs. Stocking	1873–1879
Miss Mary Jewett ††	1871–1873
Miss K. Cochran, M.D.	1871–1875

Rev. W. L. Whipple.................................	1872–1879
Mrs. Whipple.......................................	1872–1879
Rev. J. M. Oldfather ††.............................	1872–1885
Mrs. Oldfather ††..................................	1872–1885
G. W. Holmes, M.D. ††.............................	1874–1877
Mrs. Holmes ††....................................	1874–1877
Miss M. K. Van Duzee..............................	1875–
Miss A. E. Poage....................................	1875–1880
J. P. Cochran, M.D..................................	1878–
* Mrs. Cochran.....................................	1878–1895
Miss Agnes Carey..................................	1880–1883
Rev. J. E. Rogers...................................	1882–1885
Mrs. Rogers..	1882–1885
Mr. A. A. Hargrave.................................	1883–1886
Mrs. Hargrave (Miss Moore, 1884)..................	1885–1886
Rev. F. G. Coan....................................	1885–
Mrs. Coan..	1885–
Miss E. G. Cochran.................................	1885–1888
Miss Maria Morgan.................................	1885–1886
Rev. E. W. McDowell ††............................	1887–1890
Mrs. McDowell ††..................................	1887–1890
Rev. E. W. St. Pierre................................	1887–
Mrs. St. Pierre......................................	1887–
Rev. W. A. Shedd..................................	1892–
Mrs. Shedd...	1894–
Miss Anna Melton ††...............................	1888–1890
Rev. Robert Labaree................................	1888–1890
Miss Harriet L. Medbury...........................	1891–
Miss Grace G. Russell..............................	1891–
Miss Emma T. Miller, M.D.........................	1891–
Mr. E. T. Allen.....................................	1891–
Rev. Benjamin B. Labaree..........................	1893–
Mrs. Labaree.......................................	1893–
Miss M. K. Greene..................................	1890–1892

MISSIONARIES IN TABRIZ, 1873–1895.

Rev. P. Z. Easton...................................	1873–1880
Mrs. Easton..	1873–1880
Miss Mary Jewett..................................	1873–
Rev. S. L. Ward ††.................................	1876–1887
Mrs. Ward ††......................................	1876–1887
Mrs. L. C. Van Hook...............................	1876–1892
Rev. J. N. Wright ††................................	1878–1885
* Mrs. Wright......................................	1878–1879
Rev. S. G. Wilson...................................	1880–
Mrs. Wilson..	1886–
Miss M. A. Clarke ††...............................	1880–1884
Miss G. Y. Holliday.................................	1883–

PERSIA: WESTERN MISSION.

G. W. Holmes, M.D. ††	1881–1889
* Mrs. Holmes	1881–1889
Miss Mary Bradford, M.D.	1888–
Rev. J. M. Oldfather	1885–1890
Mrs. Oldfather	1885–1890
Rev. T. G. Brashear	1890–
Mrs. Brashear	1890–
W. S. Vanneman, M.D.	1890–
Mrs. Vanneman	1890–
Miss May Wallace	1894–

MISSIONARIES IN SALMAS, 1885–1895.

Rev. J. N. Wright	1885–
* Mrs. Wright	1887–1890
Mrs. Wright	1891–
Miss C. O. Van Duzee †	1886–
Rev. J. C. Mechlin	1887–
Mrs. Mechlin	1887–
Miss Emma Roberts	1887–1897
Miss J. F. McLean	1893–

MISSIONARIES IN MOSUL, 1890–1895.

Rev. E. W. McDowell	1890–
Mrs. McDowell	1890–
J. G. Wishard, M.D ††	1890–1892
Miss Anna Melton	1890–
Rev. J. A. Ainsley †	1889–
Mrs. Ainsley †	1889–
Miss L. D. Reinhart	1893–

MISSIONARIES IN TEHERAN, 1872–1895.

Rev. James Bassett	1871–1884
Mrs. Bassett	1871–1884
Rev. J. L. Potter	1874–
Mrs. Potter	1876–
Miss Sarah Bassett	1875–
* Rev. David Scott	1877–1879
Mrs. Scott	1877–1879
Miss Anna Schenck	1877–
Rev. J. W. Hawkes †	1880–1881
W. W. Torrence	1881–1891
Mrs. Torrence, M.D.	1881–1891
Miss Cora A. Bartlett	1882–
Miss A. G. Dale	1885–
Rev. T. J. Porter	1884–1885
Mrs. Porter	1884–1885
Rev. L. F. Esselstyne	1887–
Mrs. Esselstyne	1887–
Miss M. W. Greene	1889–1890

Miss Mary J. Smith, M.D............................ 1889–
Miss Mary A. Clarke................................ 1892–
J. G. Wishard, M.D................................. 1893–
Mrs. Wishard....................................... 1893–
Miss L. H. McCampbell 1892–

MISSIONARIES IN HAMADAN, 1881-1895.

Rev. J. W. Hawkes................................. 1881–
Mrs. Hawkes (Miss Sherwood, 1883)................. 1884–
Miss Annie Montgomery............................. 1882–
E. W. Alexander, M.D.............................. 1882–1891
Mrs. Alexander.................................... 1882–1891
Rev. W. G. Watson................................. 1888–
Mrs. Watson....................................... 1888–
Miss Charlotte Montgomery......................... 1887–
Miss Adeline Hunter 1889–1890
Miss S. S. Leinbach............................... 1891–
Miss Jessie C. Wilson............................. 1891–
G. W. Holmes, M.D................................. 1893–
Mrs. Holmes....................................... 1893–

INDEX.

A.

Abbas the Great, 18, 19, 316, 356.
Abbas II., on Toleration, 40 ; on Wine, 357.
Abbott, Consul-General, 338.
Abgar, King, 121.
Acacius, Bishop, ransoms prisoners, 13.
Ainslie, Rev. J. A., 84, 101.
Alexander, Dr. E. W., 260, 263, 283.
Ali, 45.
Ali Allahis, 22, 40, 317.
Allen, E. T., 75.
American rum, 358.
American mission established, 43.
Amir-i-Nizam, 163, 173, 190, 286, 337.
Amirkhaniantz, Rev. A., 107, 320 321, 343.
Amirkhaniantz, Mirza Ferukh, 319.
Anglican mission, 80, 102, 344, 345, 367.
Annual meeting, 43.
Apostles in Persia, 11.
Arabs, 16.
Armenians, 14, 26.
 colonies, 19, 21, 105.
 emigrated, 20.
 persecutions endured, 14–21.
 numbers, 104.
 character, 106–112.
 patriotism, 109.
 intemperance among, 365.
 weddings, 130–142.

Armenian Church, 112, 115.
 clergy, 112 (see priests), ignorance of, 145, 224.
 festivals, 119–128.
 church courts corrupt, 227–229.
 demands for reformation, 229–236 (see Reformation).
Armenians, missions to, 143–196.
 difficulties of, 162–167.
 persecuting spirit of, 172–179.
 Catholic missions to, 346.
Armenian versions, 104, 321–323.
Astrology, 273

B.

Babis, 23, 41, 332, 341.
Baking bread, 214.
Band of young men, 69.
Bassett, Rev. J., 250, 254, 319.
Benjamin, ex-Minister to Persia, 163, 196.
Betrothal, 131.
Bible, its influence, 91, 145, 224–225, 340.
Bible translation, 284.
 Persian versions, 304.
 Azerbaijan, Turkish, 315–321.
 Ararat Armenian, 322–325.
 Syriac, 325–326.
 Kurdish and Hebrew, 326.
Bible distribution permitted, 29.
 agents and depots, 237.
 colporteurs, 328.
 difficulties of, 329–334.
 official protection, 335.
 results, 341.

375

376   INDEX.

Bishops, 12, 62, 98, 264, 344.
  in Tabriz, 122, 124, 228.
  converted, 58, 60, 61.
Bliss, Rev. E. M., 327.
Bradford, Miss E. M., 154, 165, 189, 259, 263, 265, 266.
  in cholera time, 302–304, 308.
Brashear, Rev. T. G., 154, 188.
Breath, Edward, 80.
Bribery of ecclesiastics, 227–229.
Bridal outfit, 132.
Bruce, Rev. R., 29, 249, 253, 289, 303, 324, 330, 344.

C.

Catholics, Roman, 25, 68, 71, 72, 96–98, 102.
  history of missions of, 346–354, 367.
  murder of monks, 166–167.
Catholicos of Armenians, 112, 223, 233, 236, 325.
Cemetry, Tabriz, 161.
Child, Mr. Theodore, 303.
Cholera, past epidemics, 295.
  route of travel, 295.
  sanitation, 296.
  Mohammedans' reliance on Imams, 296.
  Mohammedans' reliance on talismans, 299.
  Mohammedans' reliance on printed prayers, 297–298.
  Armenian rites, 305.
  in Tabriz, 306–308.
  Dr. Bradford's Dispensary, 302–304.
  in Azerbaijan, 309.
  in Teheran, 309.
  Dr. Torrence's hospital work, 310.
  testimony concerning, 311.
  ingratitude of people, 312.
Christians in Persia, 11, 40.
  early history, 11–13.
  persecutions under Sassanians 14–16.
  under Arabs, 16.
  under Seljuks, 16.
  under Mongols, 17, 347.
  persecutions under Tartars, 17.
  under Safaveans, 19–20.
  under Kajars, 20.
  royal converts, 11, 12.
  oppressions of, 23, 101.
  conditions alleviated, 25, 26.
Christmas, Armenian, 117.
Church mission (Ispahan), 244, 260, 344, 366.
Clarke, Miss M. A., 154.
Cleveland, President, mentions Miss Melton, 95.
Climate of Mosul, 83.
Coan, Rev. F. G., 55, 70, 72, 89, 103, 262, 267, 368.
Cochran, Mrs. D. P., 261, 276.
Cochran, Dr. J. P., 73, 89, 262, 265, 276, 278, 282.
College, Urumia, 73, 77–80, 275.
Colporteurs, 146, 147, 328, 330–332.
Converts, 61–70, 96–97, 144, 145, 249, 247, 251, 252–253, 287.
Converts, false, 167–168, 247.
Conference of workers, 195.
Covington, John L., gift of chapel, 179.

D.

Dancing at weddings, 135.
Deacons, 54.
Deaconesses, 58.
Deen, Miss N. J., 77.
Degala, 64, 66, 70.
Doctors, native, 268–270, 308.
  foreign, 258–260, 283, 289.
  decorated by Shah, 278.

E.

Easter celebrated, 16; Armenian, 120.
Eastern Persia mission, 57, 250, 311.
Easton, Rev. P. Z., 143, 152, 153, 186.
Education among Armenians, 108, 179.
  of girls, 51, 52, 77, 84–85.
  in Urumia, 77–79.
  in mountains, 86.
  in Tabriz and Salmas, 179, 221.

Elkosh, 100, 326.
Esselstyn, Rev. Lewis, 310.
Etchmiadzin, 115, 118, 223, 226, 322, 324.
Evangelical Church, organized, 57.
  government of, 58.
  boards, 59.
  benevolence, 59, 180.
  statistics, 58, 84.
Evangelization, 156-158, 161, 170.

F.

Famine, cause of, 291.
  in Tabriz, 291.
  in Urumia, 292.
  relief work, 292.
  Mohammedans assisted, 293.
Fasts, Armenian, 128, 233.
Ferry Hospital, 259, 310.
Fiske, Miss Fidelia, 53, 77, 79.
Fisk Seminary, 73, 77.
Fire-worshipers, 27.
Food in school, 215.
Fuel in school, 214.

G.

Geogtapa, 54.
Georgians, 19, 20.
German missionaries, 320, 342, 344.
Governor of Urumia, reception by, 45; letter of, 46.
Grant, Dr. Asahel, 45, 83, 276, 283, 358.
Grant, Mrs. Asahel, 54, 77.
Grant, Wm. H., visit of, 76.
Gregor, Gnergian, Rev., 107, 147, 181, 182, 300.
Guleserian, Rev. N., 161, 211, 306.
Gulpashan, 67, 70.

H.

Haftdewan, 163, 166.
Hajiabad inscription, 11.
Hamadan, 145, 237, 254, 286.
Hargrave, Mr. A. A., 81.

Harpoot College, 206.
Hawkes, Rev. J. W., 253, 257.
Hawkes, Mrs. J. W., 145.
Health of missionaries, 261.
Holliday, Miss G. Y., 153, 154, 205, 302.
Holmes, Mrs. G. W., 201, 286.
Holmes, Dr. G. W., 52, 153, 173, 177, 259, 273, 278, 284-286.
Hospital, Urumia, 74, 258, 267, 275, 277, 287, 337.
  Howard annex, 259.
  Teheran, 259, 310.
Hypocrites, 169-171.

I.

Ibrahim Mirza, martyrdom, 31-38, 187, 189.
Industrial schools, 75.
Inner mission, 62.
Intemperance of priests, 225.
  of Jews, 243.
  tradition of origin of wine, 352.
  anecdotes about drunkenness 353, 357-359.
  Mohammed's prohibition, 354.
  Bibulous Khaliphs, 355.
  Safavean debauchees, 356-357.
  Persian poets on, 355.
  increase of intemperance, 359.
  attitude of Government towards, 364.
  attitude of Oriental Christians, 361.
  attitude of missions, 366.
  sacramental wine, 367.
  temperance revival, 367-370.
Ispahan, 19-21, 115, 344, 348.

J.

Jacobites, 15.
Jewett, Miss Mary, 143, 152.
Jews, captivities, 239.
  persecutions of, 237.
  in Hamadan, 239-241.
  separation of, 243.
  occupations, 243.
  rejectors of Talmud, 245.
  synagogues, 246.

378 INDEX.

Jews, missions to, permitted, 28.
  mission of Wolff, 244.
    of London Society, 244, 253.
    of Presbyterian Board in Salmas, 244.
    in Urumia, 245.
    in Teheran, 250.
    in Hamadan, 251, 253.
  visit to synagogue, 246.
  converts, 247, 250, 254.
Julfa (Ispahan), 20-21.

K.

Karadagh, 27, 128, 156, 224.
Khnan Eshu, Deacon, 103.
Khoi, 126, 159, 198, 205, 211, 327, 335.
Khosrov Parviz, 15.
Kindergarten, 77, 199, 204, 205.
Kochanes, 84, 103, 345, 349.
Kremian Catholicos, 114, 223, 233, 236.
Kurds, 85, 89, 276, 326.
Kurdish Sheikhs, 90, 278.

L.

Labaree, Rev. B., D. D., 48, 50, 52, 63, 70, 81, 253, 262, 320, 326, 329.
Lascelles, Sir Frank C., 37, 39.
Layah Bible Woman, 72.
Liquor traffic, 363, 364.
Lobdell, Dr., 83, 258.
London Society for Jews, 244, 253.

M.

Magianism, 12.
Malcom, Khan, 46.
Manes, 11.
Maragha, 16, 144, 172, 176, 327, 337, 340.
Marius, Persian Noble, 11.
Marriages, 139, 172, 185, 329.
Martyn, Henry, 314, 342.
Martyrs, 12, 13, 38.
Maruthas, Bishop, 13.
Mar Shimun, Patriarch 101, 102, 350.

Mary, Virgin, 120, 121, 125, 126, 138, 157, 235, 236, 305.
Mass, 122.
Mateos, Nazarian, 144.
McDowell, Rev. E. W., 84, 86, 89, 91, 92, 96, 278.
McLean, Miss J. F., 164.
Mechlin, Rev. J. C., 164, 309.
Medbery, Miss H. L., 77.
Medical Missions, where established, 258-260.
  names of physicians, 258-260 (see under names in Index).
  hospitals, 258, 259, 260.
  dispensaries, 259, 260.
  itinerating, 264.
  lady physicians, 260, 300, 309.
  benefits of, 261, 262, 265, 268, 275, 277, 283, 287.
  exemplified, 261, 262, 268, 275-277, 284.
  testimony to value of, 287.
  royal favors to physicians, 275, 278.
Medical science, Persian, 268-272, 273.
Melton, Miss Anna, 84, 92-94.
Memorial School, Tabriz, 181, 212-215.
Mercenary motives, 167-172.
Merrick, Rev., 143.
Merun (Holy Oil), 112, 118.
Metropolitan of Nochea, 103.
Mezan-ul-Hak, 29, 176, 319, 338.
Miandoab, 205, 211, 246.
Milling of flour, 214.
Miller, Dr. Emma, 259, 309.
Missions of various societies, 342.
  early Protestant missions, 342.
  Moravians, 342, Henry Martyn, 342.
  Germans, 342. Glenn, 343.
  Swedes, 344. C. M. S., 344.
  Archbishop of Canterbury's mission, 345.
  Policy of Anglican mission, 345-346.
  Roman Catholic medieval missions, 346-347.
  Roman Catholic to Armenians, 347.

Missions, Roman Catholic to Nestorians, 348.
   Presbyterian. (See Urumia, Tabriz, Mosul.)
Mobed, Christian, 12.
Mohammed on wine, 353.
Mohammedans conquer Persia, 17.
   persecute Christians, 19-21, 31-38.
   sects of, 20.
   perverts to Islam, 24, 25.
   during cholera, 296-301.
Mongols in Persia, 18, 316, 346.
Mollahs, 239, 241, 248, 307, 312, 335, 363.
Moressa Khanum, 79.
Morrison, Mr., M. A., 318.
Moshi Pastor, 172, 176, 196.
Mosul, occupation as station, 83.
   climate, 83.
   condition of work, 96, 100.
   converts from Catholics, 96-98.
Music, 133.

N.

Nakhejevan, 120, 347.
Nasr-i-Din Shah, 21, 23, 163, 165, 239, 240, 335.
Nelson, Rev. H. A., 43, 46, 48.
Nestorians, 14, 16, 17, 26, 27-29, 30, 83-86, 293, 317.
Nestorians, mission to, established, 43.
   transferred, 43.
   jubilee of, 43-49.
   sample congregations, 52, 67.
   memorial church, 55.
   organization of Reformed Church, 57.
   doctrines and government, 58.
   Presbytery and board, 58, 59.
   benevolence, 59.
   inner mission, 59-60.
   revivals in, 61-72.
   educational work, 73.
   college, 73, 75.
   industrial mission, 75.
   Fiske Seminary, 77, 79.

Nestorian press, 80, 81.
   publications, 81-82.
Nestorians, mountain, mission to, 83.
   wildness of mountains, 85.
   ignorance of people, 86.
   lawlessness, 86-88.
   attacks on missionaries, 86.
   intrigues of Anglican and Papal missions, 101.
Nestorians, Catholic mission to, 100-101, 346-349.
Nestorian chant, 55.
Nestorian church decayed, 103.
Newspaper, Syriac, 81.
   Armenian, on church, 223, 226, 229, 233, 324.
Nineteenth Century on medical missions, 289.
Nuschizad, Christian Prince, 15.
Nushirvan, 15.

O.

Oldfather, Rev. J. M., 44, 49, 154, 293.
Organs in worship, 193.

P.

Paton, Mr. A. M., 35, 183, 186.
Parsees, 27.
Perkins, Rev. Dr., 28, 43, 73, 77, 143, 258, 262, 325, 350.
Pers.-Armenia, 14.
Persian versions, 314-315.
Poets on wine, 355-356.
Potter, Rev. J. Z., 251, 310.
Pratt, U. S. Minister, 165, 180, 260.
Presbyteries, 59, 195.
Priests, Armenian, 112, 172, 195, 223, 225, 229, 305, 306.
Press at Urumia, 80-82.
Protestant Church (see Evangelical Church.)
Protestant marriage, 172.
Protestants, order for expulsion from Tabriz, 41-42.
   misrepresented, 159.
Publications in Syriac, 81.

Q.

Quarantine, 296.

R.

Rabino, Mr., testimony to missions, 311.
Raffe, 107, 111.
Rays of Light, newspaper, 81.
Reformation of Armenian Church, 222.
  demands for, 223.
  of priesthood, 223.
  of judicial procedure, 227.
  for instruction of people, 229.
  for revision of prayer-book, 233.
  for evangelical teaching, 235.
  Catholicos favorable to, 236.
Reinhart, Miss L. D., 84.
Religious liberty, state of, 22-28, 40-42, 172-178.
  for Christians, 25-28.
  for Parsees, 27.
  for missions to Christians, 28-30.
  for missions to Mohammedans, 30-31, 189, 191.
Revivals, 61-70, 219-220.
Rhea, Rev. S. A., 73, 83, 154.
Rice, Miss Susan, 53, 78.
Ritualism, 230, 231.
Robbers, 86-88, 89-90.
Roberts, Miss E., 164.
Russell, Miss G. G., 77.

S.

Sabbath observance, 194, 225.
Sacrifices, 127, 298.
Sadr-Azam, 39.
Safavean Kings, 19, 356-358.
Salmas, 18, 27, 184, 205, 220, 245, 260, 348, 350.
Salmas, station established, 162.
  opposition overcome, 163.
  murder of Mrs. Wright, 165.
  other murders, 166.
Sarah Rabi, 53, 80.
Sayad, Dr. Yohanna, 260, 283, 309.
Schools, 108, 151, 188, 220, 343.
Schoolboys' Memorial, Tabriz, started, 181, 205-206.
  curriculum of High School, 206.
  curriculum of Theological School, 206.
  examinations, 207.
  Thaw memorial, 181, 212, 213.
  sealed by government, 188.
  graduates in theology, 205.
  life of pupils, 213.
  boarding department, 213.
  native habits retained, 214.
  visits of officials, 218.
  a spiritual harvest, 219.
  girls' school, Tabriz, 199-200.
  building, 200.
  commencement exercises, 202-203.
  graduates, 201-202.
Schools, Urumia (see Nestorians), 73-82.
School for Girls, Salmas, 220.
Scriptures, 104, 314-341 (see Bible).
Seljuks, 16, 316.
Shapur II. persecutes, 12.
Shedd, Rev. J. H., 33, 48, 51, 67, 73, 162, 262, 362, 368.
Sheikhis, 41, 341.
Shiahs, 22, 23, 40.
Shirin, Christian Queen, 16.
Silar-il-Askar, 45.
Smith, Dr. Mary, 259, 310.
Soujbulak, 161, 327, 346.
Sperry, Ex-U. S. Minister, 37, 191, 310.
Stoddard, Rev., 60, 73.
Stores for schools, 215.
St. Pierre, Rev. E. W., 70, 265.
Stephanos, Bishop, 165, 166, 188, 306.
Stewart, Col., Consul-General, 165, 192.
Swedish mission, 340, 344.
Syriac versions, 325.

T.

Tabriz, 21, 25, 30, 33, 37, 104, 237, 291, 337, 356.
  bishops in, 115, 144.

INDEX. 381

Tabriz, mission work in, 143, 194, 259, 311, 320, 342, 343.
  station established, 143.
  converts, 144-145.
  establishment of schools, 152 (See schools).
  resignation of Mr. Easton, 153.
  arrival of new missionaries, 153.
  work of Miss Jewett, 153, 154.
  touring by author, 156-158.
  priestly antagonism, 144, 159, 172-174, 182.
  cemetery purchased, 161.
  Protestant marriages, 172, 185, 209.
  church, 180, 191-193, 222, 250.
  sealing of church and school, 36, 188, 218.
  evangelistic work proscribed, 190.
  deliverance, 191.
  presbytery organized, 196.
Tamurlane, 17.
Tamzarian, Mr. Vahan, 206.
Teheran mission work, 143, 250, 309, 312.
Temperance revival, 364, 365.
Terrell, Judge, 95.
Thaw, Mrs. Wm., 212-215.
Theodoret, 12.
Torrence, Dr. W. W., 278, 310.
Trial by fire, 333.
Turkish language, 161, 316-318.
Turkish versions, 315-317.
Turkish Mission's Aid Society, 80.
Tus (Meshed), 12.
Tyler, Mr. John, 189.

U.

Urumia, 24, 28, 32, 43-82, 84, 237, 244, 245, 258, 287, 292, 295, 345, 362 (see Nestorians).

V.

Vali Ahd, 286, 354.
Vartan and Satenig, 186.
Van Duzee, Miss C. O., 164.
Van Duzee, Miss M. K., 245.
Van Hook, Mrs. L. C., 49, 143, 154, 260.
Vanneman, Dr. W. S., 26, 38, 154, 188, 219, 250, 271, 287, 301, 308.
Van Orden, Dr., 258, 301, 308.
Varanes, V., persecutor, 13.
Victoria, Queen, interest in Nestorians, 24.

W.

Ward, Rev. S. L., 143, 153, 200, 310, 312.
Weddings, Armenian, 130.
  betrothals, 130.
  prohibited degrees, 131.
  age and time of marriage, 131.
  bride's outfit, 132.
  music and dancing, 132.
  blessing garments, 138.
  procession, 137.
  ceremony, 138.
  subjection of bride, 141.
  no intermarriage with Persians, 142.
Weeks, Edwin Lord, 305, 311.
Westminster Hospital, 74, 259, 267.
Whipple, Rev. W. L., 48, 52, 188, 327, 356.
Wilson, Mrs. S. G., 133, 140, 193, 206, 211, 308.
Wilson, Dr. Jessie C., 260, 264, 311.
Wilson, Rev. S. G., appointed to mission, 153.
Wine, origin of, 352.
  Koran on, 353.
  manufacture of, 316, 360.
  drinking among Christians, 360-362.
Wishard, Dr. J. G., 84, 86-89, 259, 282, 309.
Wishard, L. D., visits Persia, 76.
Woman's work, 154.
Worship, Protestant, 192.
Wright, Rev. J. N., 144, 153, 163, 292, 321.
Wright, Mrs. S., 144, 164-165.

Y.

Yezdegird, II., 13, 14.
Yoshana, Professor, 45, 53, 164, 326.

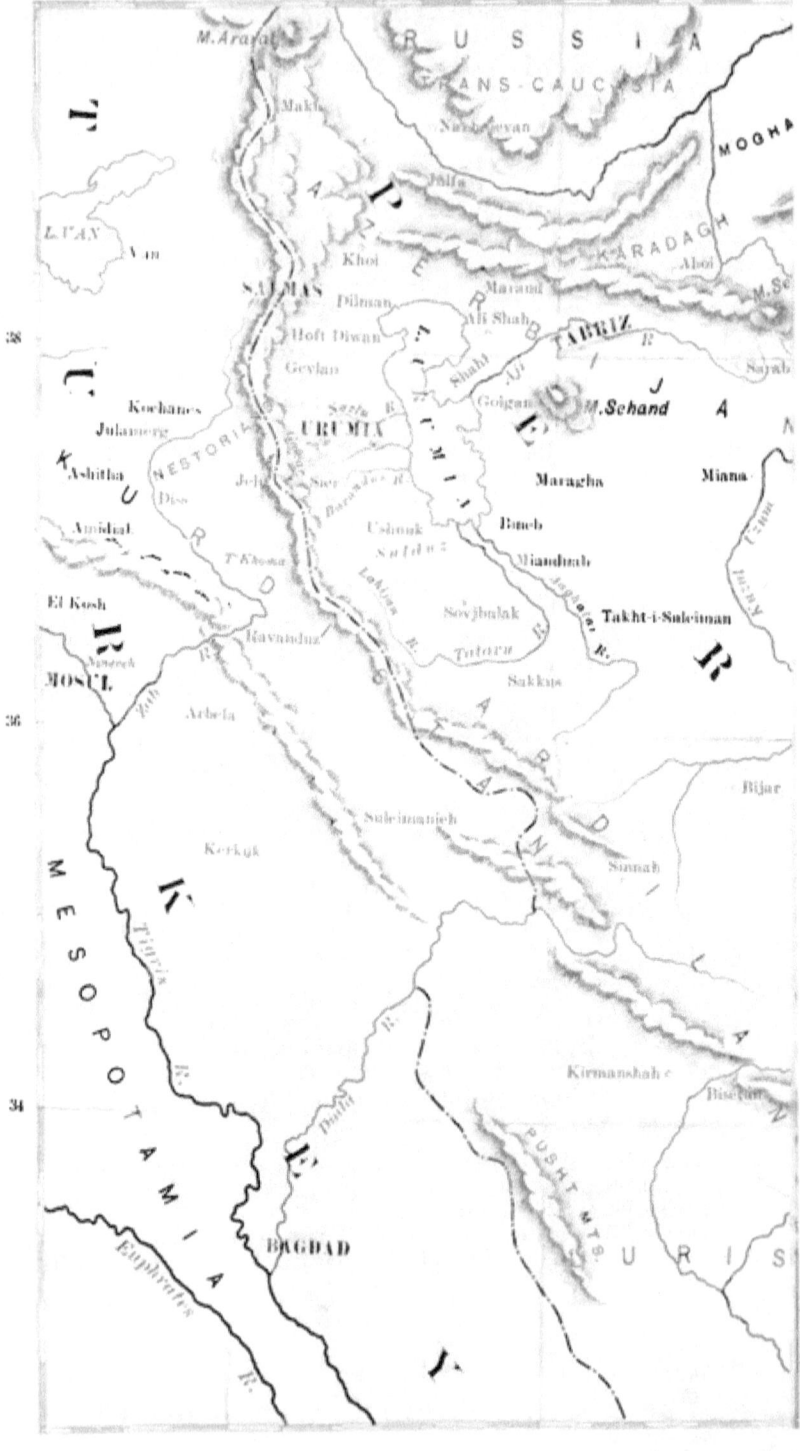

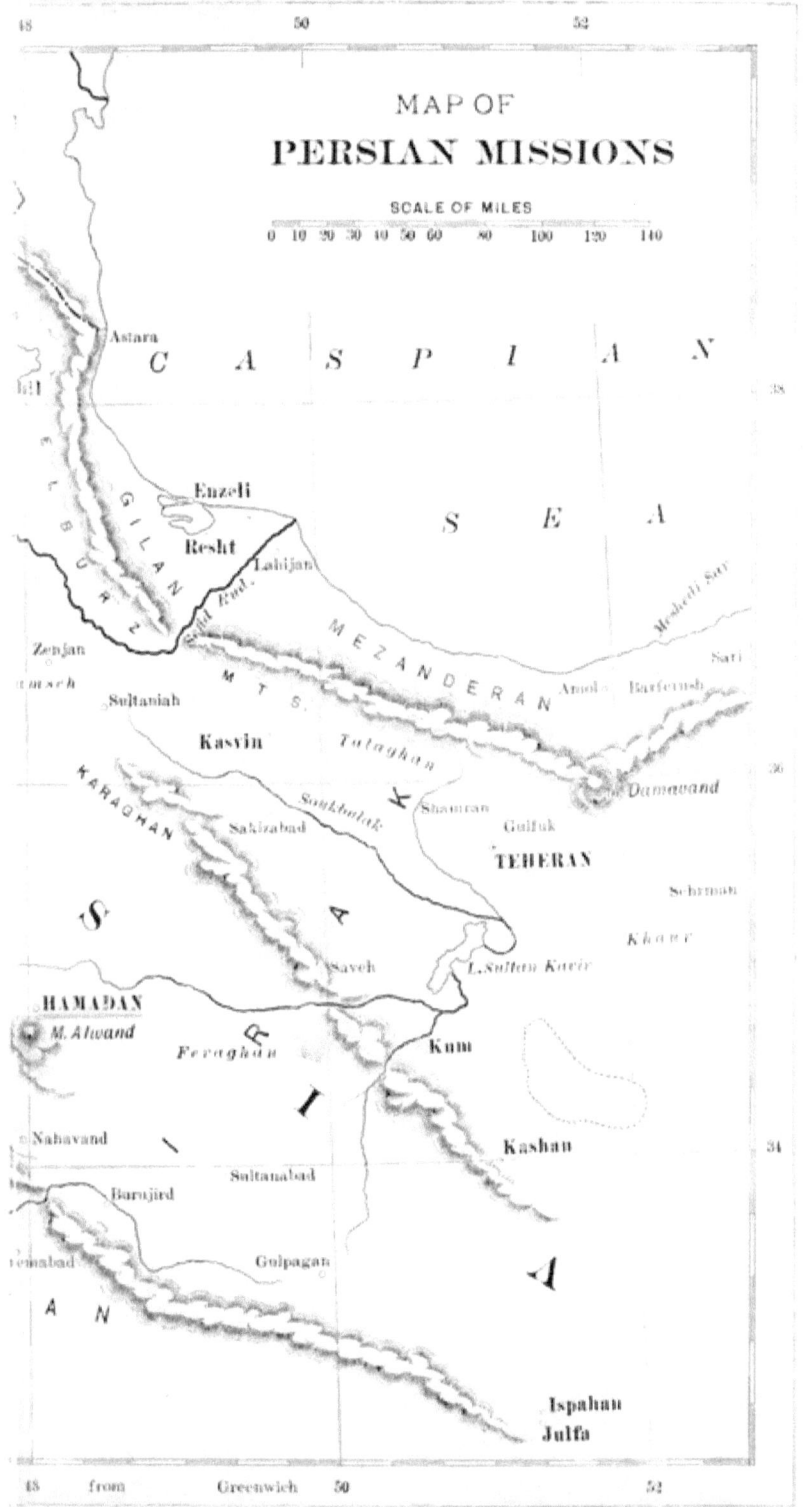

www.ingramcontent.com/pod-product-compliance
Lightning Source LLC
Chambersburg PA
CBHW032023220426

43664CB00006B/343